PACIFI
GRAVEYARD

A narrative of shipwrecks where the Columbia River meets the Pacific Ocean

By

James A. Gibbs

Binford & Mort Publishing

Portland, Oregon

TO CHERIE
who cheerfully stood by
the beachcomber who wrote
this epistle.

Pacific Graveyard

Library Of Congress Catalog Card Number: 92-74217

ISBN: 0-8323-0481-6 (Softcover)

Printed in the United States of America

Fourth Edition

ACKNOWLEDGMENTS

My sincerest thanks to the Puget Sound Maritime Historical Society and to the Oregon Historical Society. I also wish to thank those good friends who live by the sea in Pacific County; namely, Charles Fitzpatrick, Charles Nelson, and Mr. and Mrs. William Begg. Floyd M. Hecox, commanding officer of the Cape Disappointment Coast Guard Station, was most helpful—as were the Corps of Engineers of the United States Army and the United States Coast Guard.

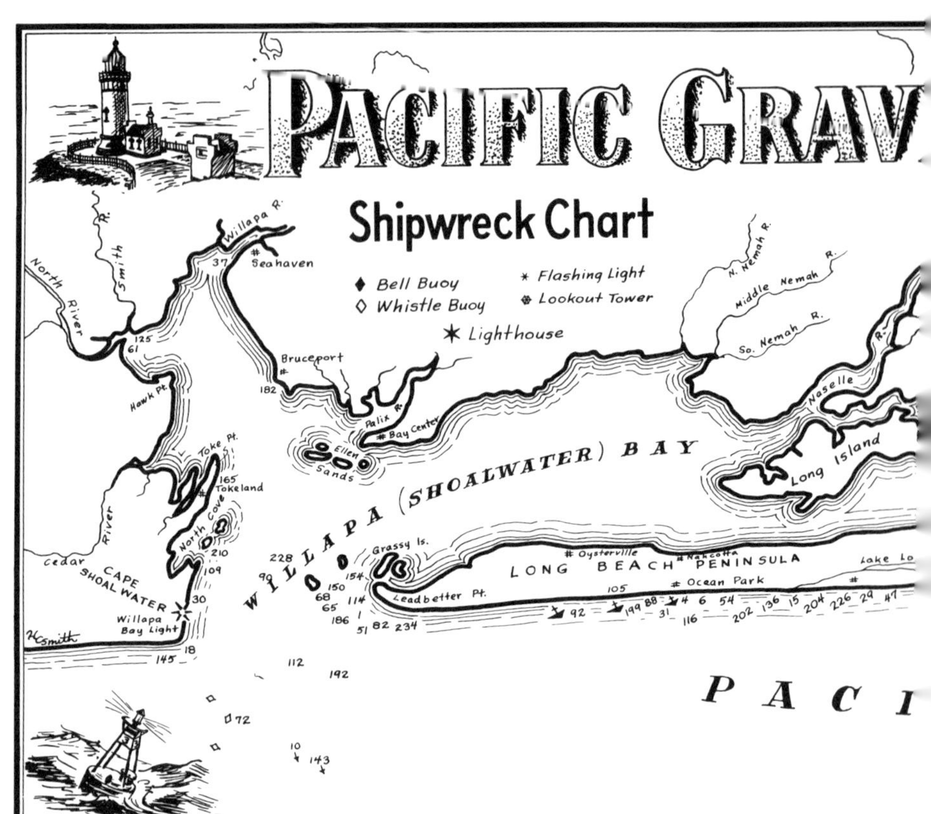

KEY TO THE CHART — Ships that have stranded, foundered, burned, or met other disaster i the Pacific Graveyard at the mouth of the Columbia River, including wrecks northward to Willapa Bay. Those marked with an asterisk (*) have been salvaged or removed.

No.	Name	Year
1.	Abbey Cowper, Br. bark	1885
2.	Admiral, Am. schr.	1912
3.	Adm. Benson, Am. S.S.	1930
4.	Alice, Fr. Ship	1909
*5.	Allegiance, Br. ship	1879
6.	Alpha, Am. gas prop.	1924
*7.	Alsternixe, Ger. bark	1903
8.	Americana, Am. schr. (11 lost)	1918
9.	Andrada, Br. bark	1900
10.	Anna C. Anderson, Am. schr. (7 lost)	1869
11.	Architect, Am. bark	1875
12.	Ariel, Am. schr.	1886
13.	Arrow, U.S. Army trans.	1947
14.	Arrow No. 2, Am. mtr. tug (1 lost)	1949
15.	Artemisia, Am. schr.	1889
*16.	Aurelia, Am. S.S.	1911
17.	Aurora, Am. packet ship	1849
*18.	Avalon, Am. S.S.	1925
*19.	Baby Doll, Am. frtr.	1955
20.	Barge, ex-Nichols I, Am.	1954
*21.	Barge No. 16, Am.	1953
*22.	Barge No. 91, Am.	1909
23.	Beaver, Am. gas prop.	1940
24.	Bell Buoy, Am. fishboat	1960
25.	Bordeaux, Am. brig	1852
26.	Brodick Castle, Br. ship	1908
27.	Cadzow Forest, Br. bark	1896
28.	Cairnsmore, Br. bark	1883
29.	C. A. Klose, Am. schr.	1905
30.	Canadian Exporter, Can. S.S.	1921
31.	Caoba, Am. S.S	1925
32.	Cape Wrath, Br. bark (15 lost)	1901
33.	Capt. James Fornance, Am. S.S.	1917
34.	Carrie B. Lake, Am. schr. (3 lost)	1886
35.	Castle, Am. River str.	1854
36.	Cavour, It. ship	1903
37.	Challenger, Am. schr.	1904
38.	Champion, Am. schr. (2 lost)	1870
39.	Chatham, HMS Br. tndr.	1792
*40.	Childar, Norw. M.S. (4 lost)	1934
41.	City of Dublin, Br. ship	1878
42.	Columbia, Am. fishboat	1928
*43.	Columbia Riv. Lightship No. 50	1899
44.	Corsica, Br. bark	1882
45.	C-Trader, Am. M.S. frtr.	1963
*46.	Decorah, Am. gas schr.	1915
*47.	Deneb, Am. M.S.	1950
48.	Desdemona, Am. bark (1 lost)	1857
49.	Detroit, Am. brig	1855
50.	Devonshire, Br. vessel	1884
51.	Dewa Gungadhar, Br. bark	1885
52.	Dilharree, Br. bark	1880
53.	Dolphin, U.S. Navy brig	1852
54.	Donna, Am. fishboat (3 lost)	1944
55.	Douglas Dearborn, Am. schr.	1890
56.	Dreadnaught, Am. sloop (7 lost)	1876
57.	Drexel Victory, Am. S.S.	1947
58.	Drumcraig, Br. bark	1906
59.	Eagle, Am. fishboat	1942
60.	Edith Lorne, Br. bark	1881
61.	Ediz, Am. gas prop.	1951
62.	Efin, Am. River frtr.	1937
63.	Eine, Am. launch	1914
64.	Electra, Am. fishboat	1944
65.	Ellen, Am. schr.	1870
66.	Elsie Faye, Am. fishboat	1960
*67.	Emily Stevens, Am. schr.	1881
68.	Empire, Am. schr.	1854
69.	Enterprise, Am. S.S.	1858
*70.	Erria, Dan. M.S. (11 lost)	1951
71.	Eva, Am. fishboat	1915
72.	Fanny, Am. sloop	1864
73.	Fern Glen, Br. ship	1881
74.	Firefly, Am. st. tug (4 lost)	1854
75.	Fishing Fleet, Am. (200 lost)	1880
*76.	Flora, Am. fishboat (2 lost)	1954
77.	Foss No. 2, Am. scow	1931
78.	Francis H. Leggett, Am. S.S. (65 lost)	1914
79.	Frank W. Howe, Am. schr.	1904
80.	Galena, Br. bark	1906
*81.	Gamecock, Am. Strnwhl. St.	1898
82.	G. Broughton, Br. bark	1881
*83.	Gen. C. H. Muir, U.S.N. trans.	1955
*84.	Gen. John Biddle, Am. dredge	1964
85.	Gen. Warren. Am. S.S. (42 lost)	1852
86.	George Olson, Am. bg.	1964
87.	Gleaner, Am. river str. (3 lost)	1888
88.	Glenmorag, Br. ship (2 lost)	1896
*89.	Go-Getter, Am. tug	1952
90.	Gotoma, Am. schr.	1908
91.	Gov. Moody, Am. pilot boat	1890
92.	Grace Roberts, Am. brkn.	1887
93.	Great Republic, Am. S.S. (11 lost)	1879
94.	Harvest Home, Am. bk.	1882
*95.	Hazard, Am. brig (5 lost)	1798
96.	Henrietta, Fr. bark	1860
*97.	Henriette, Fr. bark	1901
98.	Ida Mae, Am. fishboat	1953
99.	Industry, Am. bark (17 lost)	1865
100.	Intrepid, Am. barge	1954
101.	Iowa, Am. S.S. (31 lost)	1936
102.	Isabella, Br. brig	1830
*103.	Jane A. Falkenberg, Am. bktn.	1872
104.	Japanese Junk	
105.	Japanese Junk	
106.	J. C. Cousins, Am. pilot schr. (4 lost)	
107.	Jennie Ford, Am. bktn.	
*108.	Jenny Jones, Am. schr.	
109.	Jessie Nickerson, Am. schr.	
110.	J. Merithew, Am. bark	
111.	Josephine, Br. brig	
112.	Jupiter, Am. fishboat (4 lost)	
113.	Kake, Am. fishboat	
114.	Lammerlaw, Br. bark	
115.	Laurel, Am. S.S. (1 lost)	
116.	Lenore, Am. fishboat	
117.	Leonese, Am. bark (9 lost)	
*118.	L'Etoile Du Matin, Fr. ship	
119.	Lively, Am. fishboat	
120.	Lucky, Am. fishboat	
121.	Lupatia, Br. bark (16 lost)	
122.	Machigone, Am. schr (9 lost)	
123.	Maine, Am. whaler	
124.	Makah, Am. bktn. (11 lost)	
125.	Marathon, Am. fishbt	
126.	Maria B., Am. fishboa	
127.	Marie, Am. brig (9 lost)	
128.	Marie, Am. gas boat	
*129.	Massachusetts, U.S.S	
130.	Mauna Ala, Am. S.S.	
*131.	Melanope, Br. bark	
132.	Mermaid, Am. fishbt (2 lost)	
133.	M. F. Hazen, Am. launch	
*134.	Michigan, Am. S.S.	
135.	Mindora, Am. bark	

Compiled by James A. Gibbs

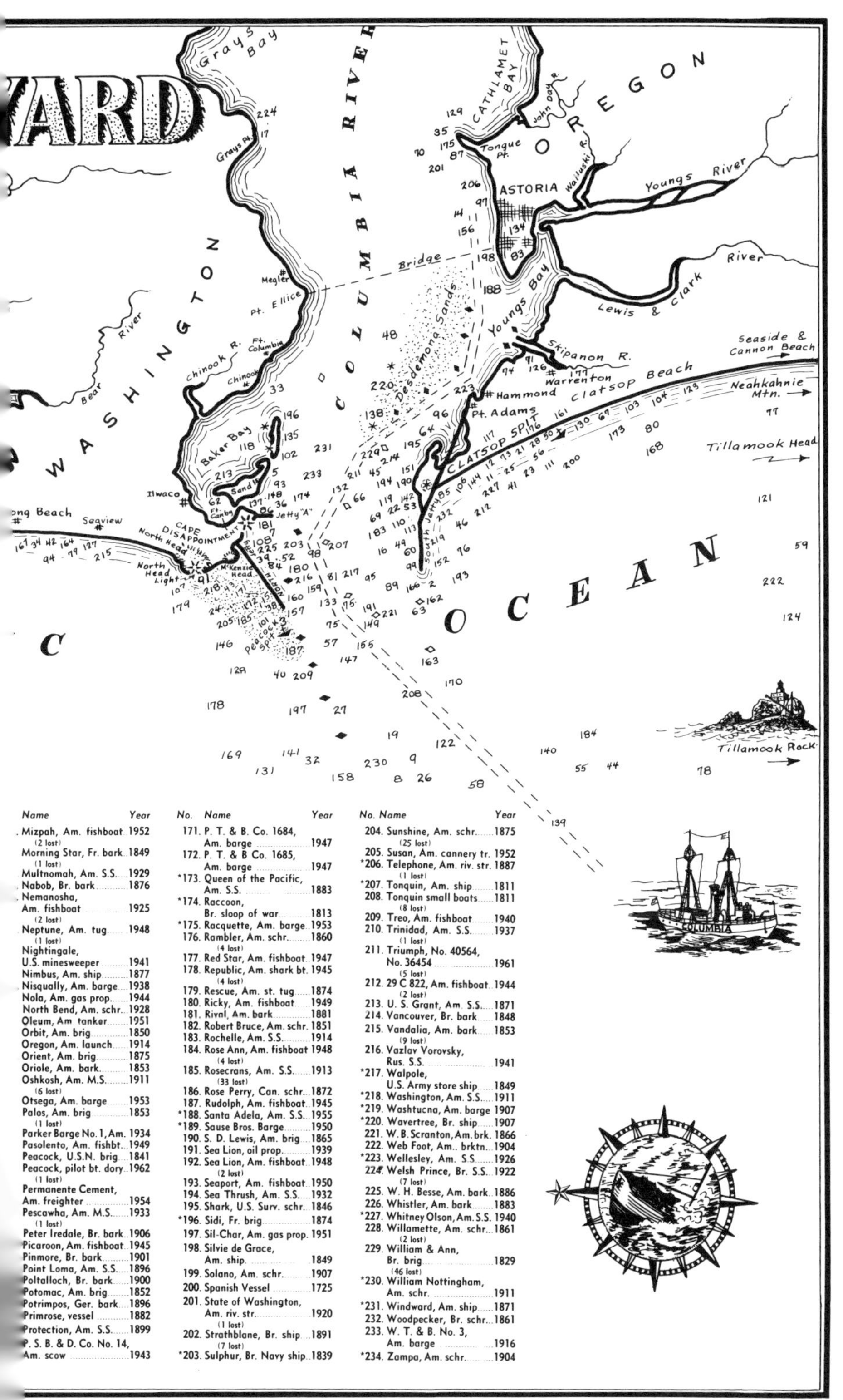

ARD
Grays Bay
Grays Pt.
COLUMBIA RIVER
CATHLAMET BAY
John Day R.
OREGON
Tongue Pt.
ASTORIA
Walluski R.
Youngs River
Lewis & Clark River
Bridge
Megler
Pt. Ellice
WASHINGTON
Bear River
Chinook R.
Ft. Columbia
Chinook
Desdemona Sands
Youngs Bay
Skipanon R.
Warrenton
Hammond
Pt. Adams
Clatsop Beach
Seaside & Cannon Beach
Neahkahnie Mtn.
Tillamook Head
CLATSOP SPIT
Baker Bay
Sand Is.
Ilwaco
Ft. Canby
Jetty "A"
Long Beach
Seaview
CAPE DISAPPOINTMENT
North Head
North Head Light
McKenzie Head
North Jetty
South Jetty
Peacock Spit
OCEAN
C
Tillamook Rock
COLUMBIA
Name Year
. Mizpah, Am. fishboat 1952
(2 lost)
Morning Star, Fr. bark 1849
(1 lost)
Multnomah, Am. S.S. 1929
. Nabob, Br. bark 1876
. Nemanosha,
Am. fishboat 1925
(2 lost)
Neptune, Am. tug 1948
(1 lost)
Nightingale,
U.S. minesweeper 1941
Nimbus, Am. ship 1877
Nisqually, Am. barge 1938
Nola, Am. gas prop. 1944
North Bend, Am. schr. 1928
Oleum, Am tanker 1951
Orbit, Am. brig 1850
Oregon, Am. launch 1914
Orient, Am. brig 1875
Oriole, Am. bark 1853
Oshkosh, Am. M.S. 1911
(6 lost)
Otsega, Am. barge 1953
Palos, Am. brig 1853
(1 lost)
Parker Barge No. 1, Am. 1934
Pasolento, Am. fishbt. 1949
Peacock, U.S.N. brig 1841
Peacock, pilot bt. dory 1962
(1 lost)
Permanente Cement,
Am. freighter 1954
Pescawha, Am. M.S. 1933
(1 lost)
Peter Iredale, Br. bark 1906
Picaroon, Am. fishboat 1945
Pinmore, Br. bark 1901
Point Loma, Am. S.S. 1896
Poltalloch, Br. bark 1900
Potomac, Am. brig 1852
Potrimpos, Ger. bark 1896
Primrose, vessel 1882
Protection, Am. S.S. 1899
P. S. B. & D. Co. No. 14,
Am. scow 1943
No. Name Year
171. P. T. & B. Co. 1684,
Am. barge 1947
172. P. T. & B Co. 1685,
Am. barge 1947
*173. Queen of the Pacific,
Am. S.S. 1883
*174. Raccoon,
Br. sloop of war 1813
*175. Racquette, Am. barge 1953
176. Rambler, Am. schr. 1860
(4 lost)
177. Red Star, Am. fishboat 1947
178. Republic, Am. shark bt. 1945
(4 lost)
179. Rescue, Am. st. tug 1874
180. Ricky, Am. fishboat 1949
181. Rival, Am. bark 1881
182. Robert Bruce, Am. schr. 1851
183. Rochelle, Am. S.S. 1914
184. Rose Ann, Am. fishboat 1948
(4 lost)
185. Rosecrans, Am. S.S. 1913
(33 lost)
186. Rose Perry, Can. schr. 1872
187. Rudolph, Am. fishboat 1945
*188. Santa Adela, Am. S.S. 1955
*189. Sause Bros. Barge 1950
190. S. D. Lewis, Am. brig 1865
191. Sea Lion, oil prop. 1939
192. Sea Lion, Am. fishboat 1948
(2 lost)
193. Seaport, Am. fishboat 1950
194. Sea Thrush, Am. S.S. 1932
195. Shark, U.S. Surv. schr. 1846
*196. Sidi, Fr. brig 1874
197. Sil-Char, Am. gas prop. 1951
198. Silvie de Grace,
Am. ship 1849
199. Solano, Am. schr. 1907
200. Spanish Vessel 1725
201. State of Washington,
Am. riv. str. 1920
(1 lost)
202. Strathblane, Br. ship 1891
(7 lost)
*203. Sulphur, Br. Navy ship 1839
No. Name Year
204. Sunshine, Am. schr. 1875
(25 lost)
205. Susan, Am. cannery tr. 1952
*206. Telephone, Am. riv. str. 1887
(1 lost)
*207. Tonquin, Am. ship 1811
208. Tonquin small boats 1811
(8 lost)
209. Treo, Am. fishboat 1940
210. Trinidad, Am. S.S. 1937
(1 lost)
211. Triumph, No. 40564,
No. 36454 1961
(5 lost)
212. 29 C 822, Am. fishboat 1944
(2 lost)
213. U. S. Grant, Am. S.S. 1871
214. Vancouver, Br. bark 1848
215. Vandalia, Am. bark 1853
(9 lost)
216. Vazlav Vorovsky,
Rus. S.S. 1941
*217. Walpole,
U.S. Army store ship 1849
*218. Washington, Am. S.S. 1911
*219. Washtucna, Am. barge 1907
*220. Wavertree, Br. ship 1907
221. W. B. Scranton, Am. brk. 1866
222. Web Foot, Am. brktn. 1904
*223. Wellesley, Am. S.S. 1926
224. Welsh Prince, Br. S.S. 1922
(7 lost)
225. W. H. Besse, Am. bark 1886
226. Whistler, Am. bark 1883
*227. Whitney Olson, Am. S.S. 1940
228. Willamette, Am. schr. 1861
(2 lost)
229. William & Ann,
Br. brig 1829
(46 lost)
*230. William Nottingham,
Am. schr. 1911
*231. Windward, Am. ship 1871
232. Woodpecker, Br. schr. 1861
233. W. T. & B. No. 3,
Am. barge 1916
*234. Zampa, Am. schr. 1904

BOOKS BY JAMES A. GIBBS

PACIFIC GRAVEYARD

Every great shipwreck in and around the waters of the Columbia River Bar, from early sailing ships to the present.

SHIPWRECKS OF THE PACIFIC COAST

Complete account of all known shipwrecks off the coasts of Washington, Oregon, and California.

SHIPWRECKS OFF JUAN DE FUCA

Stories of over 200 shipwrecks off Washington State's northwest tip—where the Strait of Juan de Fuca meets the Pacific Ocean.

SENTINELS OF THE NORTH PACIFIC

Histories of Pacific Coast lighthouses and lightships and the men who manned them—from Mexico to the Arctic.

TILLAMOOK LIGHT

Seasoned with salty drama and hilarious adventure, the complete history of "Terrible Tilly," the Tillamook Lighthouse.

CONTENTS

G. E. Plummer

French bark *Colonel de Villebois Mareuil* seems to rise from the rim of the world as she passes in from sea over the Columbia River bar, during one of her many crossings at the turn of the century.

CHAPTER 1

THE SHORE OF LOST SHIPS

Since 1792, when Captain Robert Gray sailed the *Columbia Rediviva* across its turbulent waters, mariners have battled the vagaries of the Columbia River bar. The currents over and about it have been the despair of seafarers. Those who work the bar are fully aware of the dangers, and though they curse its changeable personality, they have come to endure its nasty temper as a thing they must accept and outlast. Once proud vessels are now twisted and gnarled tombstones in this graveyard, a section without parallel in ship disaster.

A constant contention between the river and the ocean has built obstructions between them which man has tried to break down. Like the peacemaker, he has forced a truce between two unrelenting enemies; but he himself has been made to pay a costly price in lives and property.

The Pacific Ocean puts on her most striking show here at the mouth of the Columbia, and across this treacherous portal pass about twenty million gross tons of vessel traffic annually. Since the turn of the century, an estimated million craft of all types have negotiated the bar, voyaging to and from every sector of the globe.

During this period, man's continual fight to conquer the elements has limited the toll to about thirty major shipwrecks, approximately one-fourth as many as before.

The Great River

The Columbia is the largest river on the Pacific Coast of the United States. It has its source in Columbia Lake in British Columbia, and enters the United States in northeastern Washington. From there the river follows a curving course to the Oregon-Washington boundary, then travels generally westward between the two states, emptying into the Pacific Ocean about 548 miles north of the entrance to San Francisco Bay, and 145 miles south of the entrance to the Strait of Juan de Fuca—after having wound its swirling waters from the mountains to the sea over a distance of 1,214 miles.

This great river has an average flow ranging between 90,000 and 1,000,000 cubic feet per second and drains an area of around 259,000 square miles. About 220,000 square miles of this drainage area are in the United States and include most of Idaho, Oregon and Washington; all of Montana west of the Continental Divide; and small areas in northern Nevada, northern Utah, and western Wyoming.

From this huge drainage area—which is larger than all of France—the Columbia River through the ages has brought down to the bar both sand and silt. The tides of the Pacific meeting the river have built up deposits of sand covering a stretch of a hundred seacoast miles. To the south of the river entrance lies Clatsop Beach, which reaches to Tillamook Head, a

Joe Williamson

Thirty-five-mile winds from the Northwest were whipping the Columbia River bar into a frothy mass when Joe Williamson took this photo in 1961, aboard the tug *Agnes Foss*. The tug's fantail was completely awash, but she suffered no damage.

massive rock promontory. To the north spreads treacherous Peacock Spit, backed by the mighty bastion of Cape Disappointment, which is joined by North Head.

Farther north is a finger-shaped peninsula, one of the longest stretches of unbroken beach in the world—twenty-eight miles of sand indented only by Willapa bar at the northern extreme. Almost completely surrounded by water, the peninsula feels the constant roll of the ocean swell to the west, the hammering of the bars to the north and south, and the shoal waters of the bay to the east.

Such is a sketch of the shore of lost ships. Every conceivable aid to navigation has been employed in this area, and constant vigils are maintained.

Discovery and Exploration

Back of the Columbia River lies an exciting history. Rumor of such a river existed as early as 1570, when Ortelius (Abraham Oertel), a Flemish geographer, indicated such a waterway on his famous chart. Many early explorers guessed that the finding of this river would mean the discovery of the fabled Northwest Passage, the mythical Straits of Anian. Stories spread throughout Europe of great cities and riches on this river, but it evaded discovery.

The wealth of Spain for several centuries supported a powerful fleet of galleons that sailed the seven seas in quest of new lands and treasure. Those ships voyaged to the New World, filling their holds with precious cargo for the mother country. As long as rumors of the River of the West existed, Spain continued her expansion at Nueva Espana, sending exploration ships sailing up the North American Pacific coast.

The Spanish pilot, Martin d'Aguilar, as early as 1603, reported seeing an opening, or entrance, with the appearance of a great river near where the Columbia River actually is, but his records were vague. From this date there occurred a lapse of 172 years in the records of Spanish exploration along the Columbia's shores. The search continued, yet the existence of the river remained a mystery.

Then, on August 17, 1775, during his return trip of exploration along the Northwest Coast, Spanish explorer Bruno Heceta hove to, several miles off the entrance to the river. His was the first map of the Columbia River entrance. While there, he named the cape on the north side of the entrance, San Roque, the one on the south side, Frondoso; and the entrance itself, Assumption Bay. Heceta did not explore the bay, promising as it looked, because of illness among his crew. If the anchor were lowered, he reported, "we should not have men enough to get it up."

The British sea rovers came next. It was Lieutenant John Meares, who passed the fabled River of the West in 1788, in the ship, *Felice Adventurer,* after earlier charting Shoalwater (Willapa) Bay. Sailing near the coast on July 6, he named the indentation Deception Bay and changed Cape San Roque to Cape Disappointment—a title which expressed his chagrin at being unable to find an entrance.

Four years later, Captain George Vancouver sailed near Cape Disappointment. Though he sighted breakers, he attached little significance to them, heading on northward to explore the waters of Puget Sound.

Strange indeed that, with all the explorers who searched for the river, it was discovered almost accidentally by a Yankee, Captain Robert Gray, a fur trader in quest of furs for the China trade. Gray was first aware of the location while sailing southward from Vancouver Island in the early spring of 1792. As he was passing within sight of the coast in the vicinity of 46°10′ north, he noticed breakers which he concluded must mark the shallow entrance to a river. His ship, the 212-ton *Columbia Rediviva,* made several attempts to cross the bar but the outflowing current was too swift for entering. Gray then sailed for the

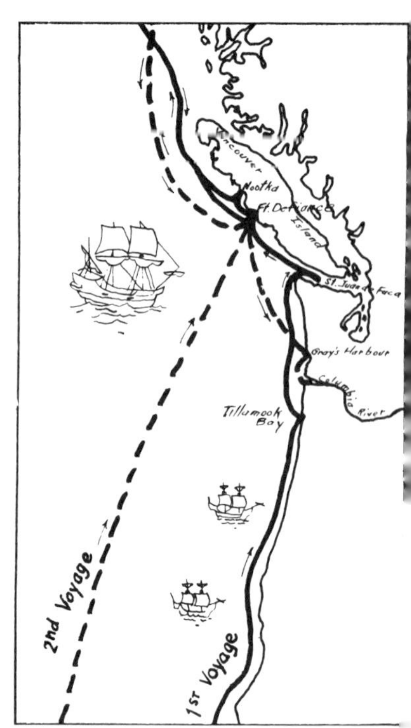

Captain Robert Gray, the shrewd Yankee mariner who discovered the Columbia River.

Gray's route during his second voyage, when he discovered the Great River of the West, on that historic spring morning: May 11, 1792.

Full rigged and 212 tons burden, Gray's famous ship, the *Columbia Rediviva*, gave the river its name.

Strait of Juan de Fuca, where he fell in company with Captain George Vancouver.

Gray and Vancouver exchanged information, but the Englishman refused to believe that an entrance to a river existed at the place where Gray had attempted a crossing.

Spurred by a greater determination to discover the river after his conversation with Vancouver, Gray again sailed southward.

On that historic voyage he discovered Bulfinch Harbor—now called Grays Harbor in his honor. Bearing still farther south, he approached Deception Bay, launching his pinnace to sound the bar depths. The *Columbia,* which drew six to eight feet of water, followed in the wake of the pinnace, threading her way into the mouth of the great river. It was Friday, May 11, 1792, when Gray proudly sailed along the north banks of the river opening, naming the north entrance Cape Hancock and the southern tip Point Adams. On the long-sought river he bestowed the name of his 83-foot command.

The American, Gray, out of Boston, had found the fabled River of the West, thereby opening it to maritime countries of the world and bringing another nation into the contest for possession of the Northwest Coast.

Upon learning of Gray's discovery, Vancouver dispatched Lieutenant William Broughton to survey the channels of the river in the armed tender *Chatham,* which was accompanying Vancouver's flagship *Discovery.* On October 21 of that same year 1792, the *Chatham* entered the river, but stranded on what is now part of Peacock Spit. Refloated with the flood tide, she continued her voyage, anchoring inside the mouth of the river.

There Broughton found James Baker, captain of the British brig *Jenny*, of Bristol, England. Vancouver reported hearing, from behind Cape Disappointment, the salute fired by the *Jenny* and the answering gun of the *Chatham*, and seeing the hoisting of the *Chatham's* colors. From this he "concluded some vessel was there at anchor."

Both vessels left the Columbia, November 10, the *Jenny* leading the way out over the bar. Baker's familiarity with the entrance indicated that he had been

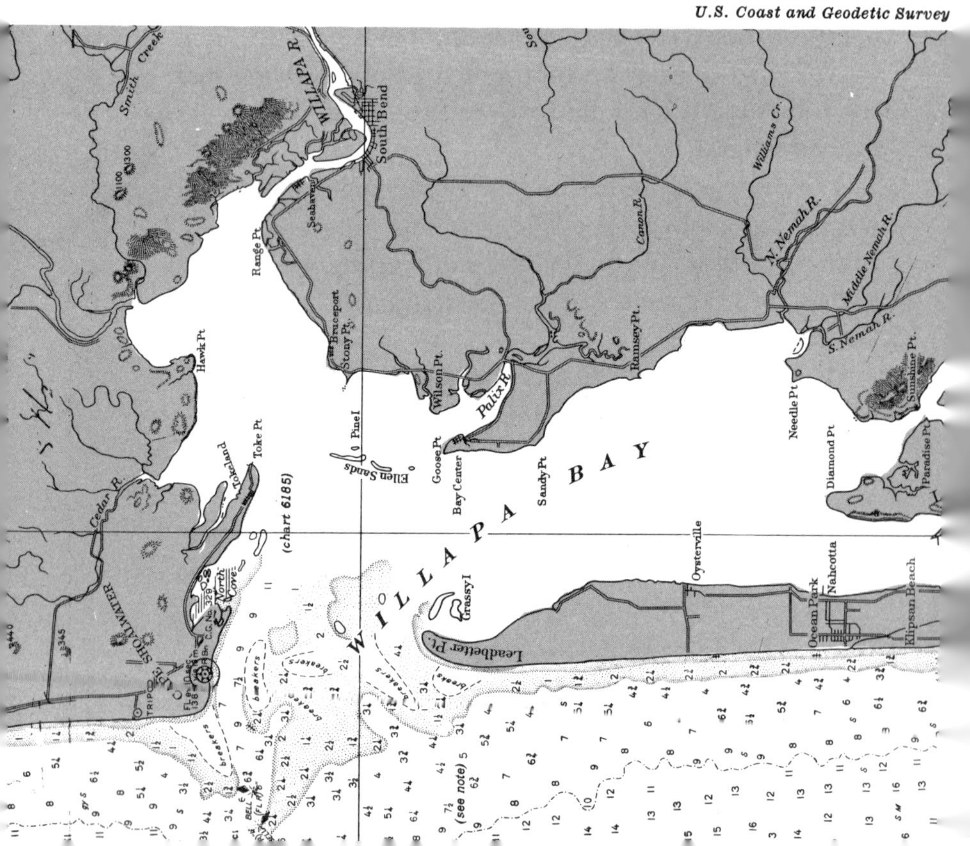

Thirty miles north of the Columbia River entrance is Willapa bar, with low, sandy Leadbetter point to the south, and the bluff of Cape Shoalwater to the north.

U.S. Coast and Geodetic Survey

there earlier that year. Probably he, like Vancouver, had heard from Gray about the river, and was checking out its fur-trade possibilities. Captain Baker, the second to enter the Columbia, received his share of glory by having the large bay at the north side of the river named in his honor.

So a Boston trader dispelled the legend and supposition that had grown up around the Columbia for almost two and a quarter centuries. Where Heceta failed because of illness, and Meares and Vancouver because of doubt, an observant Yankee captain succeeded. Gray opened a river second only to the Mississippi in volume, navigable for several hundred miles, and the only major fresh water harbor on the Pacific Coast. He also laid the cornerstone for the Pacific Graveyard.

Willapa (Shoalwater) Bay

Though not accorded as great a place in history as the entrance to the Columbia, Willapa Harbor has also played a prominent role in the maritime history of the Pacific Northwest. From its waters were picked the world-famous Willapa oysters, which long thrived in the muddy sands that fill the lengthy bay—picturesque to view at high tide and equally as ugly on the ebb. Now these sands are seeded with Japanese oysters.

Land was first settled in the Willapa Bay area in 1845. Fifty-seven years earlier, Lieutenant John Meares, sailing in the ship *Felice Adventurer,* discovered the entrance, but found it so guarded by heavy surf as not to warrant passage across the bar. Willapa Bay was originally named Shoalwater Bay, and was known as such until after the turn of the century.

In the U. S. Surveys of 1852 and 1855, under James Alden, two channels were reported, separated by a middle ground, much like the early entrance to the Columbia. By 1868, the south channel had filled, but there are now again two channels. The entrance to the south is marked by Leadbetter Point; the one to the north by Cape Shoalwater.

The south channel is undependable and charts warn mariners to take every precaution if using this channel. Warning is also given that the shoals of the bar change at frequent intervals, necessitating a constant adjustment of channel markers. Even in 1855, all shipmasters were warned to stay clear of the area, without the aid of a pilot, for the bay, as its name implied, was full of shoals, and at low tide about one half of the area was laid bare. Low water on the bay brought swift currents and dangerous eddies.

Coastguardmen shoot a line to the stranded trawler *Ray* on North Beach Peninsula, August 31, 1938. The vessel was refloated.

Ellis Photo

Flowing into the bay is the Willapa River, a lazy waterway on which the lumber towns of Raymond and South Bend are located. Across the bay on the lee side of the peninsula nestles the settlement of Oysterville, founded in 1854. That pioneer village, one of the oldest in the area, served as the county seat of Pacific County until the mushroom town of South Bend took over the honors in 1892. The rival community, pointing to promised railroad connections, swung the vote for the county seat, but Oysterville residents protested the ballot, claiming that railroad workers voted illegally. Finally the South Benders invaded Oysterville and walked off with the legal records.

Though no jetties have been constructed at the bar, dredging operations are carried on, and the controlling depths range between twenty-two and twenty-five feet. In 1950, funds were granted for dredging the Willapa Channel to a project depth of twenty-six feet. So far, more than $2.5 million has been spent on the maintenance and dredging of the bar, bay, and channels. The annual commerce on the bay was around 400,000 tons of shipping and rafting, not enough to warrant construction of jetties. It was once estimated that they would cost well in excess of $50 million.

Not the sand, but erosion by the sea has become the greatest cause of concern down through the years. More than 1,500 acres of sand have been swallowed by the sea since 1890. Erosion finally toppled the old Willapa Lighthouse in 1941. On many occasions, following heavy storms, the keepers would put the shovel to use, as if the sand were snow. Just in the past

U. S. Coast Guard

Willapa Bay Light Station in Washington shows two lights. The shorter tower, proving too low and threatened by erosion, a higher one was built at right.

decade, erosion at the north portal of the Willapa entrance has claimed many acres of land. The problem of erosion is even greater in the Tokeland area.

Government dredges continue to have all they can do to control the depths on Willapa Bar. However, in recent years the unprecedented shifting of sand and shoals prompted an end to all deepsea cargo vessel transit across the bar. Where once large lumber ships entered the river with impunity, without jetties the once flourishing ports of Raymond and South Bend have changed their images. Though the oyster industry flourishes on the bay and a small fleet of commercial fishing vessels still put to sea from the Willapa, all lumber and logs are shipped to other ports, mainly Grays Harbor, for overseas shipment.

CHAPTER 2

SAVING SHIPS—AND LIVES

Along the shores of the Pacific Graveyard, there are many safety factors to aid the mariner. These include lifesaving, lookout, lighthouse, and lifeboat stations, and especially buoyage. It has been a long and arduous task to establish the many navigation aids that exist in the area today.

Coastguardmen prepare a buoy for action, aboard the buoy tender, *Fir*, during World War II.
U. S. Coast Guard

Before the turn of the century, the lifesaving crews played a major role along these stretches. During the summer months, fair ladies flocked to the seashore to watch rugged men stage daring sham rescues; but when the storms of winter returned, the scene became stark reality.

The initial lifesaving station at the mouth of the Columbia was established at Fort Canby in 1878, although a lookout had been maintained at Cape Disappointment since the building of the light tower in 1856. When wrecks along the North Beach Peninsula increased in number, the Ilwaco Lifesaving Station was erected at Klipsan Beach in 1892. Technically speaking, the initial lifesaving station organized in the Pacific Northwest was the North Cove station, erected at the north entrance to Shoalwater Bay, in 1877.

Buoyage

Half of all the aids to navigation along the Pacific shores float on the water—shackled to the bottom by anchors and concrete. These buoys dot coastal waters and tortuous channels in critical positions where fixed lights and foghorns would be impractical, or impossible to erect. Buoyage on the North Pacific came into prominence after the middle of the nineteenth century when iron can buoys were established between the Columbia River bar and Astoria. William P. McArthur, in charge of the survey schooner, *Ewing,* in his 1850 report concerning the initial buoys at the Columbia bar, stated that the correct placing of five buoys of the iron can variety was to proceed, and that they were

U. S. Coast Guard

Coastguardmen install a battery in a huge buoy as the *Fir* stands by.

to be made at the direction of the bar pilots when changes in the channel occurred.

Because the currents are strong and treacherous at the mouth of the Columbia, much trouble was experienced in the early years with buoys slipping their

U. S. Coast Guard

The ingenious breeches buoy carries a shipwreck survivor safely shoreward. This famous rescue device has been used many times in the Pacific Graveyard.

moorings. Storms and heavy seas were just as great a hazard in keeping the buoys on station. There was the remarkable drift of the runaway buoy No. 1, which parted its moorings at the Columbia bar in a gale, January 1889. The buoy was next sighted in late June in Shelikof Strait, between Kodiak and the Alaska Peninsula, nearly 2,000 miles away. Then, after drifting 15 miles farther, it was picked up by the steamer *Al-ki,* near the mouth of the Karluk River.

As the mariner is guided by lighted buoys at night, so is he guided in fog by buoy bells, chimes, horns or whistles. The silent, fog-ridden sea becomes alive with voices, sweet and raucous, when a ship nears danger spots and harbor entrances. The primary function of the buoy is to warn the seaman of some impending danger, some obstruction or change in contours of the sea bottom, and to outline the channels leading to various points.

The Coast Guard—the organization now in charge of the lifesaving stations along the coasts of the United States—solved one lifesaving problem with their ingenious breeches buoy. This is a pair of short-legged, canvas breeches suspended from a belt-like life buoy. This contrivance, enclosing the person to be rescued, is hung from short ropes by a block which runs from a hawser stretched from the ship to the shore, and is drawn to land by hauling lines. It was the method for landing and leaving old Tillamook Rock. Occasionally elite passengers rated a basket instead of the breeches. Many times this age-old means of survival was used on the Pacific Graveyard.

Columbia River Lightship

In place of the *Columbia River Lightship*, a revolutionary super buoy was placed off the entrance to the Columbia River on October 29, 1979. Officially labled Columbia River Approach Lighted Horn Buoy CR(LNB), it it self-contained with automatic light, foghorn, radar reflector and puts out a continuous radio signal. As of that date the Coast Guard lightship *No. 604* was officially retired and eventually became a living memorial to the past in the possession of the Columbia River Maritime Museum at Astoria.

U. S. Coast Guard

Columbia Lightship **standing guard at the river entrance before being retired—guiding light, fog signal, and radio beacon to ships crossing the temperamental Columbia bar.**

It is open to the public and is kept in operating condition, after three decades of service at the river entrance. She was the last lightship to see duty on the Pacific Coast.

The *Columbia River Lightship* was very much a factor in the safe conduct of river traffic. She cost $500,000 and was completed in 1950 at East Boothbay, Maine. She replaced the 40-year old *Columbia Lightship.*

Since its establishment in 1892, four lightships have held the station: *Nos. 50, 88, 93,* and *604*.

Pilot Schooner *Columbia*

The old pilot schooner *Columbia* was retired several years ago after having made more than 40,000 crossings of the bar. She had been the official pilot boat since 1924. A staunch wooden hull, tested in the ice packs of the frozen north in her early history, made her an ideal ship for her duties.

Bar pilots now maintain two vessels to carry Columbia bar pilots to and from deep-water ships; both are based at Astoria. One of these, a new steel boat,

Latest Columbia River bar pilot boat, *Columbia*, is a staunch steel craft which can take the roughest weather the bar can dish out. Built in Portland in 1958, she replaced the old pilot boat *Columbia*.

is also called the *Columbia.* The other is a converted minesweeper named the *Peacock.* One of these is on alert near the lightship when a ship requiring a pilot is due.

Crossing the Bar

Many a captain, facing the dread entrance to the Columbia, would likely endorse a change of Alfred Tennyson's famous lines to: "I hope to see my pilot face to face *before* I cross the bar."

It was during the Gold Rush that the Columbia bar earned its title—Graveyard of the Pacific. Portland was the nearest place for San Francisco to obtain supplies, and impatient captains often took reckless chances when crossing the river's surly mouth. In 1849 alone there were four major wrecks: the *Aurora,* the *Morning Star,* the *Sylvia de Grasse,* and the *Josephine.* In 1852, five ships were destroyed on the bar: the *Dolphin,* the *General Warren,* the *Machigone,* the *Marie,* and the *Potomac.*

Wrecks became rarer with growing knowledge of the bar and with the establishment of pilot and tugboat services. The first successful bar pilot association was begun by Captain George Flavel, who came west with the Gold Rush in 1849 and made his way to the Oregon Country the following year. Flavel was given one of the first licenses ever issued to a Columbia River pilot by the State.

For almost twenty years, Flavel and his nervy pilots enjoyed a near monopoly of the towage and pilotage into the Columbia. His rates were high, but his service was excellent—and he never sent a man where he himself would not go. His Victorian mansion — from whose lofty cupola he once scanned the sea's horizon — is now the home of the Clatsop County Historical Society.

Near the turn of the century there was suddenly an amazing recurrence of wrecks. Some nautical cynics surmise that this was a way of collecting insurance on hard-pressed sailing ships in the steam age. Besides, at ebb tide, the crew could walk from a ship grounded on certain graveyard beaches.

Seen here crossing a bar in a big swell on the Oregon Coast is one of the latest Coast Guard motor lifeboats, the type now used on the Columbia River bar.

U. S. Coast Guard

Though pilots have been engaged in the transit of ships across the bar for well over a century, it was during the 1920s that the Columbia River Bar Pilots Association at Astoria was started. Qualifications for membership consist of two years as master of an ocean-going vessel and considerable experience in the immediate area. In addition, members are required to maintain the same federal and state licenses required to master deep-sea vessels. In short, the bar pilots are top men in their field. They have to be.

Prior to modern dredging procedures, large ships crossed the bar by following smaller craft which took constant soundings. Later, in the 1880s, the depths were controlled by using two boats to drag a great chain across the channel—a far cry from the huge hopper dredges which now keep the channel crossing at a 48-foot mean at zero tide.

Even now, despite modern dredging methods, piloting can sometimes be a tricky business. To the layman it might seem rather simple, but during winter months a pilot boat takes the pilot out to the lightship area, within a distance of 300 feet from the incoming ocean-going vessel. The pilot is then transferred by a smaller boat to the ship. After boarding, he guides the vessel across the bar to Astoria, or vice versa—a distance of seventeen nautical miles. At Astoria, a Columbia River pilot takes over the chores for the trip upriver.

Giant swells where the river and the ocean meet are also enemies of the pilots. Frequently these swells are from eighteen to twenty-five feet high. Older pilots tell of some exceeding fifty feet. In 1962, Captain Edgar A. Quinn, president of the bar pilots, was in a boat that capsized in rough seas while returning to the pilot boat *Peacock*. Rain squalls had set in with around seventy-mile-an-hour winds. Captain Quinn and two seamen spent seventeen hours drifting at sea, ending up at Grays Harbor, some forty miles away. One of the seamen died of exposure.

Light Stations

Of the six light stations that were established at or near the mouth of the Columbia, three have been abandoned: the ones at Point Adams, Tillamook Rock, and Desdemona Sands. Though automated,

High-powered 52-foot motor lifeboat on duty at the Columbia River bar. This vessel replaced the lifeboat *Triumph*, lost January 12, 1961.

the Cape Disappointment, North Head and Willapa Bay lighthouses are still active.

The original Willapa Bay Lighthouse, built in 1858, now lies under several fathoms of sea water. The present beacon has been moved several times. Erosion has torn asunder summer homes and other buildings. Even the old Coast Guard station has been abandoned. Appeals to the government have not helped, as surveys show that alleviation of the problem would require the expenditure of millions of dollars; and the population of the area has never warranted such an outlay.

Urgent appeals for a lighthouse on Cape Disappointment—which lifts its rugged height above the north portal of the river mouth—received attention from the government in 1853. No place on the Pacific Coast needed a beacon more urgently than did the mouth of the Columbia. Plans were drawn for a high conical tower to stand 220 feet above the water as a permanent aid to navigation.

When the funds were approved for the project, a ship was dispatched to carry building materials for the construction of the new lighthouse. The American bark *Oriole*—Captain Lewis Lentz, master—arrived off the mouth of the river, September 18, 1853.

The following day at dawn, the vessel, then twenty-two days out of San Francisco, stood in for the crossing The pilot boat came alongside, and Pilot Flavel took command of the bark. Along about noon a southwest breeze arose, causing the vessel to make slow headway; but two hours later the wind subsided and

This battery of muzzle-loading cannon at Fort Canby protected Columbia River ports from Confederate privateers in Civil War times. Cape Disappointment Lighthouse in the background appears today much as it did a century ago.

she dragged across the channel, striking the south sands in seventeen feet of water. The outgoing tide carried her seaward, banging her against the sand continually. The rudder was dislodged. Water poured through her seams. The heavy machinery and construction material she carried caused her to settle deeper. Eventually the pumps became choked, and the ship had to be abandoned.

The pilot took charge because of his familiarity with

bar conditions. The lifeboats were chained together and drifted throughout the night, as the survivors tried in vain to keep warm. In all, they contained thirty-two persons, many of whom were lighthouse construction men. Lentz had been the last to leave his ship, and none too soon; for, fifteen minutes after he had scrambled into the boat, the *Oriole* drifted off the spit, turned over on her beam ends, filled and sank in six fathoms. Only a massive whirlpool was left on the bar.

It was a happy group, when the pilot schooner *California* hove in sight the following morning to rescue the *Oriole's* survivors. Pilot Flavel had earned the gratitude of Captain Lentz for his masterful skill in safeguarding the boats throughout the night.

But the building materials were a total loss, making lighthouse construction face further delay.

* * *

Cape Disappointment Lighthouse was finally completed in 1856, to become one of the first permanent fixtures of its kind in the Pacific Northwest. It has been in constant service to the present year. The light stands 220 feet above the water and shines twenty-one miles to sea, with a beam of 700,000 candlepower on the white flash and 160,000 candlepower on the red flash. A radiobeacon is at the station.

Point Adams Lighthouse, now nonexistent, was established in 1875 at the tip of Point Adams—the south entrance to the Columbia River, but was abandoned after completion of the south jetty. Construction of the jetty resulted in the heaping of acres of sand where once the ocean had reached. The lighthouse was later ordered burned by the government.

Next-door neighbor to Cape Disappointment Lighthouse is the powerful North Head beacon, established after a rash of shipwrecks along North Beach Peninsula. The light is now automatic.

A Coast Guard station is operated on the eastern side of the point at Hammond.

Heavy loss of life and property in the Pacific Graveyard prompted the building of one of the finest lighthouses on the Pacific Coast, in 1898. Constructed on North Head, this picturesque conical tower still stands beaming out across the Pacific from an elevation of 194 feet. The light is visible for twenty miles at sea and operates with a beam of 3.5 million candlepower.

As neighboring light stations, Cape Disappointment and North Head are a scant two miles apart. They are perhaps closer together than any other primary seacoast lights on the Pacific. North Head is also known as the windiest station on the coast. Geographically speaking, it is on the extreme knob of Cape Disappointment. The mounting number of wrecks along the peninsula in the latter nineteenth century, and the limited visibility of Disappointment Light to vessels approaching from the north, were chief factors in the establishment of the North Head Light Station.

One of the most powerful beacons on the entire Pacific Coast, North Head became automatic in 1961.

The Terrible Tillamook

The most fabulous of all the lighthouses in the Pacific Graveyard is the now-abandoned Tillamook Rock Light, located a mile and a half offshore from Tillamook Head. To construct this bastion, the top of the rock had to be dynamited to hollow a hole for its foundation. Completed in 1881, and abandoned in 1957, Tillamook Light has a story that reads like fiction. Situated several miles south of the river en-

U. S. Coast Guard

Tillamook Rock Light Station at the south end of the Graveyard appears peaceful in this 1934 photograph, a few weeks after a raging gale sent seas barreling over the rock, to tear out all landing gear and do $12,000 in damage to the lighthouse.

trance, its primary purpose was to warn ships seeking entrance to the Columbia.

The Terrible Tillamook, as it was sometimes called, was a thorn in the side of the Coast Guard for many years. Cut off by its inaccessibility during many months of the year, it was one of the costliest stations to maintain in the Pacific. All personnel and supplies were landed by a derrick boom equipped to handle a breeches buoy or a cargo net. The writer, during his stint on the Rock, became familiar with that wild ride over turbulent waters to the bleak crag of Tillamook.

The beacon once glowed from 134 feet above the ocean surface with 75,000 candlepower. In 1948, lack of Coast Guard funds almost forced closure of the station, but an urgent appeal by commercial fishermen kept the historic light in operation nine more years.

Where once the light at Tillamook was directly in the course of ships approaching the river, it is now well out of the steamer lanes. Ships today set their courses with the radio beacon on the Columbia Lightship anchored well off the river entrance. Where many decades ago ships skirted the sand at the south entrance of the Columbia, now long jetties have consolidated the opening into one deep channel. Large ships keep well away from the Rock with its sheer walls on all sides. No craft, regardless of size, can get within fifty feet of it without risking destruction.

A modern radar-equipped ocean buoy has replaced the Terrible Tillamook—landfall light to mariners for more than three quarters of a century.

CHAPTER 3

CONQUERING THE BAR

One of the most difficult ocean bar problems ever attacked by engineers has been that of maintaining a channel at the entrance of the Columbia River. Its scope and the difficulties in securing accurate data for engineering computations are widely known.

The first official survey of bar conditions was made by an Englishman, Sir Edward Belcher, in the H.M.S. *Sulphur,* on his visit to the river in 1839. His findings showed some remarkable differences from Vancouver's chart in 1792. Whereas Vancouver's chart showed only one navigable entrance, the northern—Belcher's indicated two, northern and southern.

The first official American survey of the river awaited the arrival of Lieutenant Charles Wilkes of the United States Navy, in 1841. Among the findings of the Wilkes Expedition was the continual movement of the sands around the mouth of the river, which constantly changed the channel depths and river entrance. This discovery revealed why it was so difficult to make accurate navigation charts of the bar.

The Wilkes mission suffered a setback when the USS *Peacock,* a unit of the squadron, was carried onto the north spit of the river entrance and totally wrecked. Peacock Spit, named for this early wreck, claimed

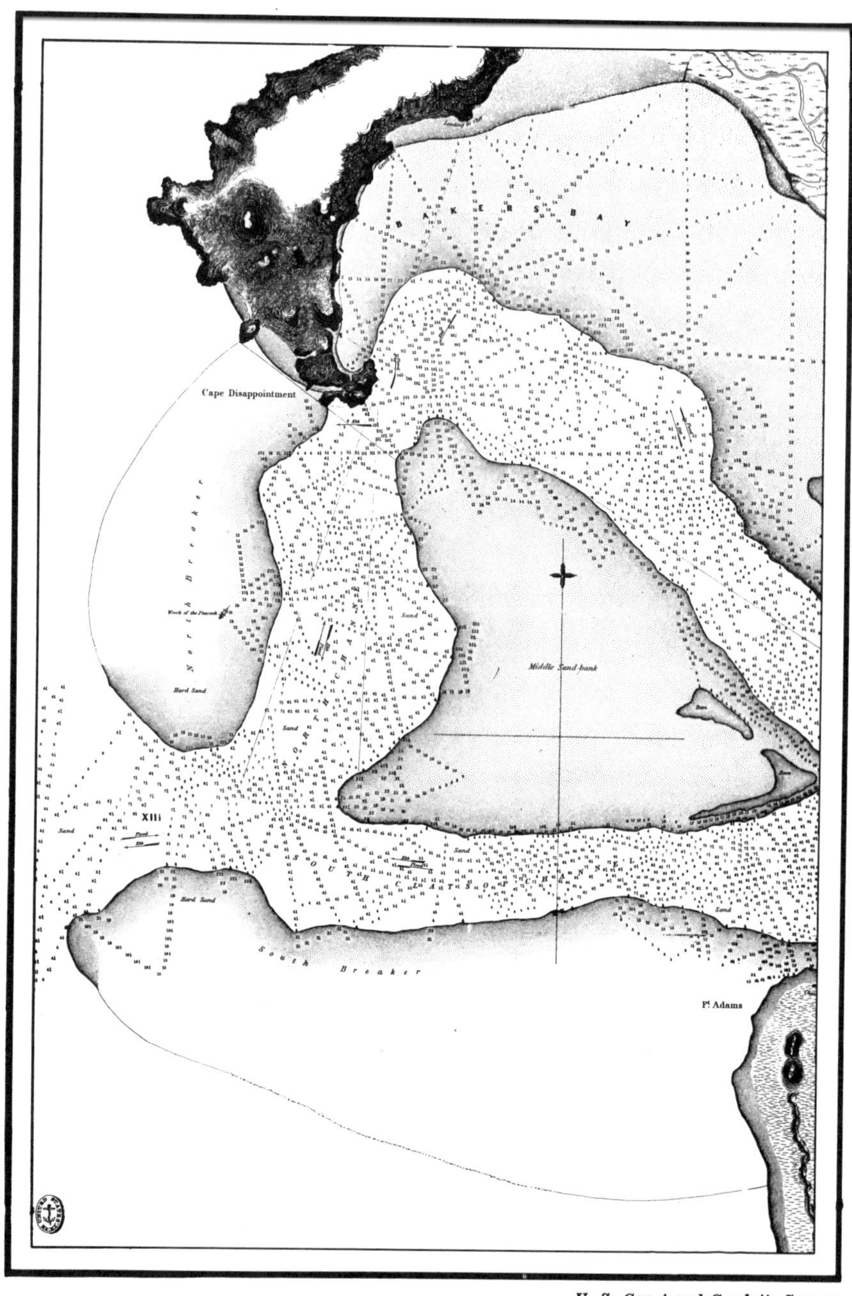

U. S. Coast and Geodetic Survey

Lt. Wilkes' 1841 chart of the entrance to the Columbia, based on the first official American survey of the river.

numerous ships in the years that followed—and left Lieutenant Wilkes less than enthusiastic about the potentialities of the Great River of the West. In his report, published in 1845, he commented:

". . . I found breakers extending from Cape Disappointment to Point Adams, in one unbroken line.

"I am at a loss to conceive how any doubt should ever have existed, that here was the mouth of the mighty river, whose existence was reported so long before the actual place of its discharge was known, or how the inquiring mind and talent of observation of Vancouver could have allowed him to hesitate, when he must have seen the evidence of a powerful flood of fresh water contending with the tides of the ocean, in a bar turbulent with breakers, in turbid waters extending several miles beyond the line of the shore, and in the marked line of separation between the sea and river water. . . .

"Mere description can give little idea of the terrors of the bar of the Columbia: all who have seen it have spoken of the wildness of the scene, and the incessant roar of the waters, representing it as one of the most fearful sights that can possibly meet the eye of the sailor."

The first examination of the Columbia River for the United States Coast Survey, completed in 1850 by Lieutenant-Commander William P. McArthur, U. S. N., showed that the north channel had altered considerably and was unsafe except for small vessels. Surveys of the Columbia in 1868 by the U. S. Coast Survey, and in 1876, by the U. S. Corps of Engineers, led to one conclusion: the need of a jetty as a permanent structure to keep the channel deep and stationary. Records over the years proved that there had been a continuous change in the channels caused by the ever-shifting sands.

After repeated petitions by Oregon citizens, the sum of $100,000 for a south jetty was finally appropriated in July 1884, through the Rivers and Harbors Bill. Considering that the actual bar area, when improvement work first began, was approximately six miles by six miles, the task undertaken was sizable. Violence of the storm forces, the tremendous volume of fresh water discharge, and the strength and variations of littoral currents reveal what the engineer had to cope with when he undertook to confine and control the river discharge and tidal flow.

The South Jetty

The year 1885 was a memorable one on the lower Columbia, for in April of that year construction got under way on the south jetty. Unfortunately, the initial appropriation little more than got the work started. Only a thousand feet of jetty was laid before funds were exhausted. Many more tons of rock would be needed to harness several unreliable channels into one safe passage.

More pressure was brought to bear on the government, and in September 1886, $187,500 in additional funds was expended for the project. This money was used to its best advantage, but the jetty was less than half completed when again the funds ran out. The boulder-mound jetty had taken shape, however, and the government now began to see its potentialities and

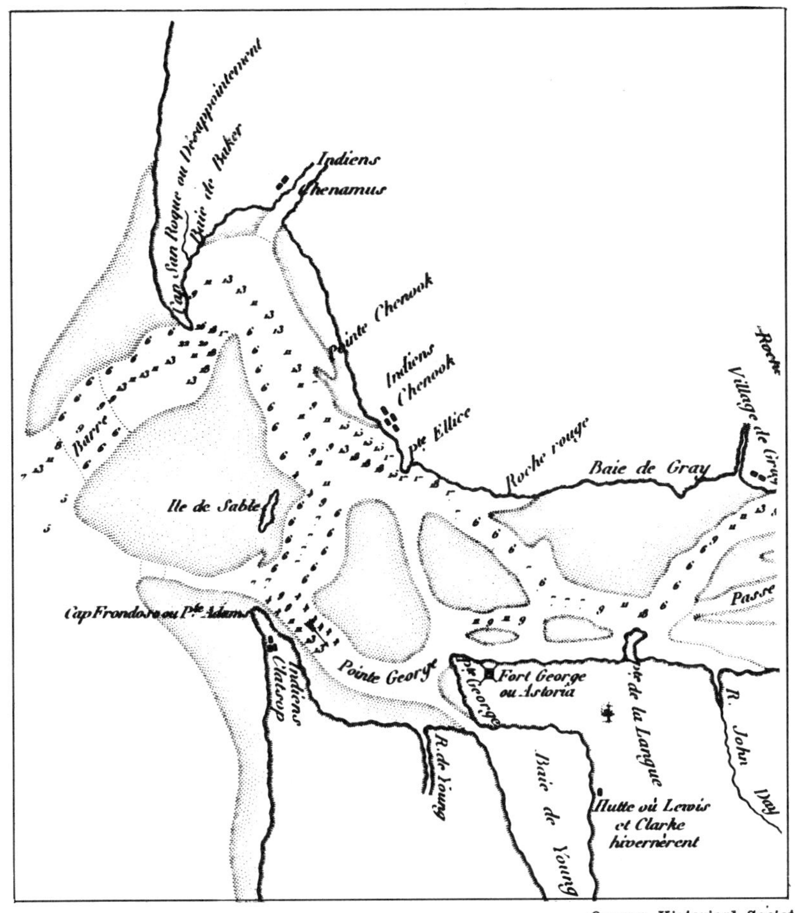

Oregon Historical Society

Chart of the river entrance in 1840, from Eugene Duflot de Mofras' "Carte du Rio Columbia," published in the atlas to his Pacific Coast travels, Paris, 1844.

to realize the necessity of the undertaking. The result was the long-awaited decision to allot $500,000 more for the project, with additional amounts to be allocated until the job was finished.

In 1888—when the engineers got the green light to resume work—the entrance to the Columbia River was five miles wide between the nearest parts of Cape Disappointment and Point Adams; but the passage was greatly obstructed by shifting shoals which extended in a curve between the entrance points. The north channel had shoaled to a depth of seventeen feet. Sailing vessels could not beat into the south channel against the summer winds blowing from the northwest, yet almost invariably could make the outward passage under similar conditions. Heavily-laden vessels used the north channel. Danger lurked everywhere.

At that early date it was recorded that once a mail steamer tried for sixty hours to find the smallest show of an opening to get across the bar when heavy weather broke from the Cape to Point Adams. Sailing vessels sometimes waited as long as six weeks offshore for safe bar transit conditions.

The summer of 1888 became a beehive of activity on the lower river as construction work on the south jetty was resumed. First, a large receiving dock was constructed near Fort Stevens; then came the rolling stock of five steam locomotives and sixty-five railroad dump cars. The sternwheeler steamer *Cascades* was assigned the job of towing the barges between the upriver quarry and Astoria. The tug *George H. Mendell* was engaged to continue the tow to Fort Stevens—where the rock was discharged, reloaded on the gondolas, then pulled by locomotives on the trestle that extended over the jetty.

Log rafts arrived in large numbers for use in fortifying the trestle. Men from all walks of life were employed in the massive undertaking; and to accommo-

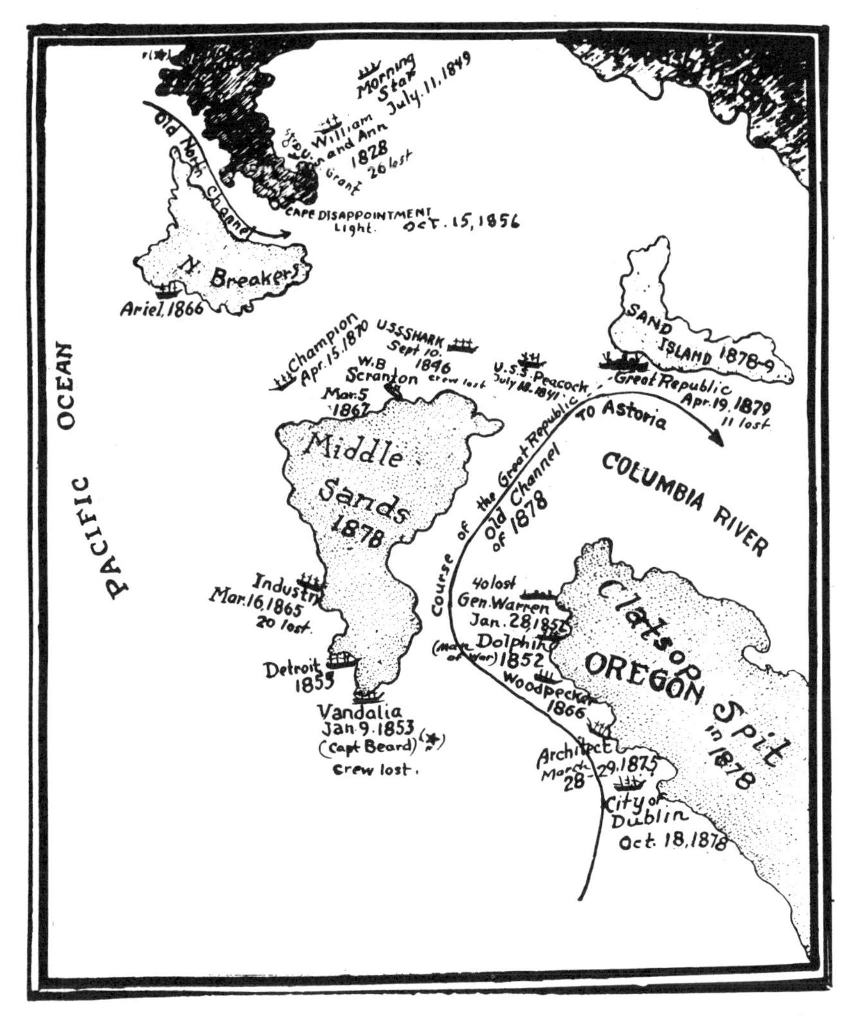

Survey of the Columbia River entrance in 1878-1879, by Captain G. M. Jessen, bar pilot, showing early shipwrecks and sand obstructions prior to the jetties. Redrawn by Charles Fitzpatrick.

date them, a fleet of mosquito launches was employed to carry workers to and from the job.

The estimated cost of the jetty was set by government officials at $3,800,000; but when the jetty was completed, the total expenditure was only $2,025,000.

It was one of the largest government projects of its kind in the United States at that period.

The jetty was nearly five miles long, and the entrance channels were dissolved into one deep passage when the last of the workers put away their tools in 1894—ten years after the first appropriation for the jetty was passed. Twenty-nine hundred acres of surf became dry sand, and the channel deepened to thirty and thirty-five feet at low water. In later years, additions were made to the south jetty; by 1914, it was nearly seven miles long.

Behind every great project are careful plans, and credit for construction of the south jetty fell to G. B. Hegardt, superintendent; J. M. Stoneman, manager; and E. M. Philabaum, chief clerk.

The jetty accomplished its purpose: the treacherous middle sands gradually disappeared, and the river entrance became more stabilized. Where the controlling depths once varied between twenty and twenty-five feet, the river opening deepened considerably. With these improving conditions though, another serious obstacle arose. As the south channel deepened, the sands piled up on the north side of the river entrance. Realizing the necessity of a north jetty, the government gave consideration to this new project.

The North Jetty

Appropriations were finally allotted, and the U. S. Army Engineers contracted with Kern and Company (Columbia Contract Company) of Portland, to build the north jetty, between 1913 and 1916. Construction actually began in 1914.

The rock was barged in, taken by steam engine over a trestle, then gradually dumped to form the jetty. Many of the boulders weighed over 50 tons. This north jetty ran more than two miles toward the open Pacific, splitting dreaded Peacock Spit. The channel entrance was soon reduced to a width of about 2,000 feet, and it steadily deepened until it afforded a splendid bar entrance.

Victory in the long battle against the elements at last appeared near.

Columbia River commerce officials were jubilant in the year 1925, when the annual bar survey made by the U. S. Army Corps of Engineers showed that, in all parts of the channel, the depth of water at the entrance to the river had deepened a minimum of one foot over the previous surveys and that the main ship channel

Grace Kern

Sternwheeler *Hercules* with barges loaded to supply the Jetty Rock Train, during construction of the Columbia's north jetty, 1914-1915.

had widened 800 feet during the year. The entrance to the river was then pronounced by the Engineers, "Eminently safe and easy of navigation." The outcome of the survey was music to the ears of merchants and shippers, but the Pacific Graveyard was yet to claim other victims.

Though the Columbia bar maintained its project depth of forty feet for two decades, the channel did not deepen to as great a depth as was originally predicted. It had been surmised that, of its own accord, the bar would deepen to fifty feet after the completion of the north jetty, but such was not the case. Annual expenditures have been necessary to keep the big Army Engineers' dredges working on the bar depths.

Deepening the Channel

A decade ago, the status of the bar was reflected in a plea from the Columbia Bar Pilots' Association. They requested that the entrance channel be dredged to a depth of forty-eight feet, complaining that it was sometimes impossible to take deep-drafted vessels over the bar in rough water without the danger of scraping bottom. On one occasion, a tanker scraped bottom while crossing the bar, puncturing some of her hull plates, thus allowing oil to filter into the river all the way to Portland. The action went unnoticed until oil had done irreparable damage along the river banks.

A bill was passed in 1953 to dredge the bar to forty-eight feet, involving an outlay of some $8.5 million. The work has since been carried out, the Army Engi-

Grace Kern

Jetty Rock Train leaving the terminal yards.

Grace Kern

The rock-laden train heads out over the "big bend."

U. S. Corps of Engineers

Huge miracle dredger *General John Biddle* is a frequent sight at the river's mouth, clearing away the always returning sands in the eternal struggle to maintain bar depths.

neers having employed one of their largest and finest dredges, the *General John Biddle,* to handle the bulk of the work. This $4.5 million dredge of the hopper type, with its twin 3,000-horsepower engines, is nothing short of a miracle dredger.

The Columbia Bar Today

The depths of the Columbia River bar are now adequate. Nearly 4,000 deepdraft ships, inbound and outbound, cross its turbulent waters annually. Lighted whistle and radar-type buoys, range lights and day markers dot the channels.

The largest vessels on the Pacific can enter and leave the Columbia River at any normal stage of the tide, and in any weather, except during the most severe storms. The Columbia River and its tributaries are navigable above the mouth by deepdraft vessels to Portland and Vancouver; and by lightdraft vessels to Priest Rapids, Washington, and to Lewiston, Idaho.

The project depths in the Columbia and Willamette rivers are 48 feet from the entrance to Clatsop Spit Lighted Whistle Buoy 14; 35 feet to Portland, Oregon; 30 feet from the mouth of the Willamette River to Vancouver, Washington; 27 feet to Bonneville, and 27 feet to The Dalles.

The hopper-dredge *Pacific* worked on both the Willapa and Columbia bars. The *Pacific* was replaced by the hopper-dredge *Yaquina* in 1982.

January 31, 1964, work began on the long-sought 40-foot channel from Portland to the sea, to replace the 35-foot waterway. Actually the Engineers will dredge from 45 to 47 feet to allow shoaling margin. Increased shipping and the larger, deeper, and faster ships now being built were major factors in support of the project.

It is impossible to maintain project depths on the bars throughout the year because of the annual freshets during the months of May, June, and July, which may cause some shoaling. However, channels are restored to project depths as soon thereafter as possible. Channel depths are maintained by dredging on the bars, and by the construction of stone and pile dikes and revetments. An estimated $50 million has been spent on improvement and maintenance of the entrance to the Columbia and the lower river channels.

The controlling depths are published frequently by the U.S. Army Engineer District in Portland, and any irregularities are reported in the Coast Guard's *Local Notice to Mariners*.

To provide public terminal and transfer facilities for deepdraft commerce, port districts have been created under state laws as agencies of the states. These port districts include those located at Portland, St. Helens, and Astoria, in Oregon; and at Vancouver, Kalama, and Longview, in Washington. Port facilities have also been provided by private interests at many other locations along the great river.

The final link in Coast Highway 101 was completed in 1966 with the completion of the Astoria trans-

Columbia River bridge linking Oregon and Washington. The four-mile bridge contains the longest continuous truss span of any bridge in the United States, 1,232 feet in length, high enough above the river to allow the largest merchant ships to pass underneath. Completion of the bridge spelled the end of the ferry service across the mouth of the river between Astoria and Megler. It also means less time for contemplation by southbound travelers of the soft outlines of Onion Peak, Saddle Mountain, and Green Mountain headland, which rise mistily from the Oregon shore, across the broad, restless waters of the Columbia.

Picturesque Astoria-Megler ferries such as this no longer work on the lower Columbia with completion of the new north-south bridge. Here *M. R. Chessman* leaves the Astoria pier for the Washington side.

Oregon State Highway Commission

CHAPTER 4

VICTIMS OF THE TRANSPACIFIC DRIFT

Moving across the North Pacific in a sweeping semicircle is a massive river within the ocean. Called either the Japanese or the Pacific Current, it is one of the mainsprings of the entire Pacific current system and is capable of carrying the most cumbersome objects on a one-way trip from Oriental shores.

It was this circular drift that brought mysterious ships to America's shores long before the recorded appearance of the white man. It is also a possible explanation why traces of foreign blood were found among the natives of the Pacific Northwest by the early explorers. On their trip west in 1805, Meriwether Lewis and William Clark saw and described Cullaby, a famous Indian of Clatsop Plains: "freckled with long dusky red hair, about 25 years of age, and must certainly be half white at least." Cullaby could have been a descendant of the lone survivor of the Indians' legendary Beeswax Ship.

Among the early Pacific sea merchants were the Spanish, who established trading between Mexico and the Philippines in the seventeenth century. It is believed by historians that their ships reached Northwest shores on several occasions after falling victim to the

Transpacific currents washed many Oriental junks such as this onto Oregon and Washington shores, long before the first recorded appearance of white men in the region.

adverse winds and the prevailing northerly currents that mark the Pacific seacoast.

Seventy-five Oriental junks are known to have been found adrift or ashore on the American side of the Pacific up to the year 1875. In 1820, two Clatsops discovered a Japanese junk cast upon the sands near Point Adams, after having drifted across the Pacific. As late as 1927, a disabled Japanese fishing boat, containing a crew of dead men, was picked up off Cape Flattery, Washington.

Several famous Indian legends of prehistoric shipwreck, and the first appearance of white man on Oregon shores, continue to delight men's imaginations.

There is the story of Konapee, the Iron-Maker, who was cast ashore on Clatsop Plains, just south of the river entrance; the story of the Treasure Ship, whose precious cargo is still being hopefully hunted; and that of the Beeswax Ship, even today the subject of controversy. All these tales have been retold many ways by many people.

In his classic *Columbia River,* William D. Lyman gives the most widely accepted versions of these prehistoric legends:

Konapee, the Iron-Maker

An old woman living near the ancient Indian village of Ne-Ahkstow, about two miles south of the mouth of the Great River, one day, after her usual custom, went to the seaside, and walked along the shore toward Clatsop Spit. While on the way she saw something very strange. At first it seemed like a whale, but, when the old woman came close, she saw that it had two trees standing upright in it. She said, "This is no whale; it is a monster." The outside was all covered over with something bright, which she afterwards found was copper. Ropes were tied all over the trees, and the inside of the Thing was full of iron.

While the old woman gazed in silent wonder, a being that looked like a bear, but had a human face, though with long hair all over it, came out of the Thing that lay there. Then the old woman hastened home in great fear.

Her people, when they had heard the strange story, hurried with bows and arrows to the spot. There, sure enough, lay the Thing upon the shore, just as the old woman had said. Only instead of one bear there were two standing on the Thing. These two creatures—whether bears or people the Indians were not sure—were just at the point of going down the Thing (which they now began to understand was an immense canoe with two trees driven into it) to the beach, with kettles in their hands.

As the bewildered Indians watched them they started a fire and put corn into the kettles. Very soon it began to pop and fly with great rapidity up and down in the kettles. The popcorn (the nature of which the Clatsops did not then understand) struck them with more surprise than anything else—and this is the one part of the story preserved in every version.

Then the corn-popping strangers made signs that they wanted water. The chief sent men to supply them with all their needs, and in the meantime he made a careful examination of the strangers. Finding that their hands were the same as his own, he became satisfied that they were indeed men. One of the Indians ran and climbed up and entered the Thing. Looking into the interior, he found it full of boxes. There were also many strings of buttons half a fathom long. He went out to call in his relatives, but, before he could return, the ship had been set on fire. As a result of the burning of the ship, the Clatsops got possession of the iron, copper, and brass.

Now the news of this strange event became noised abroad, and the Indians from all the region thronged to Clatsop Plains to see and feel of these strange men with hands and feet just like ordinary men, yet with long beards and with such peculiar garb as not to seem like men. There arose great strife as to who should receive and care for the strange men. Each tribe or village was very anxious to have them, or at least one of them. The Quienaults, the Chehales, and the Willapas, from the beach on the north side, came to press their claims. From up the river came the Cowlitz, the Cascades, and even the far-off Klickitat.

The different tribes almost had a battle for possession, but, according to one account, it was finally settled that one of the strange visitors should stay with the Clatsop chief, and that one should go with the Willapas on the north side of the Great River. According to another, they both stayed at Clatsop.

From this first arrival of white men, the Indians called them all "Tlehonnipts," that is, "Those who drift ashore." One of the men possessed the magic art of taking pieces of iron and making knives and hatchets. It was indeed to the poor Indians a marvellous gift of Tallapus, their god, that they should have a man among them who could perform that priceless labor, for the possession of iron knives and hatchets meant the indefinite mutiplying of canoes, huts, bows and arrows, weapons and implements of every sort.

The iron-maker's name was Konapee. The Indians kept close watch over him for many days and made him work incessantly. But, as the tokens of his skill became numerous, his captors held him in great favor and allowed him more liberty. Being permitted to select a site for a house, he chose a spot on the Columbia which became known to the Indians, even down to the white occupancy of the region, as "Konapee."

Among other possessions, Konapee had a large number of pieces of money, which, from the description, must have been Chinese "cash." From this some have inferred that Konapee must have been a Chinaman, and the wrecked ship a Chinese or Japanese junk. This does not, however, follow. For the Spaniards had become entirely familiar with China, and any Spanish vessel returning from the Philippine Islands or from China would have been likely to have a supply of Chinese money on board.

There is an interesting bit of testimony which seems to belong to this same story of Konapee. In his *Narrative of a Voyage to the Northwest Coast of America,* Gabriele Franchere describes meeting, at the Cascades in 1811, an old man of eighty years or so, whose name was Soto, and who said that his father was one of four Spaniards wrecked on Clatsop beach many years before. His father had tried to reach the land of the sunrise by going eastward, but, having reached the Cascades, was prevented from going farther and had there married an Indian woman, Soto's mother. It is thought likely that the father of Soto was Konapee. The two stories seem to fit quite well.

If this be true, it is likely that Konapee's landing

was as early as 1725. There is no reason to suppose that he ever saw other white men or ever got away from the region where the fortune of shipwreck had cast him. Yet he was in possession of one of the greatest geographical secrets of that country, for the hope of the discovery of some great "River of the West," the elusive stream which many believed to be a pure fabrication of Aguilar and other old navigators, had enticed many a "mariner" from many a far "countree."

In any event it is probable that the Columbia River Indians had obtained a general knowledge of the whites and their arts from Konapee long before the authentic discovery of the river was made. Especially it seems that from him they got a knowledge of iron and implements fashioned from it. Captain James Cook mentions that when he visited the coast in 1778 the Indians manifested no surprise at the weapons or implements of iron. In fact, even all whites who supposed themselves to be the first to visit this coast found the Indians ready to trade and especially eager to get iron.

The Treasure Ship

A new era of trade and business seems to have been inaugurated among these Clatsops and Chinooks dating from about the supposed time of Konapee. But he was by no means the only one of his race to be cast upon the Oregon shore. There is a story of a treasure ship cast upon the beach near Neahkahnie Mountain. This mountain, the original home of Tallapus and the chief god Nekahni, is one of the noblest areas along the shore.

Fronting the ocean with a precipitous rampart of rock and rising in a wide sweeping park clad in thick turf, and dotted here and there with beautiful spruce and fir trees, Neahkahnie presents as fine a combination of the majestic and sublime as can be seen upon a whole thousand miles of coast. It was a favorite spot with the natives. Lying upon its open and turfy slopes, they could gaze upon many miles of sea, and could no doubt light up their signal fires which might be seen over a wide expanse of beach. Very likely there, too, they celebrated the mysterious rites of Nekahni and Tallapus.

One pleasant afternoon in early summer, a large group of natives assembled upon the lower part of Neahkahnie, almost upon the edge of the precipitous cliff, with which it fronts the sea. Gazing into the distance, they saw a great object, like a huge bird, drawing near from the outer sea. It approached the shore, and then from it a number of men with a large black box put out in a small boat to land. Arriving on the beach, the men took out the box. With them was a black man whom the Indians supposed to be an evil demon.

Going a little way up the beach, the men dug a hole into which they lowered the box, and then having struck down the black man they threw him on top of the box. Then, covering it up, they returned to the ship, which soon disappeared from sight. On account of the black man buried with the box, the superstitious Indians dared not undertake to exhume the contents of the grave. But the story was handed from one generation to another and it came to constitute the story of the "treasure ship."

The ground has been dug over for sight of the regulation rusty handle which is to lead to the great iron-bound chest with its doubloons of gold and crucifixes of pearls. One search party even secured the guidance of spirits who professed to locate the treasure. But though the spirit-led enthusiasts turned over every stone and dug up the sand for many feet along the beach, they found never an iron-bound chest, and never a sign of treasure. There is, however, in plain sight now, on a rock at the foot of Neahkahnie Mountain, a character cut in the rock bearing a rude resemblance to a cross. Some think it looks more like the letters, I.H.S., the sacred emblem of the Catholic Church. There is also what seems to be a distinct arrow pointing in a certain direction. But the treasure remains unfound.

The Beeswax Ship

The next legend of the prehistoric white man is that of the Beeswax Ship. This, too, has a real confirmation in the presence of large quantities of beeswax at a point also near Neahkahnie Mountain, just north of the mouth of the Nehalem River. Early settlers have reported finding large chunks with numbers, letters, and diamonds. Some claimed at one time that this substance was simply the natural paraffin produced from the products of coal or petroleum. But, later, cakes of the substance

hunks of beeswax such as this, that have washed ashore near the Nehalem River, support the Clatsop Indian legend of the Beeswax Ship.

stamped with the sacred letters "I.H.S.," together with tapers, and even one piece with a bee plainly visible within, may be considered incontestable proof that this is indeed beeswax, while the letters, "I.H.S.," denote plainly enough the origin of the substance in some Spanish colony. In connection with this is the interesting historical fact that, on June 16, 1769, the caravel *San José* left La Paz, Lower California, for San Diego, and was never heard from again. Some have conjectured that the *San José* was the Beeswax Ship, driven far north by some storm or mutiny. As to the peculiar fact that a ship should have been entirely loaded with beeswax, it has been surmised that some of the good padres of the Spanish missions meant to furnish a new station with a large amount of wax for providing tapers for their service, the lighted candles proving a matter of marvel and wonder to the natives; and, with other features of ceremonial worship, having great power to bring them into the church.

The Indian legend runs on to the effect that several white men were saved from the wreck of the Beeswax Ship, and that they lived with the natives; but having infringed upon the family rights of the Indians, they became obnoxious, and were cast out. One story, however, asserts that there was one man left, a blue-eyed, golden-haired man, that he took a Nehalem woman, and that from him was descended a fair-complexioned progeny.

No doubt fancy has larded the facts of these legends, but doubtless much fact remains. The journals of Lewis and Clark, and those of Henry-Thompson, as well as the accounts of Ross Cox, all tell of seeing a half-breed in that picturesque Indian country below the mouth of the Columbia.

CHAPTER 5

INDIAN TROUBLES

With the beginning of the nineteenth century, a new era opened through the portals of the Columbia River. Streams rich in beaver attracted traders to gather furs highly valued in world markets. Later, tall timber and productive valleys brought settlers.

Within a quarter century of Gray's discovery of the Columbia, traders were sailing their ships into its waters. The Astor party had founded Astoria, and the Hudson's Bay Company had established Fort Vancouver, one hundred miles upstream.

Between the natives and the white men occasional misunderstandings arose which often had bloody aftermaths.

The Ship *Tonquin*

Astoria was established through the plans of John Jacob Astor, business tycoon and fur trader of New York. He organized one party to go overland and another by sea to locate a suitable spot for a trading post at the mouth of the Columbia.

The ten-gun *Tonquin,* under command of Captain Jonathan Thorn, sailed from New York on September 8, 1810, loaded with supplies for the establishment of the new Astor colony, and carrying a thirty-three-man crew made up of Scots Highlanders, gentlemen's sons, and rough Canadian voyageurs. Such a motley group would have been hard for any captain to handle; for Thorn it was virtually impossible.

Thorn, a naval officer on leave from his regular commission, wore no velvet gloves to soften his iron-handed rule. His harsh discipline led to open trouble soon after the voyage began. Before his ship had reached the Sandwich Islands, mutiny and murder threatened the expedition.

When the *Tonquin* and her surly crew finally arrived at the Columbia River entrance, March 22, 1811, the bar was rough with breakers from a strong southwest wind. A less headstrong commander would have waited for milder weather, but not Captain Thorn. He ordered William Fox, his first officer, along with several others, to man the whaleboat and take soundings.

Knowing the whaleboat was in need of repair and justly fearful of the angry seas, Fox protested bitterly. Thorn merely taunted his cowardice:

"If you are afraid of the sea, Mr. Fox, you should never have left Boston."

So the damaged whaleboat, with Fox at the tiller, went over the side of the *Tonquin* into the raging waters—soon to disappear in the heaving swells. Neither craft nor crew was ever seen thereafter.

Night came on and the ship rolled violently in the sea. The following day the wind subsided and the *Tonquin* found anchorage in fourteen fathoms near the north entrance of the river—but she had yet to cross the bar.

From Gabriel Franchere's Narrative of a Voyage to the Northwest Coast of America

Sketch of Astoria, made in 1813, two years after the city was founded by the men of the *Tonquin*.

The presence of the *Tonquin* aroused the attention of the natives along the shores, who were preparing their canoes to come out and barter, should the ship enter the river.

Because the ship lay in a dangerous position, it was decided that Alexander McKay and David Stuart of the Astor party should man the pinnace and sound the bar channel. The boat was lowered, but within a few minutes it swamped in the surf, the two men narrowly escaping with their lives.

The pinnace was bailed out and repaired; then another attempt was made to sound the bar, but this also ended in failure. As the *Tonquin* was slowly being carried toward shore, Captain Thorn found his position growing more perilous by the minute.

Among the cargo carried on the vessel was the frame of a small schooner which was to have been assembled at the new establishment. All hands set to work; shortly they had the craft fitted together. John Aiken was put in charge, assisted by the ship's sailmaker and the ship's armorer. When the work was completed, the vessel was manned for one final attempt to guide the *Tonquin* into safe waters.

The schooner proved to be more successful than the smaller boats; it eventually located the safe channel. After carefully marking the area, the crew headed back to join the *Tonquin,* but the currents swept their craft broadside into a curling breaker, tossing her on her beam ends and spilling the crew into the chilling waters.

Thorn would not risk sending aid to the struggling men, as he needed every hand to save the ship from being carried onto the spit. Suddenly the *Tonquin* struck. Water surged over her decks, and loose gear floated free of its fittings. Shrouds and halyards snapped as the vessel kept poking her prow on the shoal. Foundering seemed imminent, and fear filled the vessel's company.

Then almost miraculously the *Tonquin* drifted free with the tide and was carried over the bar after having struck it repeatedly without sustaining serious damage to her hull.

At daybreak the natives came alongside in their canoes. Barter, however, failed to interest the crew, for they mourned the loss of their shipmates. Immediately they set out to comb the shore in the hope of finding them alive. Stephen Weekes, the armorer, and one of the Kanaka sailors who had joined the ship in the islands, were found near Cape Disappointment, suffering from exposure; but the search failed to locate the others. The schooner was washed ashore and later rebuilt at the new settlement. It was named the *Dolly.*

While the *Tonquin* lay at anchor off the north bank

of the river, the Astor party set out in search of a suitable location for a post. Finally a site was selected midway between Tongue Point and Point George (now Smith Point). That location on the south bank offered protection from the winds as well as a sheltered moorage.

For the next several days all hands were busied unloading the cargo of the *Tonquin,* while the natives gathered near, filled with curiosity. By June 5, the stevedoring duties were completed and the vessel weighed anchor. Bidding farewell to the colonizers, the ship's company departed for Vancouver Island in quest of a cargo of furs. En route to sea, a native came alongside in a small dugout to ask to be taken on the voyage as interpreter. He gave his name as Lamazee, claiming to be well acquainted with the tribes to the north. Considering him a valuable addition to the crew, Captain Thorn granted him passage, and the ship continued her voyage.

More than two years later, this same native arrived in Astoria, where he claimed to be the sole survivor of the *Tonquin* party. According to his story, the *Tonquin* anchored off the village of Neweetee, and a number of natives, filled with anxiety, hurried out in their canoes to meet the ship.

When bartering began, a wrinkled old chief named Nookamis was allowed to come aboard to display his pelts. Nookamis, who had become shrewd in his methods of bargaining after dealings with earlier white traders, refused all offers made by Thorn. Becoming angered with the presistent chief, the shipmaster threw him overboard.

Cottrell Collectio

In 1811, Captain Jonathan Thorn of the Astor ship *Tonquin* sent a manned whaleboat int wind-whipped seas at the bar mouth, to take soundings. In minutes, both craft and crew disap peared forever in the engulfing waters.

Pretending to continue bartering the following day, the natives, enraged by the incident of the preceding day, boarded the *Tonquin* with their skins. At a given signal they commenced an attack on the crew which left the ship's decks running with blood. Only four escaped by managing to reach the after cabin and holding the savages off with rifle fire. Captain Thorn and the others were murdered.

Being a native, Lamazee was unharmed, but was forced to flee with the attackers to escape the bullets fired by the surviving crew members.

Lacking sufficient manpower to operate the vessel, three members of the crew attempted an escape by the ship's boat during the night. Repelled by a strong wind at the harbor entrance, they sought refuge in a cave on the shore, but were discovered by the natives and taken back to the village where they were tortured to death.

Mr. Lewis, the ship's clerk, kept a lonely vigil aboard the *Tonquin*. Wounded in the skirmish, he had refused to join his shipmates in their escape. Intent on revenge, he paced the debris-laden deck hour after hour, making friendly signs to the natives to come on board.

Growing increasingly confident, the savages swarmed up over the sides of the vessel from scores of canoes and set about to strip the ship of its wares. While the decks teemed with excited red men, Lewis, unnoticed, slipped down to the ship's powder magazine and ignited it.

For an instant there was a twisting flame with a puff of smoke. Then came a tremendous explosion. Bodies went spinning through the air and fell into the sea. The *Tonquin* was blasted into pieces along with the near-by war canoes. Bodies washed up on the beaches for days afterward.

At the conclusion of his story, Lamazee estimated that more than five-score natives were killed and many others were maimed for life as a result of the explosion.

Brig *William and Ann*

Firmly established in 1825, Fort Vancouver, the Hudson's Bay Company post, became a mecca for fur traders in the nineteenth century. Numerous ships from the United Kingdom arrived on the river to bring supplies and return home with furs. American ships were sent to the river by eastern merchants who carried on a thriving trade with the Orient.

There was cause for celebration each time a vessel arrived from far ports; but when disaster was reported, gloom fell over the settlers, for it meant the loss of essential supplies.

In early March of 1829, the British brig *William and Ann,* owned by the Hudson's Bay Company, arrived off the mouth of the Columbia, after a long voyage from London. Falling in company with the American schooner *Convoy,* of Boston–Captain Thompson, master–the two vessels maneuvered for the crossing of the bar. Coming in on a port tack, the *Convoy* entered first, with her crew sounding the depths at frequent intervals. When the schooner had cleared the bar, the velocity of the wind had increased two-fold, and refuge was taken in Baker Bay.

The *William and Ann,* in command of Captain Hanwell, was nowhere in sight. After several hours of scanning the horizon, the schooner's lookout yelled from aloft, "The Britisher's in trouble, sir."

Without hesitation, Captain Thompson called for volunteers, and soon the ship's boat put out to sea to aid the stricken vessel. Pulling to within a quarter of a mile of the *William and Ann,* the would-be rescuers became exhausted in their battle against the sea and were forced to abandon the effort and return to the *Convoy* .

All night the storm raged. Trapped in the sands off Clatsop Spit, the *William and Ann* was pounded by overflowing walls of water and her total complement of forty-six persons was carried into the sea.

When the *Convoy* anchored off Fort George–as Astoria was then called–word was received that the Clatsops were salvaging large quantities of goods washed on the beach in the aftermath of the wreck. When that news was sent to Fort Vancouver, a party was immediately organized for a visit to the Clatsop village to recover the goods. The natives made no attempt to hide their gifts from the sea, for when the Hudson's Bay Company party entered the village, they found a grand array of supplies as well as wooden crates stamp-marked, "London, England." A demand was made of the chief for the return of the goods, but it was denied. Instead, the high-ranking native handed the white leader a tattered old broom, instructing him to return it to Dr. John McLoughlin, then in charge of Fort Vancouver.

"You tell white leader he receive no more," muttered the chief.

Too small to enforce their demands, the party departed. They presented the broom to McLoughlin on their return, after which plans were made to send an armed party to the village to regain the merchandise by force if necessary.

Meanwhile McLoughlin was informed that an abandoned lifeboat from the *William and Ann* was in the possession of the Clatsops, and gossip that the natives had murdered the survivors was circulated at the settlement. As the stories gained impetus, the men at the post plotted revenge.

By the fall of the year, plans were complete. A small river schooner was armed with cannon and filled with company men, ready to do battle with the Clatsops. The scheme called for one group to go by land and another by water. When the schooner approached the area, it sent a volley from the cannon into the center of the village. The Clatsops were taken by complete surprise. They fled to the forests to protect themselves, but in the cross-fire from the land army, one of the natives was killed and two others injured.

The battle was over and the Fort Vancouver party walked into the village and recovered the loot.

Some of the tribe were taken as hostages and questioned over the murder of the survivors of the *William and Ann,* but each emphatically insisted that the lifeboat was found abandoned.

The attack on the village was severely criticized by the Americans, but the conquerors stressed the fact that the incident taught the natives respect for the Hudson's Bay Company's power and property.

CHAPTER 6

SAND

Noah Webster defines sand as more or less fine debris of rocks—usually of quartz and common to beaches. The hard-shelled skipper of an old square-rigger, on finding his ship aground on a shoal, likely had a slightly different definition.

Sand, as harmless as it appears, has been a prime factor in the destruction of most of the ships lost in the Pacific Graveyard. It is capable of sucking its prey down and devouring the remains like a hungry animal.

An enormous sand deposit was found at the mouth of the Columbia by the early navigators. This deposit was constantly shifted by the conflict of river flow and ocean storm. Channels varying in depth from nineteen to thirty feet were formed and again effaced. Tens of millions of cubic yards were moved into a given area, or out again, within a few seasons.

Along the coastline southward, a steadily narrowing sand spit or beach extends from the Columbia River to Tillamook Head, beyond which it all but disappears. The beaches to the north, however, increase in importance. Submerged bars and spits project prominently at Willapa Bay and Grays Harbor entrances, having been formed without the assistance of silt- or sediment-carrying rivers emptying into these entrances. Therefore the Columbia River becomes the artery of the sand conditions along the shores of Oregon and Washington.

The fine sand found around the Columbia's portal, readily shifted by the combined action of wind, tide, and current, is carried northward by a prevailing northerly drift.

British Brig *Isabella*

Among the fleet of ships supplying the Hudson's Bay interests on the Columbia was the British brig *Isabella*, commanded by Captain Thomas Ryan. Arriving off the river in 1830 with cargo for Fort Vancouver, the following account was written in the ship's log.

"May 3, 1830...At 4. Saw a very great Swell & Broken water ahead, but thinking there was always broken water on the Bar, did not imagine there could be any danger, the Weather being so very fine. At 5PM Struck on a Sand bar in the Enterance of the Columbia River and carried away the rudder. Broached to with her head to the Northward the Vessel became unmanagable in the heavy Sea and Strong Flood tide. The Vessel Driving on to the Breakers very fast, we let go the anchor in 2½ fathoms. Striking very heavy. Got the boats out, Stove the water Casks upon Deck and Cleared away the Lumber. Vessel Still Striking very heavy, we hove a great part of the Cargo and Stores overboard to lighten her. At 9PM, the Vessel Still Striking heavy and dreading the Indians and Expecting the Vessel to go to pieces during the Night, we agreed to abandon her and proceed in the Boats to Fort Vancouver...."

The wreck, largely buried in the sand, lies about 30 feet below the surface off Sand Island, near Baker Bay. The wreck was first discovered in September 1986 when gillnetter nets fouled the obstruction. She was a two-masted brig of 195 tons, estimated to be a little over 90 feet in length, and was the second recorded wreck at the mouth of the Columbia, the first occuring the previous year when the *William and Ann*, another Hudson's Bay brig, was wrecked on Clatsop Spit with the loss of her entire company. The *Isabella* was purchased from Gilmour and Richardson for 2,900 pounds to replace the ill-fated vessel. Sailing from Blackwall, England for the Columbia on October 30, 1829, under Captain Ryan, the crew consisted of two officers, a surgeon, 11 seamen, a cabin boy and a few Hawaiians picked up in the islands.

Sloop of War *Peacock*

Another decade slipped by before serious disaster again occurred on the Columbia bar. On July 18, 1841, the U.S. Naval brig *Peacock* ended the period of safe bar transit. The eighteen-gun sloop of war was a unit of Lieutenant Charles Wilkes' Expedition employed in sounding and charting Pacific Ocean waters.

When the *Peacock*–Captain William L. Hudson, master–arrived off the mouth of the Columbia from the Sandwich Islands, the sky was clear and flaked with puffs of cloud. The bar was favorable for crossing, but the ship's master carried only inaccurate bar charts given him, while in the islands, by Captain Josiah Spaulding of the ship *Lausanne*.

The charts were followed closely, but the main channel was erroneously marked and the vessel struck the sands with a terrific impact. The tide was ebbing and the freshening breeze sent volumes of water smashing against the ship. Her beamy hull pounded on the sand like a sledge hammer. A comber leaped over the vessel and crushed the ship's cutter. The crew was ordered to jettison all excess cargo in an attempt to free the ship. Over went the cannons, the shot, and the stores. The port anchor was dropped, and by herculean efforts the vessel's head was turned toward the open sea.

Any hope that may have come at the moment faded as the anchor chain snapped, forcing the *Peacock* to turn broadside, yawing in the surf. By midnight the crew were sloshing around in three feet of water on the gun deck. They were cold and exhausted and all chances of escaping in the ship's launch were useless in the face of the rising sea. The pumps, which were manned continuously, finally became clogged with debris and had to be abandoned.

By 6 a.m. the sea had calmed considerably and a native war canoe carrying a pilot from Fort George pushed its way out to the side of the vessel. The pilot's arrival was to no avail, for during the night the brig's hull had broken under the strain of working on the shoal and all hands had elected to abandon ship.

While carrying the crew members ashore on the second trip, the *Peacock's* launch capsized in a breaker and ten seamen were thrown into the swell, narrowly escaping with their lives.

Captain Hudson was the last to leave the ship and with him went the *Peacock's* articles and navigation instruments.

The following day, the *Peacock* broke up and her wreckage was scattered along the shore. Her grave was marked only by her bowsprit, which protruded from the sands.

When Lieutenant Wilkes arrived at Fort George

aboard the USS *Porpoise,* he chartered the American schooner *Thomas H. Perkins,* at anchor off the settlement, and placed the *Peacock's* crew aboard to continue survey work on the river.

Before departing the Columbia, Wilkes found that there was no space to carry the *Peacock's* launch. He decided to leave it at Fort George where it could be maintained as a rescue boat for the relief of vessels in distress.

U. S. Naval Survey Schooner *Shark*

The U. S. Naval Survey schooner *Shark* gave permanence to her name in the area surrounding the mouth of the Columbia. A rock at Astoria bears her name, and one of her cannon was responsible for the naming of an Oregon coastal town. After leaving a memorable chapter in history, she bequeathed her bones to Clatsop Spit.

The 300-ton *Shark,* in command of Captain Schenck, and part of the surveying fleet under Lieutenant Neil M. Howison, U.S.N., arrived off the mouth of the Columbia River after a 25-day passage from Honolulu, in August, 1846. Not being familiar with the bar, the shipmaster picked up a Negro cook who had come out in a small boat and declared himself to be a pilot. A survivor of the *Peacock* wreck five years earlier, he claimed to have a knowledge of the bar.

His role as a pilot, however, was short-lived; for, twenty minutes after he took over the piloting chores, he put the vessel on the sands, while negotiating the passage. Fortunately the weather was calm. With the incoming tide, the vessel drifted free, virtually undam-

Shark Rock has been moved from its former place as seen above to the Columbia River Maritime Museum, Astoria, Oregon. The original cannon salvaged from the *Shark* was responsible for the name of the city of Cannon Beach. The cannon and capstan are located at the Clatsop County Historical Society Heritage Center, Astoria, Oregon.

aged. John Lattie, one of the few in the area with a genuine knowledge of the bar passages, was summoned to the ship to guide her into safe haven off the Astor colony.

Trouble of another kind next plagued the arrival of the ship. Anxiety over the boundary question—involving the United States and Great Britain—had started rumors among the settlers that war was near and that the arrival of the *Shark* was a war precaution and not a survey mission.

The crew members, weary from long months at sea, began deserting, and replacements were unobtainable. Thus the survey had to be rushed and much valuable information bypassed in a hasty effort to finish the job before other crewmen deserted. Hard as they tried, the officers were unable to bribe the townsmen of the settlement to divulge the hiding places of the deserters.

On September 10, without taking proper precautions, the vessel weighed anchor. Crossing the bar, she struck the outlying fangs of Clatsop Spit, this time with a death-dealing blow. The waters were not calm as on her inward trek, and the ship shuddered and trembled while mounting breakers drove into her wooden hull. With her weight fastening her to the bottom, she was working on the sands.

Captain Schenck was gravely concerned. He ordered the three masts chopped down and all twelve of the ship's cannon jettisoned, in an effort to get the ship off the spit.

Before these acts could be carried out, the ship began to break up, and all hands were ordered to the boats. During the night, the wreck was battered to pieces, parts of it drifting out over the bar. Evidently the crew did not jettison all the cannon, for a large section of the wreck came ashore just south of Tillamook Head, bearing a ship's cannon and the capstan. The cannon and capstan today are a tourist attraction near the town of Cannon Beach, named for the *Shark's* cannon. A man named John Hobson, dismantled the wreckage.

Meanwhile the crew of the *Shark* all reached safety and were looked after by the citizens of the Astor Colony. Eventually they were able to get passage back to San Francisco on the old *Cadboro,* which was chartered from the Hudson's Bay Company for the trip. Before the survivors left, however, they inscribed the incident of the wreck on a large rock, which today is on display in Astoria. It is known as Shark Rock.

Lieutenant Howison maintained the wreck was due to channel alterations not shown on the charts the *Shark* carried. He managed to save the ship's colors, presenting them to the Astor Colony, which long flew "Old Glory" over the former British settlement.

French Bark *Morning Star*

She flew the French flag and in bright gold across her counter was the name *Morning Star.* She hailed from Le Havre and had arrived off the mouth of the Columbia, the first week in July, 1849, after a seven-months' passage.

A week passed and the vessel still waited outside the river for the arrival of a pilot, but none came. Her master, Captain Francis Menes, grew impatient. He was a big man whose ruddy face was framed from ear to ear with a flaming red beard. On the eighth day, he spoke to an American brig outbound from the river and was informed that no pilot was available.

Meanwhile, a coastwise schooner arrived off the river and again the *Morning Star* exchanged information. Menes learned that a few months earlier one of the bar pilots had grounded the British bark *Vancouver* on the middle sands and, to avoid embarrassing questions, had departed for San Francisco.

That was the last straw. The French skipper on the first favorable wind got his command under way. Not entirely unfamiliar with the bar, Captain Menes had successfully crossed it on a voyage two years earlier. He had kept notes on his first crossing, but was unaware of the changing conditions of the bar entrances. On July 11, the *Morning Star* started the inbound trek, heavily laden and drawing sixteen feet. Off Sand Island, the vessel struck the bottom. The enraged skipper, who had been following his charts with precision, stormed to the taffrail, gazed overboard and tossed his charts into the surf.

For ten hours the vessel was hung up on the spit. Working on the sands, the timbers were loosened and water began pouring through her seams. The boats were lowered but as fast as they hit the water they were destroyed in the tempest. When the last remaining lifeboat went over the side, a seaman volunteered to hold it steady until his shipmates could man the craft. He was unaware of a giant wave that rolled toward the boat as it dangled precariously, and the howl of the wind blotted out the warnings of the crew. The comber struck with such force that it literally swallowed up the boat and its occupant.

With the last boat gone, all hope for rescue faded. The wreck was at the mercy of the buffeting seas. Stern first on the shoal, the rudder cracked under the strain and drifted free of the vessel. A moment later a section of the keel parted, and to the amazement of the crew, the bark released its grip on the spit and drifted into the channel as if guided by an unseen hand. She came drifting into Baker Bay several hours later with her exhausted crew draped over the rigging, seemingly more dead than alive.

John Lattie—the bar pilot who had guided the *Shark* in safety to the Astor colony—sighted the derelict and made haste to the vessel's side with several natives in a canoe. Following him came the crews of three sailing vessels that were at anchor in the river, the ship *Walpole,* the brig *Undine,* and the bark *John W. Cater.* The salvagers scrambled aboard the *Morning Star* and began clearing the tangled rigging in an effort to get at the pumps and save the ship from sinking. The exhausted Frenchmen were taken ashore while the salvage gang worked ceaselessly for twenty-four hours before the vessel's holds were finally emptied of water. When the task was completed, a box rudder was installed and the ship taken upriver to Portland, where the damaged cargo was disposed of at high prices. The hull was later sold to the firm of Couch and Flanders, of Portland, who afterwards resold it to California interests.

That she ever went to sea again is doubtful.

American Bark *Mindora*

On January 12, 1853, double tragedy occurred on the Columbia bar with the loss of two American vessels, the barks *Mindora* and *J. Merithew.*

The more important of the two wrecks, from a historical standpoint, was the loss of the *Mindora,* a 400-ton coastwise vessel, which was en route to Portland from San Francisco when disaster occurred. While some of the most severe weather of the year blew itself out, the *Mindora* was compelled to wait outside the bar for twenty-eight days. One gale after another lashed the shores, and the bar was a foaming mass of swells. Food and supplies ran short on the vessel, and her master, Captain George Staples, was forced to ration the water, hardtack, and beans. The crew became quarrelsome, and all that kept them in line was the presence of a few other vessels that had arrived off the bar and were undergoing similar trials.

On January 12, a temporary calm prevailed and the *Mindora* trimmed sail for the crossing. Making good headway with a running sea, the vessel pitched gently at four knots when suddenly the wind died completely, forcing the square-rigger to anchor off Sand Island. Her position was exposed to the currents, which started her anchors dragging in spite of efforts by the crew to hold her position. The currents carried the vessel toward the middle sands and beached her on a shoal. The *Mindora* shuddered under the strain, and no sooner had she struck than the breakers swept her decks, smashing the housing aft and flooding the fo'c'sle forward.

The crewmen held their stations until Captain Staples gave the order to abandon; they then manned a boat and launched out into the tempest. Icy water poured into the craft as fast as eager hands could bail it out. With a sailor's will they rowed, tossing about as the darkness closed in around them. All the way to Astoria they went, backs and arms at the breaking point and the boat with only a few inches of freeboard.

When help arrived with food and warm clothing, the crew members were so exhausted that for several hours they slept stretched out around the potbellied stove in the town hall.

In the morning, Captain Staples summoned the pilot schooner and shoved off from Astoria to find the wreck. When they arrived at the scene, all that greeted their eyes was an empty stretch of sand. The *Mindora* was nowhere to be found. First conclusions were that she had foundered and was buried in the sands; the true story was not learned until several days later.

The *Mindora* wasn't ready to terminate her career of roaming the seas. After being abandoned, she decided to set her own course. During the night the vessel pounded on the sands until her anchor cables parted. The sands were hollowed from her hull by the surging tides; then the currents swept her out to sea. Like a ghost ship she drifted in the murk. Her masts were severed from their fittings and wreckage covered her decks, but the vessel drifted on, nobody ever knowing how far.

The *Mindora* might have joined the legendary world of phantom ships, but that several days later her battered hulk plowed its way through the breakers and came to rest on the beach several miles north of Shoalwater Bay.

An interesting conclusion to this story is the tale of the bark *J. Merithew,* lost at the bar on the same day as the *Mindora.* Earlier the two vessels had loaded side by side in San Francisco Bay, and both departed for the river within a few days of each other. They crossed the bar on the same day and both came to grief. No loss of life occurred in either wreck. As did the *Mindora,* the *J. Merithew,* which grounded on Clatsop Spit, drifted to sea after being abandoned. The latter vessel's trip was curtailed when she was swept against the rock walls near North Head.

American Bark *Desdemona*

Many of the spits and sand bars at the mouth of the Columbia have been named for the ships that have stranded on them. One such unlucky ship was the bark *Desdemona.* Though many of these shoals have been effaced, Desdemona Sands are still in existence today. They were charted after the *Desdemona* left her bones there on New Year's Day in 1857.

Captain Francis Williams made a wager before his vessel departed San Francisco. It was the price of a new Sunday suit to be given him by the vessel's owner, Thomas Smith, if he could get his cargo to the river by New Year's Day. Williams had faith in the *Desde-*

mona, and her owner stood to gain a handsome price from the consignee if the cargo arrived on time.

The *Desdemona* was one of the most familiar ships in the coasting trade and one of the most dependable. She was built at Jonesboro, Maine, in 1847, and had been operating out of the Columbia River since 1851.

Captain Williams didn't spare an inch of canvas on the northbound trip and arrived off the mouth of the river in good time. It was New Year's Eve, towards midnight, but the *Desdemona's* master preferred not to cross the bar until dawn. Deep in the water with a heavy load of general merchandise, the vessel would need to be handled with great precaution in bar transit. At daybreak, the *Desdemona* signalled for a pilot. When the pilot boat failed to come, Williams decided to save the vessel's owner the fee and take her into the river himself. His knowledge of the bar was adequate, but his vessel sat deep in the water and the swell on the bar caused her to labor heavily. Suddenly the ship struck at a point where the charts had indicated deep water.

Concerned over the valuable cargo, Williams ordered a boat lowered and he and some of the ship's crew went to Astoria to seek aid. While they were away, the U. S. Revenue Cutter *Joe Lane* hove to and got a line aboard the stricken craft. For hours the cutter strained to free the *Desdemona,* but abandoned the effort after the third hawser had parted.

When Williams returned to his ship, he brought several men from the Parker Sawmill to help refloat her, but much to his dismay discovered that his vessel had bilged and was sinking deeper in the sands. All hands set to work removing the cargo in lighters. They worked night and day until January 3, when the pilot boat arrived and warned them of an approaching storm. The crew went ashore until the winds had died, and then returned two days later to finish the job with the aid of a wooden scow. Anxious to complete the task, the crew overloaded the scow. A snorting tug from the mill had difficulty controlling it against the strong currents. It began to roll at dangerous angles; then it swamped and capsized, throwing its cargo and several of the *Desdemona's* crew into the water. One of the seamen was trapped beneath the scow and drowned, but the others struggled in the water until the tug managed to pick them up.

At a public auction in Astoria on January 6, the wreck of the *Desdemona* brought only $215. She was sold to Moses Rogers, who stripped the hull of everything removable.

For many years the ribs of the *Desdemona* were pointed out to passengers crossing the bar. Finally one hard winter, the wreck sank out of sight in the sands and has never been seen since.

Before a hearing involving the loss of his ship, Captain Williams claimed that the wreck was caused by the absence of the lower bar buoy which was reported missing from position when the *Desdemona* was inbound.

Whether or not he ever got his new Sunday suit has always remained a mystery.

American Bark *Industry*

Inscribed on Shark Rock, on Niagara Street in Astoria, is an epitaph telling of the wreck of the American bark *Industry,* lost, as was the brig *S. D. Lewis,* in March 1865, making this a double-tragedy month on the Columbia bar.

The *Industry* was a coastwise trader built at Stockton, Maine, by Captain Paul Corno, who earlier had amassed a fortune with his initial vessel, the brig *Susan Abigal.* The new Corno addition had paid for herself within a few months of her arrival on the Pacific Coast. Her record was unmarred until her fatal voyage from San Francisco to Portland, in command of Captain I. Lewis.

Departing the Golden Gate, February 23, the *Industry* shoved off on a hectic voyage up the coast. After a two-weeks' struggle with foul weather, she arrived off the river badly battered by the succession of gales she had encountered. Some of her crew had been injured by the heavy seas, and her fresh-water tanks had been smashed.

The bar was rough and the pilot boat was nowhere in sight, but the barkentine *Falkenberg* was sighted nearby and hailed by Captain Lewis. He made an urgent plea for fresh water. After the seas had calmed, a boat was lowered and eventually returned with casks full of the precious liquid.

No pilot came, so Lewis, determined to assume the responsibility for his vessel, on March 15, ordered the sail trimmed and moved her in for the crossing.

"Sail ho!" yelled a seaman from aloft.

"Where away?" came the answer from the ship's master.

"Two points off the starboard bow."

It was the pilot boat and, as it approached the *In-*

dustry, a signal flag was raised. Assuming that he was to alter his course, Lewis waited for the pilot schooner to come alongside, but instead it turned about and started back across the bar. It was evident that the *Industry* was expected to follow in her wake.

When well under way, the wind failed, and the bark was obliged to drop her anchors and stay clear of the sands. Within fifteen minutes the breeze returned and the hooks were weighed. For five minutes more the vessel groped her way along the bar, when the wind died once again. Again the anchors went over the side, but the vessel had already lost steerageway and was drifting into shallow water. A moment later she struck, stern first, near the middle sands, severing her rudder.

The vessel finally freed herself and began drifting over the spit. Desperate attempts were made to clear the sands, but less than 100 yards farther on, she drove ashore again, this time dislodging her false keel.

Fearing for the lives of his passengers, Captain Lewis ordered a boat lowered and placed first officer Coppin in charge. Before the passengers could man it, a giant swell flipped the craft skyward, tearing out the bottom and sweeping Coppin to a watery grave. No further attempts were made to lower another boat as the sea was running and the wind increasing.

As night approached on the wings of a gale, all hands took to the rigging like spiders in a web. The rising seas stove in the boats, uprooted the capstan and carried the steering wheel and the binnacle into the deep. Tons of water cascaded over the vessel as she settled. After seemingly eternal night, morning shed its light on a battered and broken ship inhabited by gaunt figures of human life.

Though they were chilled to the bone, Captain Lewis ordered the crew and passengers to set to work building rafts as the one remaining means of saving their lives. With the decks awash, they worked ceaselessly, constructing one raft from fallen yards and another from wooden pumps.

The first conveyance was set adrift with five persons aboard and was carried over the bar where a lifeboat manned by soldiers from Fort Stevens rescued them. The second raft met with ill fortune when four men were swept overboard and drowned; a fifth died of exposure. A pretty twelve-year-old girl was also carried overboard, perishing after frantic efforts to save her had failed. Only two of the passengers, out of the eight that took passage on the *Industry,* reached shore alive.

Some of the ship's crew remained with the wreck so that the others could have a place on the rafts. They too met death when the vessel broke up shortly after the second raft set out to cross the bar.

Probably the incident is best described on Astoria's Shark Rock, in these simple words: "The bark *Industry* was lost March 16, 1865; lives lost 17, saved 7."

American Steamer *Great Republic*

One of the wrecks long talked about by old-time captains was that of the side-wheel passenger steamer *Great Republic.* She entered the coastwise run in 1878, as the largest passenger steamer on the Pacific Coast. She was owned by P. B. Cornwall and successfully operated until she stranded on Sand Island, April 19, 1879, with a loss of eleven lives.

The *Great Republic* was constructed at Greenport, Long Island, New York, in 1866, for the historic Pacific Mail Steamship Company. Built of white oak and chestnut, the vessel was strengthened with copper and iron fastenings. She measured 378 feet in length and registered 4,750 gross tons.

For several years the vessel was in the China trade, but she was a costly ship to operate, and as her owners could not meet expenses, they decided to lay her up at San Francisco.

Cornwall, an adventurer as well as a promoter, eyed the *Great Republic* and decided to purchase her for coast passenger service. He acquired her for a fraction of her original cost. His plan was to worry the other coastwise steamship companies into paying him to keep his ship off the run. The scheme failed to materialize, however, and his only alternative was to give the vessel a face-lifting and place her in the passenger and freight service between San Francisco and Portland.

Cornwall found to his surprise that business was booming. On the *Great Republic's* initial voyage she carried 225 passengers and more than 400 tons of freight.

On her arrival at Portland, June 19, 1878, the big vessel was given a warm welcome. Portlanders turned out in large numbers to salute the big ship and to fete her master, Captain James Carroll.

She carried 236 passengers on the return trip to San Francisco, and for the next six passages more than 600 passengers and 500 tons of freight, in spite of a rate war promoted by her competitors.

The *Great Republic* was also a fast carrier. Her vertical beam engine, fed by four massive boilers, made more than one old river skipper scratch his head in amazement when he heard she had run from Portland to Astoria in five hours and fifteen minutes.

It was a happy crowd of some 896 passengers that departed San Francisco in the spring of 1879. The *Great Republic,* including her crew, carried more than a thousand persons.

At midnight on April 18, the steamer arrived off the mouth of the Columbia. The pilot boat was awaiting her arrival and pulled alongside to put pilot Thomas Doig aboard. Doig decided to await daylight before taking the steamer across but later changed his plans. At 12:30 a.m., the vessel's course was set.

Passengers were sleeping soundly in their berths, oblivious to the ship's slow pitch in the long swells. It was high tide and the sea was calm. The pilot guided the steamer as far as the Sand Island buoy, where suddenly the ship came to a stop with a jolt.

Only some of the more curious passengers bothered to come up on deck to see what had happened. The *Great Republic* was aground on Sand Island, but word was spread among the tourists that the vessel would be refloated with the following tide. Unfortunately the ship hit the shoal at the extreme tide, and the ebb left her in a position that severely tested her hull. She was such a cumbersome vessel that the strain forward and aft played amidships, disconnecting the steam pipes.

The sea was rising; and the bilge pumps, clogged

with silt, were failing to function properly, allowing the water to gurgle through the ship's bottom unchecked. The black gang worked continuously below deck, but as fast as one pipe was connected, another would burst.

The following tide succeeded only in sending breakers scudding against the steamer, damaging her upper works and straining the hull. Passengers were ushered into their staterooms and a mild form of panic broke out down in steerage.

On the following day, when the sea modulated sufficiently, rescue ships arrived and the passengers were immediately transferred. The crew remained aboard the *Great Republic,* awaiting an opportunity to refloat her. From the shore she appeared to be virtually undamaged, but the elements took only two days to begin their destruction.

The most authoritative account of the wreck was given by Captain James Carroll, the ship's master, who testified at a special hearing following the loss of the ship. Stating that he had placed the vessel in charge of pilot Thomas Doig at 12:30 a.m., on April 19, he gave this account of the disaster:

"There was not a ripple on the water, and we came over the bar under a slow bell all the way, crossing safely and reaching the inside buoy. The first and the third officers were on the lookout with me. I had a pair of glasses and was the first to discover Sand Island, and found the bearings all right. I reported it to the pilot, who as yet had not seen it. We ran along probably two minutes, and I then told the pilot that I thought we were getting too close to the island and that he had better haul her up. He replied, 'I do not think we are in far enough.' A minute later I said, 'Port your helm and put it hard over, as I think you are getting too near the island.' He made no reply, but ran along for about five minutes and then put the helm hard aport, and the vessel swung up, heading toward Astoria, but the ebb tide caught her on the starboard bow and, being so near the island, sent her on the spit.

"She went on so lightly that few knew of the accident, but as the tide was falling we had no chance to get the vessel off that night. The next tide was a small one, and we could do nothing, and as the barometer was falling, indicating a storm, I sent Mr. Peck, the purser, to Fort Canby for assistance. The tugs *Brenham* and *Canby* arrived, followed soon afterward by the *Shubrick* and the *Columbia.* With the aid of small boats the passengers were transferred to these steamers and taken to Astoria, the *Brenham* making two trips. The entire crew remained on board and I made arrangements with Captain Flavel to have three tugs there at high tide. In the meantime the crew was at work discharging coal in an effort to lighten the vessel. At 8 p.m. a southwest gale started in, making a heavy sea, chopping to the southeast about midnight. Up to this time the ship was lying easy and making no water, but the heavy sea prevented the tugs from rendering assistance and also drove her higher on the spit, and shortly after midnight, she began to work, breaking the steam pipes and disabling engines. The few remaining passengers were put ashore on Sand Island at 6 a.m. on Sunday and were followed by the crew, the ship commencing to break up so that it was dangerous to remain on board. The last boat left the ship at 10:30 a.m., and in getting away, the steering oar broke and the boat capsized, drowning eleven of the fourteen men it contained.

"About this time a heavy sea boarded the ship and carried away the staterooms on the starboard side, gutted the dining room, broke up the floor of the social hall, and carried away the piano. Several seas afterward boarded her forward and carried away the starboard guard, officers' room and steerage deck, also a number of horses. I remained aboard until 5 p.m., when the pilot and I lowered a lifeboat and came ashore."

At the time of the disaster the *Great Republic* was insured for $50,000, and her cargo at an additional $25,000. She carried 1,059 tons of general freight valued at $75,000. Among the cargo were twenty-seven horses, and only seven managed to reach the shore after they were dumped overboard.

Thomas Doig, pilot of the *Great Republic,* was called at the hearing to give his version of the disaster. Under oath he stated:

"I took charge of the ship at the automatic buoy at 12:30 a.m. It was a starlight night, and I had no doubt about keeping the course and getting in all right. After taking charge, I headed her for the bar which I crossed in safety at 12:55 a.m. I kept the lead going constantly from the time I took charge, and after crossing the bar, I put the ship under a slow bell, and ran her that way until she grounded. After crossing the bar I took my course for the middle of Sand Island with a bright lookout kept. Captain Carroll reported Sand Island to me, and I answered him and said, 'That's all right.' He then said, 'Port your helm, Doig: she is getting too near the Island.' I answered, 'I don't think she is far enough in from two to four minutes.' About that time I sighted Sand Island and put her helm hard over, she answering her helm and coming up on her course headed east northeast; but immediately on getting her on her course she brought up on the spit with her port bilge.

"On her starboard quarter I had five fathoms by the lead, and the only reason I can give for the disaster is that, when I took charge of the vessel, I did not figure on the ebb being so strong. I knew the tide had been ebbing for at least an hour and a half, but had no fear as to her not having water enough, as she was drawing but seventeen feet, and I knew there was plenty of water for that draught at that stage of the tide. The ship working under a slow bell, and the ebb tide striking her on the starboard quarter, had set her down for at least a quarter or a half mile from where I thought I was on my course. When she brought up on the spit, her headway was so slow that the jar was hardly noticeable by those who were standing on deck, and both the Captain and myself thought she would go off at the next high tide."

The decision of the marine inspectors' inquiry resulted in the suspension of pilot Doig's license for one year and Captain Carroll's license for six months. Upon hearing the decision, Carroll immediately appealed to the supervising inspector and had no trouble in getting the decision against himself reversed.

Passengers aboard the *Great Republic* commended the able way in which Carroll had handled the complex situation after his vessel struck the sands.

The wreck was purchased by Jackson & Meyers from the underwriters, who were represented by Captain George Flavel. The salvage firm paid $3,780 for the wreck and took into partnership J. H. D. Gray, W. S. Kinney and W. S. Gibson, of Astoria, who formed the Great Republic Wrecking Company.

They set to work immediately salvaging the remaining cargo. A month later the hull aft of the walking beam crumbled into the sea and the fore and mainmast went over the side. In another ten days the walking beam and the two large paddle wheels alone remained intact. Parts of the wreckage could be seen at low tide as late as the turn of the century. The steamer's grave was marked on navigation charts thereafter as Republic Spit.

The months following the loss of the *Great Republic* were both prosperous and disastrous on the Columbia River.

On the brighter side of the ledger were events like the arrival of the steamers *Oregon* and the *State of California,* which marked a new era in coastwise passenger travel. The newly formed Oregon Railway and Navigation Company offered rail and sea connections at Portland and other ports in the area. More towns popped up along the river banks. Lumbering, fishing, and farming became large industries. Both Astoria and Portland prospered. But the portal to world trade through the Columbia's entrance was still a treacherous waterway about which little had been done. It became increasingly apparent that if the Columbia were to meet the growing demands of maritime traffic, steps would have to be taken to improve the bar conditions. The combination of sand and sea would have to be challenged.

It was during this period, the 1880s, that plans for the construction of a jetty passed the talking stage and became a reality.

As the years rolled by, traffic negotiating the Columbia bar was afforded greater protection but the grim reminders of the past were still in existence.

British Bark *Peter Iredale*

The final anguish of a great vessel—whether or not she is carrying down with her the men who served her—is a spectacle that, once seen, is never forgotten. Even the last agony of an abandoned ship, or of a hopelessly stranded one, is more impressive, more solemn than most land burials—but like man, a ship is soon forgotten.

Occasionally, however, the wreck of a ship cast up on a lonely beach refuses to die, her will to live seemingly uncrushable. Such a ship is the *Peter Iredale.* For 55 years her bowsprit pointed to the sky, while her carcass lay on the beach, her rusting iron and steel hull a prey to the surging tide—and also the ebbing tide, when sand filled each nook and cranny.

Bit by bit she was eaten away. Then, in the fateful year of 1961, early autumn storms caused the supports for her lengthy bowsprit to break loose and fall into

British bark, *Peter Iredale*, a costly calamity on Clatsop Beach, October 25, 1906.

the surf. This was the last reminder that the *Iredale* was once a great windship. What remains is no longer the picturesque sight it once was, but her iron and steel bones have withstood the onslaught of nature perhaps better than any other wreck marking West Coast beaches.

The *Iredale* was in line of fire from the Japanese submarine that shelled the Oregon Coast in the early months of World War II. The coastal blackout was in effect, and the submarine fired blindly toward Fort Stevens, but the shells cleared the wreck, landing in the open acres beyond without inflicting damage. As a protection against possible invasion, the entire beach along Clatsop sands was lined with barbed wire, which was also spread over the remains of the *Iredale*.

This wreck was once a handsome British sailing vessel, a large, dependable sailer. She was ruggedly constructed with steel plates over iron frames, a partial iron deck, and steel masts. Ritson & Company of Maryport, England, built her in 1890, for P. Iredale and Porter. She made her homeport in Liverpool. Of 2,075 gross tons, a length of 287.5 feet, and a beam of 40 feet, she was one of the larger sailing ships of her day and one of the finest.

The *Iredale* was a familiar sight in Pacific Northwest ports in her early years, becoming especially well known on the Columbia River. After sixteen years of service, concern over her loss was widespread.

It was at 6 a.m., October 25, 1906, that the *Peter Iredale,* 28 days out from Salina Cruz, went ashore on Clatsop Beach, a few miles south of the jetty. Her distress signals alerted the Point Adams Lifesaving crew, who were joined by the Fort Canby (Cape Disappointment) crew and soldiers from Fort Stevens in moving their rescue equipment to the scene of the wreck. Fortunately, evacuation of the crew came off without incident, and there were no injuries.

William K. "Ken" Inman, a member of the Fort Canby crew and resident of Ilwaco, recalled wading out waist-deep to the last of the surfboats and carrying in Captain H. Lawrence, master of the *Iredale.* The captain told Inman that he thought his ship was fifty miles offshore when he encountered trouble, and had been trying for a fast run up the coast. He had offered his crew a bonus, if five days could be cut from the usual sailing time.

When Lawrence came ashore, he carried the ship's log, a sextant, and a bottle of whiskey. After thanking his rescuers, he placed his salvage on the sands near him, and stood at attention, gazing silently at the battered wreck of his ship. He then saluted the *Iredale* with a simple,

"May God bless you, and may your bones bleach in the sands." Picking up the bottle, he passed it among the men about him, offering each a drink.

Captain Lawrence later gave this account of the stranding of his ship:

"I picked up Tillamook Light at 2 a.m. and immediately called all hands to set all sails, intending to stand off for the mouth of the Columbia and pick up a pilot by day. A heavy southeast wind blew and a strong current prevailed. Before the vessel could be veered around, she was in the breakers and all efforts to keep her off were unavailing.

"The first shock sent the mizzen top hamper overboard, and when she struck again, parts of other masts snapped like pipe stems. It was a miracle that none of the crew was killed by the falling masts as the ship pounded in the surf. After the crew had escaped the danger of the falling debris, all hands were summoned aft as the vessel ran up on the shelving sands with little violence. I told them to abandon ship. The Point Adams surf boat was soon alongside and took all hands quickly and safely ashore."

The survivors were taken by train to Astoria. There they were turned over to the British vice consul, P. I.

Oregon State Highway Commission

The remains of the *Iredale*, as they appeared nearly a half century after the ship was wrecked. Since then, the famed bowsprit has tumbled into the sea.

Cherry, until the wreck was investigated and the insurance matters adjusted with the owners, Iredale and Porter of Liverpool. Meanwhile salvage attempts were undertaken, but all proved futile. Following her abandonment, the *Iredale* was whipped by gales and heavy seas. As the sands built up around her listed hull, her rigging became a tangled mass of wreckage.

With each passing year, the pathetic plight of the *Peter Iredale* has grown worse. Depending on the strange pranks of the shifting sands, her hull is seen each year in varying degrees. Yet, she still attracts thousands of visitors and has probably been the subject of more photographers and artists than any other wreck along the coastline of the United States.

French Ship *Alice*

To be sealed in a coffin of cement, was the fate of the once-graceful sailing ship *Alice.* This tall ship, which flew the French Tricolor, was another of the many victims that succumbed to the hungry sands along the North Beach Peninsula.

Bitter cold and a strong gale on the fifteenth day of January 1909, had made the fringes of the 28-mile-long peninsula a solid mass of white fury. Out there in that stormy murk, the *Alice* was fighting her way in a bid to gain safer waters. She wanted to pick up a pilot and enter the Columbia River, after her lengthy passage from London via Hobart, Australia.

It was still early morning, pitch-dark and foreboding. Captain Aubert was frankly worried for the safety of his crew, his ship, and her full cargo of cement—some 3,000 tons of it. All hands were sea weary following their 176-day passage, but the sight of land was obscured that black morning. There had been little sleep for any aboard, for all were employed in handling the ship and trimming her sails.

Then suddenly the ship lurched forward as her bottom struck the sand amid roaring breakers. Fear masked the faces of the crew, well aware of the sinister reputation of the Graveyard.

Meanwhile, a dog had wandered down to the dunes on the beach, near where the wreck had come ashore. As soon as the ship hit the beach, about 4:10 a.m., he began howling as if in great pain. He kept this up until his master, a boy named Willie Taylor, was attracted to the scene. The dog himself had been a shipwreck

Charles Fitzpatrick Collection

A howling gale drove the French ship *Alice* onto the sands of North Beach Peninsula, January 15, 1909. Her coffin was sealed by a cargo of 3,000 tons of cement. Note the crewman on yardarm and one at crosstrees, in this picture taken a few days after her loss.

victim two years earlier when the *Solano* was wrecked. Ironically he was now responsible for alerting his master of impending disaster.

Willie quickly spread the word; and Captain Conick, with his crew from the Klipsan Lifesaving Station, hitched the horses, placed the surf boat on the beach cart, and took off for the scene of the wreck. It was a difficult job to reach the ship because the soft sand and adverse weather made the horses balky. As it turned out, most of the efforts of the lifesaving crew were futile. The crew of the *Alice* had defied the elements, launched their own boats, and made a successful run through the high surf. All hands reached shore safely.

The wreck was lying head-on to the beach, three hundred yards offshore, her fore and main top-gallant masts gone, her lower topsails and foresail in tatters. She was listing heavily to starboard and settling by the the bow, as seas swept her decks. It was four days before the ship could again be boarded.

Finally Captain Aubert and some members of the lifesaving station did get aboard the wreck, but the tangled mass that greeted them was an unpleasant sight. The tremendous weight of her cargo had pulled the 2,509-ton vessel down into the sand. Virtually a new ship—having been built at Bordeaux in 1901—she was one of the largest sailing vessels under the French flag.

One of her masts remained above the surf until 1930, when it finally crashed into the sea. At this writing a vestige of the wreck can be seen on minus tides, but the bulk of her hull has been sucked down into the sand—held together by hardened cement.

American Freighter *Mauna Ala*

The story of the *Mauna Ala* shows the necessity of aids to navigation and what happens when they become inoperative in treacherous waters.

On December 7, 1941, the news of the Japanese bombardment of Pearl Harbor reached continental United States. Three days later the entire coast was blacked out. Under-sea marauders were taking their toll of American ships in the Pacific, and all radios were silenced.

The Matson Line Christmas ship *Mauna Ala* was en route to Honolulu when she received a dispatch to return to the nearest port immediately. The vessel had received vague reports of the bombing of Pearl Harbor, but her officers were ignorant of the fact that the coast was under total blackout.

Several days later the following report on the loss of the *Mauna Ala* was forthcoming from the Bureau of Inspection and Navigation:

"The blackout of navigation aids, lights, and the silencing of radio beacons at the mouth of the Columbia River under wartime restrictions caused the wreck of the *Mauna Ala,* which stranded on Clatsop Spit, December 10, 1941."

At the hearing, O. S. Anderson, ship's officer of the wrecked freighter, testified that thirty minutes before breakers were sighted, the *Mauna Ala* was ordered to halt by a blinker light from a passing vessel. He stated that a light fog made it impossible for him to determine whether the third letter of the message was actually "L," but that the radio operator definitely believed the message to read "halt." Anderson further

Blurred in the mist, the American freighter *Mauna Ala* drove hard aground on the sands of Clatsop, December 10, 1941, after all ships were ordered back to port following the Pearl Harbor disaster.

said that Captain C. W. Saunders, Jr., master of the freighter, had been informed of the blinker warning and had accordingly ordered "dead slow" for several minutes, but later ordered full speed ahead, expecting momentarily to sight the lightship. Shortly after, breakers were sighted and the freighter piled up on the sands at 6 p.m., two and one half miles south of the position of the lightship. Observers on the beach said they could see the vessel's running lights before she hit the sands.

No one aboard the *Mauna Ala* was aware that the vessel was near the beach until she struck. She drove aground, her screw still spinning, and came to rest 700 feet from the shore. She pushed her bow hard on the sands and several hours later was turned broadside by the surf. It was then that the breakers began their destruction.

The Coast Guard lifeboats removed the crew of thirty-five and took them to Point Adams, while tugs and salvage craft stood by the freighter.

Lashed by high winds and heavy seas, the steamer broke in two several days later, most of her $750,000 cargo being lost. Besides the 60,000 Christmas trees, she carried a large shipment of turkeys, meats, general cargo, lumber and shingles. The holiday essentials were for Hawaii's Christmas from Pacific Northwest ports.

On December 17, the Columbia Salvage Company began operations to save parts of the ship's cargo, but the efforts were short lived.

Captain Saunders testified that the *Mauna Ala* was 750 miles at sea when orders were received to return to port. She carried no pilot and the proximity of land could not be determined when the ship went aground in the blackout.

The big freighter, built at Bath, Maine, in 1918, as the *Canibas*, grossed 6,256 tons, and was one of the largest lost around the Columbia bar, with a length of over 420 feet.

American Freighter *C-Trader*

The ocean graveyard long provided rich booty for those who dwelled along its shores. Before the advent of superhighways and bridges, tourists were a rarity. The permanent year-round dwellers reaped most of the treasures that wrecked ships cast ashore.

When the cry "shipwreck" echoed among the dunes, there was first a concerted drive to bring the tempest-tossed mariner safely ashore. Not only the lifesaving crews helped, but so did practically every man, woman, and child in the vicinity. With rescue taken care of, shore dwellers frequently watched day and night for the wreck to succumb to the elements and scatter its treasure.

Competing with the beachcombers, before the turn of the century, were wreckers who purchased abandoned craft from the underwriters and recovered whatever they could. The underwriter's agent, or wreck commissioner, would hastily check prospects for refloating the wreck while local citizens hovered greedily around, awaiting the verdict. If the wreck was abandoned, the agent would sometimes vie with the beachcombers in pilfering the sea booty.

As wrecks became rarer, an aura of romance vanished with them. Gallant lifesaving crews, faithful lighthouse keepers, straining horses pulling the beach carts, glowing fires by night, breeches buoys, Lyle line-throwing guns, excited crowds and barking dogs—all these have become part of an era that has ended. Replacing them are the wonders of radio, radar, and Loran—the latter a system of long-range navigation for finding the geographical position of a ship. Then there are the great salvage tugs, the helicopters, the high-powered rescue craft, and other modern innovations.

When a wreck occurs nowadays—as it still occasionally does — and a helpless vessel disgorges into the Graveyard, that same old-time excitement returns in the thrill of collecting graveyard treasure.

One such modern incident, on December 6, 1963, was the wreck of the coastwise lumber vessel, *C-Trader*. She was a 2,392-gross-ton freighter, 256 feet long, with a 43-foot beam and a draft of 23 feet. In her depths was a large diesel engine with an output of 1,300 horsepower. A few years earlier, the vessel had been specially converted and modernized by her owners, W. R. Chamberlin & Company of Portland and San Francisco, for the haulage of coastal lumber. She carried a small crew and deck cranes for handling the lumber quickly and efficiently. The *C-Trader* was built in 1944, at Camden, New Jersey, and launched as a small wartime government freighter with the designation *BAK-2*. With the end of the war, she was sold surplus and given the name *Laughlan McKay,* before coming out west as a lumber packer. As one of the last of a once great coastal fleet, she was a holdout in a day when land transportation has virtually driven such vessels from the face of the waters.

The *C-Trader* had loaded a full cargo of 2.4 million feet of lumber at Raymond, Washington, in the Willapa Harbor area. The vessel was a mass of lumber piled several feet high in an uninterrupted stack, from the superstructure aft, clear to the forecastle.

Storm flags had been flying at Willapa Bay, but the ship was loaded, ready to sail, and Captain Francis Leary, a swarthy, experienced master mariner, was anxious to get under way. His port of destination was San Pedro, California. He checked with Chief Engineer George Steiner and found all was well, below. Furthermore, the tide was right on the bar.

Yet, the winds were creating heavy swells, and the ship was down to her marks.

With little fanfare, the *C-Trader*'s lines were dropped at the lumber dock, and she pulled out into the stream as she had done hundreds of times before, at various ports along the coast. When the *Trader* neared

Les T. Ordeman

Lumber carrier *C-Trader* was taken in tow by the *Salvage Chief*, December 1963, when she began leaking off the Washington Coast. In this photo she still carried most of her 2.4 million feet of lumber.

Willapa bar, the wind began to stiffen, and the heavily laden craft pitched and rolled.

Captain Leary showed some anxiety but gave little thought to serious trouble. Then suddenly the steering mechanism began to act strangely; the ship grew sluggish in answering the helm. Laboring and shuddering, she dug her snout into a huge swell, then dropped into a trough. There was a scraping sound as the vessel thumped over the shoals. The crewmen—above and below—were tense, listening. A hasty check showed the ship was taking water.

Five miles off the Willapa entrance, water began pouring through the started plates. The engine room filled rapidly. Pumps were going full capacity—1,000 gallons per minute—but they could not check the inflow. They scarcely slowed it down. The time was 4:30 p.m., Friday, December 6, a day Captain Leary would not soon forget. Within an hour the rising waters stopped the pumps and drove the engine room crew from the recesses of the ship.

Aboard the *C-Trader* were twenty-two men, their lives in jeopardy if the ship went down—and the lashings were beginning to weaken on the huge deck load. Captain Leary ordered an SOS sent out. Emergency radio frequencies came alive with activity. Waves struck the vessel's side like ramrods—a symphonic rendition that sounded of death. The Coast Guard picked up the message and immediately the cutter *Mallow* and the 52-foot motor lifeboat from Cape Disappointment hurried to the stricken ship. When the *Mallow* arrived, her skipper, Lt. Commander A. G. Taylor, knew that the *C-Trader*'s situation was serious. Her crew was taken aboard the motor lifeboat in an orderly evacuation. Captain Leary and Chief Engineer Steiner remained with the ship. The *Mallow* stood by, awaiting the powerful tug *Salvage Chief*, famed savior of many a ship in distress.

The experienced crew worked fast to get a towing hawser aboard the floundering vessel. Destination was the haven inside the Columbia River bar, but time was running out. As a precaution, the *C-Trader*'s skipper and chief engineer finally boarded the salvage ship.

Riding low in the water and drawing almost 27 feet, the cumbersome freighter became increasingly difficult to tow. However, the *Salvage Chief* was equal to the task—if she could just get her charge to port before it gulped up too much ocean. But the *C-Trader* had an insatiable thirst; she settled deeper and deeper.

Minutes ticked slowly by as the long haul continued. The tug crewmen kept a close eye on the towing haw-

Les T. Ordeman

The *C-Trader* struck sands outbound over Willapa bar and again while she was being towed into the Columbia. Stern down, sea and sand soon fatally trapped her.

ser, watching every erratic movement of the freighter. By this time the ship had taken a noticeable list. Water was swirling over her main deck. Lumber was breaking loose, banging and splitting.

On the bar, they breasted each swell with a spray of spume; and success seemed certain when, suddenly, the *C-Trader*'s submarine-like stern struck and the ship was hung up on a shoal just out of the main channel. It was the end of the line. The *Salvage Chief* helped her get a good grip on the sand so that she would not go down into deep water; then took up a tight line so that the sand would not suck her down.

The wreck was in a shifting position, 1,600 yards, 271 degrees true, from Desdemona Sands Light. Heeled to port, her stern and pilothouse were soon completely submerged. The lumber on her decks broke loose and drifted away in cargo lots—onto the beaches, into the channel, and out to sea. Small boats from every direction swooped in to reap the bounty of the sea. Beach dwellers searched the shore in trucks to haul the loot. Others came in family automobiles, or just on foot, to salvage the lumber.

Fearing that the stranded hulk might cause another wreck, the Coast Guard placed a red buoy with a quick flashing light near the stern of the vessel. Mariners were urged to proceed with caution and would-be poachers were warned to stay away. Meanwhile the lumber roundup continued with gusto, and the fate of the *C-Trader* hung in the balance. Was the ship to be abandoned? Lloyd's agent pondered the matter and decided that there was still hope of patching her. Pacific Inland Navigation Company then offered to take the wreck on a "no cure, no pay" basis, hired the *Salvage Chief* to keep a strain on the ship, and dispatched two tugs and a barge to the scene. But after removing some of the ship's lumber cargo on December 17—11 days after she hit—they gave up in despair. The wreck had assumed a 38-degree list, making salvage work not only highly dangerous but almost impossible.

Both the owners and underwriters now abandoned the ship. Whose responsibility was it?

C. Alan Rees, agent for the Salvage Association of London, which represented the underwriters, said it had become economically impossible to refloat the ship or to unload the lumber cargo. Strong and dangerous tides and eddies produced a scouring action around the hull.

"It's too dangerous for men to work there," Rees said.

The government at first refused responsibility for the wreck, stating that it was not in the channel proper and did not represent an emergency. Then the U.S. Army Engineers, Portland district, under Colonel Sterling K. Eisiminger, found a loophole whereby the government could issue bids to remove the wreck, under provision of an old act dating back to 1899, which grants the Engineers authority in an emergency situation. This was a borderline case.

While bids were called for removing the wreck, the unwanted hulk reposed uneasily, the Coast Guard keeping a vigil over her. At nightfall the bright lights of Astoria illuminated the sky, silhouetting the grim, twisted remains of the ill-fated vessel that had been so close to salvation. Only a few days earlier she had been a live ship insured for $800,000, carrying a fine load of lumber reputed to be worth $125,000. Now her value could be counted in pennies.

A few days later, a strange thing happened. As the insurance company prepared to pay the loss on the vessel, the *C-Trader*'s sistership, the *Alaska Spruce,* was crossing the Columbia bar, packed with lumber for Los Angeles. As she neared the vicinity where her running mate lay hopelessly aground, her steering cable broke, leaving her at the mercy of the elements. Fortunately a favorable tide carried the ship to sea while her crew feverishly constructed a jury rig, which permitted her to maneuver during the night. Except

Hopelessly wrecked, the *C-Trader* was abandoned as a total loss.

for a turn of luck, the *Alaska Spruce* might have ended up on a shoal right next to her sistership. Throughout the night, the Coast Guard cutter *Yocona* stood by the troubled freighter, and the next day the tug *Mohawk* took her in tow, bringing her safely back to Astoria.

Another strange twist to this story is the fact that a third sistership, the *Alaska Cedar,* was wrecked on the Coos Bay, Oregon, jetty when her engine failed while she was crossing the bar—just one year, lacking a few days, before the *C-Trader* came to grief. All three vessels were built at the same yard in the same year, and all came to the Pacific Coast for the same type of operation. It would almost seem that their compulsion to live and work together nearly brought them to death together.

In January, the Army Engineers chose a contractor to remove the wreck of the *C-Trader.* The successful low bidder was the R. L. Matthews Logging Company of Coos Bay, Oregon; the price was $143,000. The terms called for removing or lowering the vessel so that no portion extended above the removal line—23 feet below mean low water. To complete the job, the company was given 75 calendar days from the date of the awarding of the contract.

All of the wreck's equipment and contents were to become the property of the Matthews Company. The "take" consisted of 50 barrels of diesel fuel oil, between 600 and 700 gallons of lubricating oil, and 1.8 million feet of fir and hemlock lumber stowed below deck. The salvage job was difficult and the working conditions deplorable in this battle between human ingenuity and the warring elements of nature, for possession of the spoils—and winner take all.

The wreck was cut to the prescribed depth within the required time. The Coast Guard ceased its vigil, removed its buoy, and announced—along with the Army Engineers—that the wreck was no longer a navigation hazard.

CHAPTER 7

STORM

Few months in the year pass without the storm flags flying from the local weather tower at the mouth of the Columbia, warning ships of impending danger. Ugly weather is no respecter of ships and sailors, and when the barometer falls and the wind kicks up along those stretches, mariners know it is time to get out the oilskins.

Proving that the Pacific Graveyard is a place to be feared, is an article that appeared in the *Seattle Times* on January 30, 1920.

"North Head, Wash.—The hurricane which yesterday swept over this section was by far the most severe storm that ever visited the North Pacific, based upon wind velocity which, according to the official weather estimates, attained the speed of 160 miles per hour.

"According to records here, no such wind velocity has ever before been reported anywhere along the Pacific Coast.

"The anemometer tower at the weather station was razed by the gale after government instruments had recorded a wind of 132 miles per hour. All movable things in the path of the storm were swept away and damage to government buildings and property was large.

"When the hurricane was at its height, the government wireless antenna was blown away, and the cottage which housed the family of the operator in charge was demolished. All telegraph and telephone lines were swept away and roofs of all buildings on North Head were razed and blown away. Fully eighty per cent of all matured trees on North Head were razed and all roads were blocked by fallen trees and debris."

Forty-two years were to pass before the Pacific Northwest was hit by another such gale. The Columbus Day Storm of 1962 will probably be remembered as the most famous wind disaster in West Coast history, but it bypassed the mouth of the Columbia. On reaching the Portland-Vancouver area, its "eye" was off the Graveyard.

Funneling through the Willamette Valley, its hurricane winds met the winds from the Columbia Gorge head-on. As ships broke loose from their moorings in Portland's Harbor, and tugs, barges, and boats were hurtled over the waves, citizens clocked the howling gusts to a shocking peak of 116 miles per hour. In Hebo, Oregon, they peaked at 170, topping the North Head official estimate of 160.

Steamer *General Warren*

Forty-two lives were sacrificed in the tragic loss of the steamer *General Warren* on Clatsop Spit, January 28, 1852. The vessel departed Portland with fifty-two persons aboard and a capacity load of grain. A long trail of black smoke belched from her stack, as the "steam kettle" moved down river, leaving a frothy wake behind. Folks gathered at the river settlements to watch the vessel pass by, for, in that early day, steamboats were still a novelty.

Formerly a Bangor packet steamer, the *General Warren* was artistically furnished. Her main lounge presented an array of carved woodwork and plush furniture, and at the top of the grand staircase hung a life-size portrait of the general for whom she was named.

General Joseph Warren, who lost his life in the battle of Bunker Hill, was the man who, on April 18, 1775, sent Paul Revere and William Dawes on their famous ride.

Captain Flavel piloted the steamer down the river and across the bar on what was to be her final trip. After he was picked up by the pilot schooner *Mary Taylor,* the packet's master—Captain Charles Thompson—assumed command and pointed the vessel's bow to the southwest in late afternoon on January 28. Under an overcast sky she moved slowly under steam and a light spread of canvas, but towards evening the wind had reached gale-like proportions and the foretopmast was carried away. Water seeped into the hold, soaking the grain and choking the pumps.

Captain Thompson stood on the bridge maintaining his vigil all through the night. When darkness faded, the vessel was put about with great difficulty and her course set for returning to the Columbia. Signal flags called for a pilot to come out and guide the vessel into calm waters, but it was 3 p.m. the following day before the pilot schooner could battle her way across the bar and put pilot Flavel aboard again.

Toward evening a strong ebb tide was running on the bar and the swells were mountainous. Flavel was not willing to make the crossing until the conditions improved, but the frightened passengers gathered around him and pleaded for him to change his decision for fear that the vessel might founder. Later came threats and shaking fists, but the pilot still refused. Even the ship's master desired to risk the crossing and told Flavel that his vessel was incapable of staying afloat much longer. Again the passengers moved in on the pilot, taunting him with cowardice.

In desperation, Flavel said, "Very well, if you insist on going, I will take you in, but I refuse to be responsible for what might happen."

He signalled the pilot schooner to accompany the *Warren,* but the wind changed and the schooner drifted away from the steamer.

The vessel made little headway and water was gaining rapidly in her holds. The pilot ordered the anchors dropped, but Thompson insisted that his ship should be beached immediately if it were to be saved. Respecting the captain's desire, the course was altered and the steamer was run hard aground on the spit at 7 p.m.

All hands huddled forward. Some prayed, some cursed, and others sang to keep fear from gripping them as the seas buffeted the vessel without mercy.

The ship was breaking up fast and most of the lifeboats had been demolished by the seas. Finally Thompson called for volunteers to man an undamaged lifeboat and go in search of help. There followed a long pause, for each felt his chances of survival would be better by remaining with the steamer. Finally ten men stepped forward.

With the pilot's superior knowledge of the bar, Thompson requested that he take charge of the boat. Flavel agreed, and the craft was put over the side, nothing short of a miracle keeping it from swamping.

As the feeble cheering from the passengers on the steamer faded in the distance, the men pulled the oars until across the bar. With the aid of the tide they made a remarkable run to Astoria in less than three hours. They came alongside the bark *George and Martha,* at anchor in the harbor, and persuaded Captain C. Beard, master of the vessel, to send a boat to aid the shipwrecked victims.

Immediately a large whaleboat was provisioned and set out with a fresh crew to find the wreck. Fighting against odds, the boat finally reached the reported scene of the stranding, but nothing was visible. The *Warren* had been leveled by the tireless surf and forty-two persons were missing. The only vestige of the steamer was a few pieces of wreckage scattered along the beach.

The following day the shore was combed in the hope of finding some survivors, but instead only dead bodies floated in with the tide. Among them was that of Captain Thompson.

The tragic tale was climaxed with the discovery of a young married couple found dead on the beach, hands tightly locked, her wedding ring still on her finger. Even death could not part them.

Steamer *U. S. Grant*

On the banks of the Willamette, at a river vantage point known as Brooklyn, a suburb of East Portland, one of the Pacific Northwest's early propeller steamboats was constructed. She was launched in 1865, amid the fanfare of a group of farmers. Strange indeed, her builder was a farmer by trade, named Clinton Kelly, and his one secret ambition had always been to build a steamboat. He named his ambition *U. S. Grant.*

Competition was heavy on the upper Columbia and lower Willamette rivers, but the field was yet green down river, so off went the *Grant* to establish the first regular passenger and freight service between Astoria and Baker Bay. The business was seasonal, however, and the vessel did a variety of jobs up and down the Columbia, carrying the mails and occasionally towing a vessel across the bar. Later she became the summer tourist boat between Astoria and Ilwaco, gateway to the ocean beaches.

On the winter day of December 19, 1871, the *Grant* was berthed alongside the wharf at Fort Canby. Under wind-whipped rain the little steamer strained at her mooring lines. Only Captain J. H. D. Gray and his brother, A. W. Gray, the vessel's owners, were aboard.

They were below greasing the engine, when suddenly they became aware that the vessel had gone adrift. Nobody was on the wharf and the steamer was carried away unnoticed. The two men tried to get up steam, but the boilers were cold and the ship was drifting at an alarming rate towards Sand Island. They ran forward to drop the anchors, but the powerful wind soon put the steamer on the sands.

Hastily a boat was put over the side, and the two men tumbled into it before the surf could smash it to pieces. Unable to land in the surf, the craft drifted in the fury of the storm all through the night. The following day the two men were discovered huddled together in the boat, nearly frozen to death. They were picked up and brought ashore, and in spite of their experience, lived for many years afterwards.

The *Grant* proved a total loss, and her bones cluttered the beach for several months before the tide washed them out to sea. Her name board was hung on the wall of the Fort Canby Lifesaving Station, where it remained for many years among the relics of other shipwrecks.

British Bark *Lupatia*

Having once served as a lighthouse keeper on historic Tillamook Rock, the author has heard the story of the *Lupatia* told many times by the retired lightkeepers.

The tale could well be entitled, "The Portrait of a Dog," for the only survivor of the wreck was a small Australian shepherd.

According to the late Captain H. S. Wheeler, superintendent of the lighthouse construction on Tillamook Rock, the weather was nasty and a strong southeast wind was blowing on January 2, 1881. At 8 p.m., the lighthouse crew heard loud voices which penetrated the darkness in ghostly fashion. One stood out above the others, shouting the strident command, "Hard aport!"

Realizing that a ship must be in trouble near the rock, Wheeler ordered lanterns lighted and a blazing fire built to warn the seafarers of their dangerous position.

As the wind fanned the fire in the black night, the image of a great sailing ship appeared through the murk, less than 600 feet away from the rock. For a few moments the ship's port running light was visible, and Wheeler was of the opinion that the vessel had heeded the warning and had stood out to sea.

When dawn broke, the construction crew scanned the mile and a half between the rock and the shore. There silhouetted against dour-faced Tillamook Head was a mizzen topmast jutting from the sea. It was then that Wheeler realized that the ship had not heeded the warning but had crashed into the rocks.

Searching parties later found five thinly clad dead men in a rocky cove near the cliff. A half mile farther down the beach, they located another group of seven in a similar condition.

It was surmised that the men had either stripped off their clothes in attempting to swim to land or were asleep when the vessel struck and were swept into the swirling eddies and carried ashore.

When the disaster occurred, the *Lupatia* was en route to the Columbia River in ballast from Hiogo, Japan, having commenced her voyage at Antwerp. She was in command of her first officer, B. H. Raven; his brother, Captain Irvine Raven, having died at sea nine days out of Antwerp. The captain's wife was aboard at the start of the voyage but had left the ship in Japan.

When the searching party returned to the beach to give the bodies proper burial, they found a shabby dog, his eyes swollen shut from the salt water. Whining incessantly and shivering with the cold, the year-old animal was the sole survivor of the wreck. The dog was sent to a friend of Raven, residing at Astoria, and became the pet of its new owner.

The twelve men of the *Lupatia's* crew were carried a mile and a half inland and buried. Four other crew members, reported to have been aboard the ship, were never found. In the aftermath of the tragedy, Captain Wheeler ventured his theory for the loss of the *Lupatia*. He claimed that the weather was too thick to take bearings and that if the shipmaster had been going by dead reckoning, the compass might have been affected by the proximity of the shore.

The *Lupatia* was reported to have been sighted off the mouth of the Columbia, the day prior to the wreck, by the British bark *Dovenby*, whose master claimed that all appeared well aboard the vessel.

British Ship *Strathblane*

A row of tombstones now entwined in undergrowth at the Ilwaco cemetery is a worn reminder of the lives lost in the wreck of the British ship *Strathblane*, November 3, 1891.

Captain George Cuthell, master of the vessel, cupped his hands to his lips and called to first officer J. D. Murray, in charge of the lifeboat as it pulled away from the wreck:

Seven lives wer2 lost in the angry surf when the British ship *Strathblane* was wrecked south of Ocean Park, November 3, 1891. The vessel shows dimly through the fog.

"Give my love to my wife and family back home." After a slight pause, he added,

"I suppose this will be put down as just another case of reckless navigation, but, God knows, I did the best I could."

Just twelve hours earlier the log book entry read: "Thick fog, barometer falling fast, course northeast by east, 19 days out from Honolulu for the Columbia River, crew employed reefing sails and all pumps attended to."

Unaware that he had been navigating with an erratic chronometer, Cuthell had figured his position to be sixty miles offshore at the time the vessel struck the beach. The weather had been so thick that it was impossible to take observations.

After the first lifeboat had left the *Strathblane,* the remaining boats were stove in by the seas, and one of the frightened seamen flung himself into the surf and attempted to gain the shore, but was drowned in the attempt. His body was never recovered.

Hundreds of people gathered on the beach to watch rescue operations. The lifesaving crew from Klipsan arrived on the scene and made desperate efforts to reach the remaining seamen, but each lifeline that they fired fell short of its mark. Continual attempts to launch a surf boat were made, but all were repelled in the angry surf.

The seas became a heaving mass of wreckage as the *Strathblane* broke up. Those still aboard the wreck made one final attempt to reach shore after repairing the ship's damaged launch. Ten feet from the side of the ship, however, the craft capsized, drowning all hands.

Captain Cuthell, who had elected to remain with his ship, kept his post until the decks buckled beneath his feet, waiting till all hope of saving his ship was gone. Then, true to the law of the sea, he went down with his ship.

When the fury of the storm had abated, six bodies were washed ashore, including Cuthell's. The survivors were kindly cared for by the people of Ilwaco, and the dead were buried in the cemetery there, where local residents placed flowers on their graves for many years.

The *Strathblane* struck the beach on the ebb tide at 5 a.m. and had completely disintegrated by 3 p.m. the following afternoon.

For many years prior to the wreck, the *Strathblane* had operated between the United Kingdom and Portland, as a unit of the grain fleet. She first entered the

Charles Fitzpatrick

A savage southwest gale drove the American schooner, *Frank W. Howe*, onto the sands near Seaview, Washington, February 22, 1904. She soon fell victim to the relentless surf.

river in 1878, and was one of the best known vessels in the trade.

American Schooner *Frank W. Howe*

The wrath of a southwest gale was responsible for the loss of the schooner *Frank W. Howe,* which was en route to San Pedro from Ballard with a cargo of railroad ties in 1904.

The first news of the *Howe* in distress was received at 10 a.m. at the North Head Lighthouse, when flares were sighted directly west of the station. Word was relayed to the lifesaving stations, and both the Fort Canby and Klipsan crews were directed to the beach.

Out beyond the surf, a waterlogged schooner moved toward the shore. As the surf was too high to launch a boat, the lifesaving crews patiently waited for the vessel to strike the sands before attempting a rescue. Finally she struck, and immediately two line-throwing guns were set up on the sands. After several futile attempts, three lines hit their mark. A few hours later, Captain A. Keegan and six crew members came ashore by breeches buoy.

"Thank God, it's all over," said the shipmaster. Bundling up in a warm blanket, he addressed the chief of the lifesaving crew:

"We left Ballard on February 12, and all went well till the afternoon of Thursday last. . . . We were off Yaquina Bay, about 1:30 p.m., when the vessel suddenly filled. A strong southwest gale was blowing at the time and the seas were mountain high. Since then the schooner had been waterlogged and all that kept it afloat was the cargo in her hold. We had lived in the rigging and on the deck since that time without a wink of sleep and almost nothing to eat. Realizing our desperate condition, I determined to reach the Columbia River or Cape Flattery, if possible. Sail was set and we sailed and drifted before the gale until we were off the Columbia River. About 10 a.m., on the morning of February 22, the schooner's back broke clear across under the hatch. I could not enter the Columbia, and finding the schooner would weather Cape Disappointment, I headed her for a sandy beach in order to save the lives of the balance of the crew. During the terrible ordeal, a Norwegian seaman was swept from the rigging and drowned in the seas, and the cook, while taking his trick at the wheel, was crushed to death by a massive wall of water that cleaned the deck. Thank God, it's all over," he repeated.

* * *

The *Frank Howe* floated free on the next high tide but drove hard aground again with two bewildered men aboard who had come to look over salvage prospects. It didn't occur to them that they could have made sail and brought the ship into Willapa Harbor for a fat salvage claim. Owned at Boston, the *Howe* was valued at $35,000.

American Schooner *C. A. Klose*

On the night of March 26, 1905, a derelict drifted onto the beach ten miles north of Fort Canby, on North Beach Peninsula. Discovered the following day by beach dwellers, the vessel was the immediate subject of speculation.

The deserted hull came on the beach bottom up, and all theory led to the belief that the entire crew had been drowned. When the tide receded, the name *C. A. Klose* was plainly visible in black letters across the vessel's stern.

Checking with the pilot station at Astoria, it was learned that the vessel had passed over the Columbia bar several weeks earlier, bound for San Francisco from Vancouver, Washington, in command of Captain Nicholas Wagner.

Later reports revealed that the hulk had been sighted adrift by the tug *Dauntless*, off the mouth of the Columbia, before the wreck was washed up on the beach. The tug was unable to approach the derelict because of the heavy seas. On the same day, the lookout at Cape

Disappointment sighted the vessel, but by the time his report was relayed to Astoria, it was dusk and the sea was so heavy that no tug was willing to go out after it.

Early in the morning two bar tugs started out after the hulk but were summoned back when it was learned that the wreck had drifted ashore on North Beach.

The fate of the crew remained a mystery for several weeks, and after all hope had been abandoned for their safety, word was received at Astoria that they had taken to the boats several miles southwest of the Columbia River, on March 21, after their ship had given indications of foundering. Later they were picked up by a southbound vessel, but their whereabouts was not learned till the rescue ship made port several days later.

American Schooner *Admiral*

While homebound from Valparaiso for Grays Harbor, the four-masted schooner *Admiral* finished her career, January 13, 1912, after striking the south jetty of the Columbia bar in a gale that drove her sixty miles off course.

It was nearly eight bells when the telephone on the wall of the Point Adams Lifesaving Station rang. Captain O. S. Wicklund, officer in charge, answered the call and heard the voice of the keeper from one of the neighboring light stations.

"I received a wireless message from a tanker this morning stating that a four-masted schooner was in trouble off the south jetty," said the voice.

Outside, the weather was bitter, and the rain slanted down from the gray clouds hanging low over the mouth of the river.

The career of the American schooner *Admiral* ended on January 13, 1912, when she struck the south jetty of the Columbia bar in a driving gale that swept her sixty miles off course.

Clicking up the telephone receiver, Wicklund alerted the life-saving crew and then called the wireless station for any additional information, but to his dismay found that the wires had blown down.

Since the bar was impassable, he accordingly made arrangements to go to Fort Stevens and run the steam locomotive, used for repairing the jetty, out to the ship. With communications damaged, Wicklund set out on foot for the fort, bucking the wind and rain for three miles until he had reached his destination. Both the engineer and fireman who operated the locomotive volunteered to aid in the rescue, and after getting up steam, started the steel horse down the track. In the terrible wind and high seas there was danger that the trestle had been carried away. The accompanying fog all but obliterated the track from view, and the engine crept along at a snail's pace. All eyes strained forward.

Suddenly, on the track ahead, the engineer sighted the dim outline of a uniformed man carrying a bundle. The figure was down on his hands and knees slowly crawling. The engine jerked to a stop and the three men jumped out of the cab to aid the man who later identified himself as Captain Joseph Bender of the schooner *Admiral*. The bundle in his arms was his infant child, which he held close to his body to keep it from freezing.

Gasping for breath, the captain pointed down the track. "My wife! My wife!" he cried. "Go get my wife."

A short distance ahead, the engine clanked to a halt again, and there was the captain's wife clad in a thin nightgown which revealed her youthful form. Wicklund picked her up and carried her back to the cab where she fainted after asking for her baby.

A hundred feet farther on, the ship's cook was found on the trestle.

With the cab filled, the little engine back-tracked three miles to Fort Stevens, to get medical aid for the survivors.

When the locomotive arrived, the lifesaving crew was waiting with the breeches buoy and line-throwing gun, which they had loaded on a flatcar. The engine, connected with the flatcar, started across the trestle with the lifesaving crew and their gear.

Before the engine left on its second trip, Captain Bender told Wicklund that the schooner had been carried into the jetty, and he believed that the trestle had been smashed somewhere along the line. Thus caution was exercised to prevent the locomotive from plunging into the sea.

Passing the three-mile mark, they sighted the gap. Not only was the trestle smashed, but a 200-foot stretch of open water separated the two segments of the jetty.

At the opposite side of the break, the murk lifted sufficiently to sight the remainder of the shipwrecked sailors. With accuracy, a line was fired across the gap and made fast, and one by one the shivering survivors were brought to safety.

All hands were accounted for, but the schooner was nowhere in the locality. Later it was learned that the seventy-mile wind and heavy seas had driven the *Admiral* overtop of the rock-strewn jetty into the channel, where she drifted with the currents towards Peacock Spit. In an attempt to salvage the schooner, the bar tug *Wallula* had three members of her crew board the wreck to make a towline secure. As the men pulled the line aboard, the schooner capsized and they were thrown into the sea and nearly drowned. The vessel was carried onto the spit where she broke up shortly afterwards.

The *Admiral* was owned by the Pacific Shipping Company of San Francisco at the time of her loss, and had been engaged in various Pacific trade lanes since her building at North Bend, Oregon, in 1899.

British Bark *Melanope*

On a bright morning in December 1906, a curious-looking craft floated into the prevailing currents several miles off the Columbia. A lookout perched in the crow's nest of the steamer *Northland* was scanning the horizon when his glasses fell upon the strange-appear-

Woodfield Photo

Dismasted in a heavy gale, the British bark *Melanope* was abandoned off the Columbia River entrance, December 1906. Discovered by the *Northland*, the drifting wreck had only one survivor aboard—a very hungry little dog.

ing craft. After a critical examination he scrambled down the shrouds to announce his find. In a few moments a boat was swung over the side and her crew pulled toward the reported location.

Fifteen minutes later, details of the craft began to show more clearly. There was no sign of life aboard; her yardarms were dangling in their fittings and the masts were broken at the hounds. The hull bore a color of brown and dingy gray, which as they drew near showed as iron rust. Under the tattered bowsprit projected the weather-worn figurehead representing a god of the sea. The vessel strained under a severe starboard list. Aft on the starboard quarter were iron davits with blocks intact—but no tackle and no boat. On the port quarter a boat still rocked to and fro. In the deadeyes in the channels could be seen frayed rope-yarns and ragged sails draped here and there on the slanting decks.

As the boat rounded the stern of the derelict, the crew read in raised letters, flecked here and there, the name *Melanope.* Badly mauled by the storm, the vessel had come in from the mysterious sea to tell her story.

The seamen from the steamer climbed the channels, fastened the painter, and peered over the rails. Only the creaking of the loose tackle filled their ears.

Then from the fo'c'sle came a strange cry. The men worked their way forward and crept into the dank quarters. There sat a small dog nearly starved to death. He was the only living thing aboard the derelict. What had happened to the crew?

Eyeing the prospects of salvage, the *Northland* took the wreck in tow, and after encountering considerable trouble bringing her over the bar, finally got the derelict to Astoria, where she was pumped out and eventually sold to Captain James Griffiths, through her operators, J. J. Moore & Company, of San Francisco. Her new owner cut the vessel down to a barge.

Several weeks later it was learned that the *Melanope's* crew had hurriedly abandoned the ship after she was dismasted in a gale and took on a heavy starboard list. They left in such a rush they forgot the little dog that was the ship's mascot.

The master of the *Melanope,* Captain N. K. Wills, expressed amazement when he heard that his vessel had not foundered, and also that the little dog had weathered the ordeal.

Sailors who at one time or another had shipped out in the *Melanope* pointed to the incident as just another in the life of a ship that had had a curse placed upon her.

On the *Melanope's* maiden voyage from England in 1876, she stood out to sea under the banner of Potter & Company of Liverpool. She was bound for Australia, well freighted and with a large passenger list. Before the tug had cast off, an old woman was discovered peddling apples to the passengers. Nobody on board knew where she had come from.

When Captain Watson discovered the woman, he ordered her to leave his ship at once. The action so infuriated her that she blasphemed him with a torrent of curses. It took three burly seamen to control the screaming, clawing apple peddler, as they lowered her down to the tug, while the passengers looked on in amusement.

From the deck of the tug, the woman yelled, "I curse you, ship *Melanope*, for as long as you shall sail the seas," and then she shook her fist at Captain Watson as the tug steamed back to port.

Sailors of old never treated a curse lightly. It was not without precedent that the *Melanope* was dismasted in a gale on her initial voyage, and in subsequent passages met with other troubles. On one occasion her master sailed away with an Indian princess, who drank herself to death after tedious days at sea. Soon afterwards, the captain went insane and threw himself to the sharks. The mate took charge of the vessel and landed the crew at San Francisco, penniless. The ship had to be sold to pay them off. One of the seamen complained that he had seen the mate counting gold coins which he had stolen from the captain's cabin after the latter was drowned.

Then came the incident off the Columbia River, and

finally her role as a barge. The old iron hull, which reminded one of an old witch of the sea, was afloat in Canadian waters until a few years ago, but has since been scrapped.

American Tanker *Rosecrans*

In the year 1913, three ships were lost in the Pacific Graveyard.

The most tragic was the loss of the tanker *Rosecrans,* which plunged to the bottom off Peacock Spit, taking the lives of thirty-three. Only three survivors were removed from the wreckage.

If ever a luckless vessel sailed the seas, it was the *Rosecrans,* launched at Glasgow, Scotland, in 1884, as the *Methven Castle,* of the Union Castle Line. A few years later she was sold and renamed *Columbia,* and eventually came under American registry.

During the Spanish American War, the ship joined the United States Army as the transport *Rosecrans,* but so displeased was the military with her high operating costs, that she was disposed of shortly after.

Next the *Rosecrans* came to the Pacific Coast to be converted from a troop ship to a tanker for the Associated Oil Company, of San Francisco.

On March 12, 1912, after fighting a furious gale off the California Coast, she became unmanageable and was tossed broadside on the rocks at Alcatraz, twenty-two miles north of Santa Barbara. Two crew members were drowned. After she was abandoned to the underwriters, the Whitelaw Salvage Company performed an amazing salvage job and ushered the tanker off to San

Francisco, to patch up a twenty-five foot hole in her hull.

Six months later, the *Rosecrans* was completely gutted by fire while loading oil at Gaviota, but again her hull was salvaged and rebuilt at a tremendous cost.

Captain L. F. Johnson was her master during both mishaps, and the same skipper was in command when the vessel was lost for good on the morning of January 7, 1913, at the mouth of the Columbia.

The *Rosecrans* was en route to Portland from San Francisco with 20,000 barrels of crude oil valued at $200,000 when she sailed into a sixty-mile gale off the mouth of the Columbia River. Captain Johnson lost his bearings and let his ship overrun the channel entrance, coming head on with the tip of Peacock Spit.

A distress message was picked up at Cape Disappointment at 5:15 a.m.:

"Steamer *Rosecrans* on bar, send assistance, ship breaking up fast; can stay at my station no longer."

Then everything went silent and the race against death was on. By 8 a.m., the tanker broke in two and the crew was forced into the rigging for safety from the angry sea. One by one they gave up the struggle and were swept into the boiling surf. Finally only four remained, and the mast to which they clung was all that rose above the surface.

Under the most hazardous conditions, a surf boat from Point Adams reached the wreck. As the boat maneuvered near the mast, one of the four survivors became over-anxious and threw himself into the water in an effort to reach the rescuers, but before his exhausted body was pulled aboard, he had drowned. The other three were rescued.

So rough was the bar that the boat was unable to make the return crossing and, after several hours, the shore stations gave it up as lost in the tempest. Instead, the boat reached the lightship and all hands were taken safely aboard. During the attempt to lift the surf boat onto the deck of the lightship, the lines parted and the boat went adrift, still bearing the lifeless body of the seaman who had flung himself from the mast.

It wasn't until two days later that the tug *Oneonta* made her way across the bar and picked up the survivors on the lightship.

Upon reaching Astoria, the three survivors, Erick Lindmark, ship's carpenter, Joseph Lenning, quartermaster, and another man named Peters, claimed that Captain Johnson had mistaken North Head for the lightship and had never regained his bearings. Shortly after, the vessel struck the spit.

Meanwhile, the nation's newspapers screamed headlines telling of the disaster, one of the worst of the year.

American Steam Schooner *Caoba*

On the beach five miles north of Ocean Park, lies a rust-riddled boiler, the last remembrance of the steam schooner *Caoba,* cast ashore February 5, 1925, in a severe blow.

Outbound from Willapa Bay, and laden with lumber, the *Caoba* ran into a sudden gale of such velocity that her 400-horsepower engine was incapable of mak-

An ocean storm drove the American steam schooner *Caoba* ashore north of Ocean Park, February 5, 1925, abandoned by all hands.

ing any headway. Laboring under her twenty years and a heavy deckload, the steamer developed a most unholy appetite for salt water. She spat all the oakum from her seams, and all hands could note the course she made by merely watching the track of spent oakum astern. Three or four feet of bilge wash was nothing to worry about, but when it rose to nine feet despite the efforts of all hands pumping, it was time to make quick decisions.

The water put out the boiler fires, and the vessel appeared to be afloat by the deckload, which gave indications of popping the gripes under the strain.

"All hands man the lifeboats," barked Captain Alfred Sandvig. "It's black and stormy out there, but we'll take our chances."

Two boats put out into the heaving sea and for thirty-eight hours were tossed about like matchsticks. By morning they had drifted apart; the first boat was found by the tug *John Cudahy,* but the other was listed as missing with ten souls. Then from out of the misty dawn appeared a ship, which turned out to be a Canadian rumrunner, named the *Pescawha,* commanded by Captain R. Pamphley.

The grateful survivors were taken aboard, suffering intensely from the cold, but extracts from the Canadian ship's cargo soon warmed their spirits.

Before the crew of the *Caoba* could be landed, the *Pescawha* unfortunately fell in company with the Coast Guard cutter *Algonquin,* which promptly seized the vessel for carrying liquor inside the limits of the United States boundaries. The government vessel ran down the *Pescawha* and towed her back to Astoria with some 1,200 cases of liquor stacked in her holds. When the vessel was docked, her officers were immediately placed under arrest and a guard put around the vessel. It was believed that three-quarters of the cargo was dumped before the vessel was seized.

The Coast Guard was bitterly assailed in the press by those who felt strongly that traditions of the sea had been observed by the crew of the rumrunner in rescuing the seamen and that they should not have been interned. As a result of the seizure, however, twenty-three shore operators of the bootleg enterprise were picked up and convicted.

U. S. Customs Inspector Harry J. Strowbridge took over the *Pescawha* in Astoria. The cargo was discharged at the dockside and reloaded again for evi-

Charles Fitzpatrick

Final remains of the 683-ton *Caoba* were only this rusted boiler, target of sand and sea.

dence in Portland. During the stevedoring operations, twenty-seven cases of liquor were found missing.

Meanwhile the *Caoba,* held afloat by her cargo of lumber, was driven ashore near Ocean Park, on February 5. Her wooden hull lay on the beach for many years and gradually disappeared until only her rusted boiler remained to break the level contour of the acres of sand.

Sudden & Christenson, of San Francisco, were the owners of the *Caoba.*

American Motor Vessel *Pescawha*

After her brush with the law, the *Pescawha* became a black sheep among seafarers. She was sold and resold and spent much of her time straining at her lines for another chance to go back to sea.

The following scene took place eight years after her capture by the *Algonquin*:

The *Pescawha* now had the American flag flying from her staff, and had become a reformed unit from illegal trades. She shoved off from her berth on what was to be her last voyage. The date was February 27, 1933 and the place was the lower Columbia.

The *Pescawha,* a few months earlier, had been sold to an adventurer who proceeded to interest a party of ten young men in what was said to be a whaling expedition. The vessel was fitted with special gear and equipment for capturing and rendering whales.

Her crew of amateur mechanics installed a balky Maxwell car engine on the deck, where they could administer to its humors. A makeshift belt transmitted power to the propeller.

Despite the fact that a southwester was blowing, the *Pescawha* put out to sea, her sails clewed down and the Maxwell purring. Her course was down the middle of the channel. She should have hugged the south edge of the waterway to allow for drift.

The Maxwell faltered and died off buoy No. 10, and the set of the ebb tide put the vessel into the north jetty. Her skipper was crushed against the housing as the lifeboat was knocked from the davits while the crew was attempting to put it over the side.

The other crew members survived, reaching the jetty on debris. Their escape was regarded as remarkable, for the ebb was sweeping along the huge boulders of the jetty with considerable force. The *Pescawha* was reduced to splinters, with the wheel being the largest piece of wreckage found by beachcombers.

The body of the skipper, Captain Victor H. Riley, of Oregon City, was recovered in Deadman's Cove.

When gray dawn broke over the bar, the *Pescawha* was no more; and there off the jetty, her pranks of dodging the law and her attempts at reformation had their closing chapter.

American Freighter *Laurel*

The eyes and ears of the world were on a die-hard shipmaster who refused to abandon his ship after it had broken in two and was given up as a total loss. His tenacity in remaining with his ship afforded front page newspaper material, but his role as a hero angered the Coast Guard.

It all came about in a howling southwester when the Quaker Line-operated freighter *Laurel* was outbound across the Columbia bar with seven million feet of lumber destined for New York and Philadelphia, on June 16, 1929.

As the high seas buffeted the ship, the steering engine became disabled, and she was swept onto Peacock Spit. Mammoth breakers pounded the vessel unmercifully, and calls of distress crackled over the wireless asking immediate assistance.

The Coast Guard managed to get a boat over the bar, but it was unable to approach the stranded ship. The deckload had been carried overboard and the surf was a solid mass of lumber. In early morning the steamship broke in two just forward the bridge, and a nineteen-year-old seaman named Russell Smith was carried to his death. The thirty-two other crew members gathered on the after half of the vessel to await rescue.

By this time the cutter *Redwing* was standing off the wreck, waiting to pick up the survivors, should the lifeboats manage to navigate through the lumber-laden

Her deckload of lumber crashed overboard when the *Laurel* was swept onto Clatsop Spit in 1929, victim of savage breakers and a howling southwester.

sea. After several futile attempts, the lifeboats worked in near the after section of the *Laurel* and managed to remove twenty-four shipwrecked seamen, but were unable to save those remaining until the following day when the seas had moderated.

While the rescue work continued, word was received that the steam schooner *Multnomah* was in trouble on the bar. It was reported that she had lost 600,000 feet of lumber from her deckload after boiler trouble had been encountered. Torn between two rescue missions, the Coast Guard dispatched the pilot schooner to go to the aid of the *Multnomah.* Fifteen passengers were removed from the steam schooner, but shortly after they were evacuated, temporary repairs were made on the ship's boiler. The Coast Guard was relieved to learn that the vessel had reached Astoria under her own power.

Turning their efforts back to the *Laurel,* Coast-guardmen rescued all hands, with the exception of Captain Louis Johnson, master, who refused to leave his ship despite pleas by the rescue crew. The *Redwing* finally shoved off for Astoria to get medical aid for some of the survivors.

From Cape Disappointment, a steady watch was maintained over the freighter as the crashing sea licked at her remains. Planes flew over the ship and snapped pictures of the skipper pacing the deck in defiance of the conquering elements. For fifty-four hours he remained on the bridge as another gale hammered the ship, placing his life in grave peril. As the swells rolled across the bar, the forward section of the wreck was carried fully 800 feet from the after half of the freighter.

When hope was about to be abandoned for Johnson's life, a white flag suddenly appeared on the ship's bridge, indicating that he was ready to come ashore.

Several hours later the motor lifeboat fought its way to the side of the wreck, and the captain, bearing the ship's papers, money, and a few personal belongings, slid down a manila rope to the rescue craft.

Upon reaching shore, Johnson was quizzed concerning his refusal to abandon the ship several hours earlier.

"I didn't want to be a hero," he smiled, "I stayed on what was left of the ship to protect its cargo from salvagers. I had hoped that the after section of the ship would be washed on the beach so salvage would be possible, but the bulkheads gave way, which prompted me to fly the white flag."

He had kept a fire going the entire time he was aboard the wreck and had sufficient food and water to last him indefinitely.

So ended the story of a shipmaster's vigil and the life of a freighter.

American Freighter *Iowa*

Peacock Spit claimed the freighter *Iowa* and her entire complement of thirty-four men, January 12, 1936. The tragedy was one of the blackest marks against the Columbia River bar.

The vessel, owned by the States Steamship Company, was outbound from the river when a gale, estimated to have had a velocity of seventy-six miles per hour, struck. The steamer crossed the bar shortly after midnight and fought against the gale until she was swept onto Peacock Spit, early Sunday morning.

Only one faint SOS message emanated from the *Iowa's* wireless room, but that was enough to get the Coast Guard cutter *Onondaga* under way. The cutter experienced the worst the bar could offer before it finally came in sight of the wreck. Only the *Iowa's* masts and samson posts were above the sea and all signs of life had vanished. Massive whirlpools swished around the grave of the ship.

No survivors, no solution! Nobody will ever know the direct cause that led to the loss of the *Iowa,* because dead men tell no tales. Competent authorities surmised that the vessel was caught broadside by the gale's fury and carried from her course in the main channel through loss of steerage, either by a damaged rudder or injury to her steering engine.

The *Iowa* was commanded by Captain Edgar L. Yates, veteran shipmaster, who was familiar with the

The SS *Iowa* as she appeared shortly before her tragic demise in a gale at the entrance to the Columbia.

Columbia bar, having piloted many ships across its reaches during his seafaring career.

For days after the wreck, the beaches were strewn with oil-smeared lumber, sacks of flour, rope, shingles, matches, and a hundred other items which had been loaded at Puget Sound and at Longview, her final port of departure. Among the wreckage only six bodies were recovered.

From the sailors' union hall in Portland, came a storm of protests demanding an immediate investigation as to why the *Iowa* had crossed the bar in the face of a fierce gale. The wreck was probed, but evidence was lacking. The ship was resting in Davy Jones's Locker, and there were no witnesses.

American Steam Schooner *Trinidad*

On May 7, 1937, one of the most widely heralded rescues of the North Pacific took place off Willapa bar when the steam schooner *Trinidad* stretched her ribs across the sands.

Only the *Iowa's* masts and samson posts marked her grave when the Coast Guard Cutter *Onondaga* sighted her. Peacock Spit claimed her entire crew of thirty-four.

The *Trinidad* was outbound from Willapa Bay, with a load of lumber for San Francisco merchants. Head on into a sixty-mile gale went the vessel, staggering like a drunken man. Like the rest of the wooden lumber fleet, her flexible hull had yawning seams, and her master would have bet on a stack of holystones that his crew had pumped the entire North Pacific through her hull twice.

Her departure port of Raymond lay astern, and only the Pacific's fury was ahead, but the ship had crossed the bar and for several hours had tried in vain to outwit the gale. She retreated under the strain and was driven hard on a submerged shoal off North Spit, a mile due west of Willapa Light, between buoys 6 and 7.

There was a crash of splintering wood which shivered the vessel from stem to stern as snapping gripes loosened the deckload and sent it sprawling. Timbers struck end on or broadside to, smashing and tearing. The crew gathered on the bridge as Captain I. Hellestone pondered the fate of his ship and crew.

Elsewhere on the scene, the Willapa Bay motor lifeboat was out on the Pacific, aiding a distressed fish boat. When the lookout at the tower sighted flares from the spit at 8:15 p.m., there was nothing to do but summon help from the Coast Guard at the Westport Station on Grays Harbor.

At the height of the gale, the Grays Harbor boat immediately got under way. Five men in a thirty-six-foot motor lifeboat started down the coast with H. J. Perssons, the boatswain, in charge.

For fourteen miles, lifeboat *"3829"* battled walls of water, shaking herself like a wet poodle and going back for more. About 3 a.m., Perssons was greatly relieved to sight a flare from the otherwise black night. The wreck had been found at last.

The lifeboat maneuvered in close to the *Trinidad.* Each breaker brought with it the power to crush the lifeboat against the side of the wreck, but by moving in at the opportune time and pulling out with each swell, the lifeboat somehow managed to remove twenty-one crew members from the bridge. Only the second mate, Werner Kraft, was carried to his death.

For this act of heroism and ability, the crew of the *"3829"* was awarded the gold Congressional Medal for the most outstanding performance of lifesaving during the year 1937.

The luckless steam schooner had stranded so far out on the bar that she was a direct target for the full fury of the gale, which knocked her to pieces within a few hours.

Russian Freighter *Vazlav Vorovsky*

The only Russian ship ever claimed by the sands of the Columbia bar was the 374-foot steamship *Vazlav Vorovsky*. She was pounded to pieces after stranding on Peacock Spit, April 3, 1941, outbound with a $1,750,000 cargo of heavy machinery for Vladivostok.

It was midnight when the Russian ship commenced her ill-fated voyage. As she moved toward the open Pacific, a driving forty-mile gale moved in from the south. The vessel rolled and pitched and so rough was the sea that the ship was forced back and attempted to gain calmer waters. Her steering mechanism jammed and both anchors were dropped in an effort to keep her from drifting. The anchors, however, were no match for the seas and the vessel drove on the spit, southeast of Cape Disappointment Lighthouse.

Three motor lifeboats went to the aid of the stricken freighter, successfully removing the crew of thirty-seven, two of whom were women. The survivors were taken to the Coast Guard station at Point Adams, until arrangements could be made for them at Astoria.

The *Vorovsky's* master, Captain J. Tokareff, refused to leave his ship and signalled the lifeboat to shove off.

As the wind whistled across the sea, it became increasingly apparent that the vessel was in a dangerous position and was working hard on the bar. Tugs stood

Joe Williamson

Outbound with machinery and general cargo for Vladivostock, April 1941, the Russian freighter *Vazlav Vorovsky* succumbed to the fury of the Columbia bar.

Joe Williamson

Gale winds and giant breakers drove the *Vorovsky* onto Peacock Spit, where she broke like an accordion, with two cracks buckling her steel hull.

by the wreck, but thought of refloating the freighter was abandoned when she began to break up.

Twenty-four hours after the stranding, Tokareff signaled the shore station with blinker light that he was ready to quit his ship. The surf boat promptly went out to rescue him.

The following day the vessel folded like an accordion, with two giant cracks buckling her steel hull. One break was fully eight feet wide. The local fishermen had a holiday picking loot from the wreck but the water was too shallow for larger vessels to salvage any heavy machinery.

By the summer of 1950, only a few of the frames of the ship were visible on the low tide.

U. S. Army Transport *Arrow*

Digging her own grave in the sands near Cranberry Road, two miles north of Long Beach, the deactivated Army transport *Arrow* lay while Army guardsmen kept a stern eye on 1,500 souvenir hunters. Such was the situation surrounding the stranding of the *Arrow* on February 13, 1947.

The vessel was under tow from Puget Sound to the Columbia River, where she was to have been placed in the reserve fleet, near Tongue Point. Severe seas were encountered by the Army tug, and the towing line parted twice, but each time was retrieved by the tug's crew. As the seas mounted, the hawser snapped again, and the *Arrow* was carried toward the shore and trapped in the surf, driving hard up on the beach.

Ideas of getting the 320-foot vessel off soon diminished as the sand filled in around her hull. When

In this photo, the fury of the storm has abated but the swells continue to work on the hull of the *Vorovsky*.

Wade-Fitzpatrick

Thousands of cases of lard and other foodstuffs from the wrecked *Vazlav Vorovsky washed* ashore on the sands below Cape Disappointment.

Ellis Photo

From palatial luxury liner to army transport to total wreck—such was the career of the *Arrow*, trapped in the sands north of Long Beach, February 13, 1947.

hopes of salvage were dismissed, the *Arrow* was put up for sale on an "as is, where is" basis. Several salvage companies looked over the wreck, but most of them agreed that the vessel would be completely swallowed by the sands within the period of a month.

Nobody wanted the ship. Finally the Army withdrew their guards and left the *Arrow* to any who wished to pick at her remains. She settled deep in the sand but stayed intact until the summer of 1949, when local steel cutters removed what remained above the sands between tides. Some of the peninsula fishermen were slightly irritated, for they had enjoyed fishing off her rusty fantail. The wreck had also become a first-class tourist attraction.

Like great people whose success is forgotten in their sunset years, so it was with the *Arrow*. Few knew she had once been a palatial luxury liner on the east coast. Built at Bath, Maine, in 1909, as the steamer *Belfast*, she had operated as a unit of the Colonial Navigation

Company of New York. Painted a brilliant white on her exterior, she had lavish appointments on the interior, which would have stood out in contrast to the dull gray paint and steel bulkheads of her latter days. Her glamorous career ended when the Army took her over, for everything on the luxurious side went by the board.

Serving the military throughout World War II, the *Arrow* was operated as an inter-island ferry in the Hawaiian Islands, where her 4,000-horsepower engine had churned thousands of miles, carrying troops and supplies.

To keep the memory of the *Arrow* green, the citizens of Ocean Park removed her masts and placed them as a war memorial at the town's entrance to the beach,

Joe Williamson

Until local steel cutters removed what remained above sands between tides, peninsula fishermen enjoyed casting from the *Arrow's* rusty fantail.

centrally located on the twenty-eight-mile-long peninsula.

American Fish Boat *Rose Ann*

In February, 1948, the object of a wide search by the Coast Guard was the sixty-four-foot fishing vessel *Rose Ann,* reported missing after departing Astoria with a crew of four men. Though planes searched a wide area and ships had been on a constant lookout, no clue to the vessel's whereabouts was found. Finally the craft was given up for lost.

Two months later, the dragger *Jack Junior* caught her nets on some large object in several fathoms off the mouth of the Columbia. So heavy was the object that it could not be lifted, but the position was marked.

Speculation led to the theory that the obstruction might be the steel hull of the *Rose Ann*. A few weeks later, the drag boat *Princess Aho,* skippered by George Moskovita, got her net fouled in the same area and promptly sent to Astoria for a diver.

Great interest was aroused as the diver descended. Instead of the *Rose Ann,* he found the object to be an ancient hand-wrought anchor weighing about three tons.

The *Rose Ann* has yet to be located, but it is interesting to note that the old anchor might have been lost from one of the many wrecks that have occurred off Clatsop Spit. Perhaps it belonged to the *City of Dublin,* the *Edith Lorne,* the *Fern Glen,* or one of the many other victims of the Graveyard storms.

The Loss of Three Coast Guard Craft and a Fishboat

One of the saddest tragedies of local Coast Guard history occurred in the storm-tossed Columbia River bar on January 14, 1961. The toll was seven dead, plus loss of three Coast Guard craft and a fishboat. The disaster began when the fishboat *Mermaid,* manned by Bert and Stanley Bergman, lost her rudder and radioed for help.

Help came fast.

The Coast Guard 40-footer and the 36-footer went out from Cape Disappointment Lifeboat Station, and the *Triumph* from the Point Adams Lifeboat Station. The *Triumph* and the 40-footer (CG-40564) soon had towlines aboard the troubled fishboat, but the hazardous, wind-whipped seas caused the line from the *Triumph* to snap. As the waters hissed and snarled, for the crewmen it was one hand for the boat and the other for themselves.

The *Triumph* attempted to come about in an effort to retrieve the line, but the raging waters without warning flipped the motor lifeboat over, trapping her gasping crew. Only one of them managed to jump free, and the fishermen on the *Mermaid* pulled him aboard their own troubled craft. Suddenly the 40-footer rolled over in almost the same manner as had the *Triumph.*

Plowing head-on into the nightmare came the 36-footer (CG-36454), to join in the rescue effort. In a daring piece of seamanship, she managed to pick up three men on the 40-footer, but was able to do little else. She took them out to the heaving *Columbia River*

Lightship. There she received such a terrible beating while lashed to the side of the lightship that she, too filled and sank.

Meanwhile, the *Mermaid* was being torn to pieces by the barreling seas. The frantic men vainly awaited rescue. Finally the craft broke up beneath their feet, carrying them into the whirling vortex and drowning all three.

Only those aboard the 36-footer were saved—with the exception of Gordon Huggins, who was washed ashore after the *Triumph* went down. Found dazed on the beach by attendants at the North Head Light Station, he was revived at a local hospital. The veteran 52-foot motor lifeboat *Triumph* had participated in many rescues in the Graveyard, and boasted a brilliant service record.

The deceased Coastguardmen who gave their lives were Joseph E. Petrin, Gordon F. Sussex, Ralph E. Mace, John S. Hoban, and John L. Culp. Culp's body was later picked up on the beach. Both Bert and Stanley Bergman, the lost crewmen of the *Mermaid,* were from nearby Ilwaco.

CHAPTER 8

VICTORY OVER THE ELEMENTS

Seldom indeed did a ship gain her freedom, once she was trapped on the shoals of the Pacific Graveyard. The exceptions were a victory over the elements.

Canadian Schooner *Jenny Jones*

The schooner *Jenny Jones*—James "Jimmy" Jones, master—several days out of Victoria, B.C., for Portland, stood off the mouth of the Columbia River, May 13, 1864. On board were twenty-one seasick passengers and five crew members. The vessel carried a cargo consisting of ten casks of ale, one box of codfish, one pipe of brandy, 615 bundles of pig iron, twenty-eight crates of crockery, 200 bars of sugar, and five crates of glassware.

Amid cantankerous seas, several casks of ale had broken open and a pungent odor permeated the schooner, causing her to reek like a floating brewery.

Rolling in the trough of the seas, the vessel awaited the arrival of a pilot all day, but the bar schooner failed to appear. The *Jenny* had a small makeshift engine, but it was not in use this trip.

Towards late afternoon of the following day, the bar showed signs of moderating and Jones decided to attempt the crossing without a pilot. He chose the north channel, but when the ship was on the bar, the wind blew itself out, leaving the schooner at the mercy of the currents. She drifted broadside into Peacock Spit, where the surf engulfed her.

All hands, including the passengers, were mustered at the hatches to pass up cargo and toss it overboard to lighten the vessel's burden. Seamen and landlubbers worked hand in hand for hours, until at last the pilot boat appeared off the starboard quarter.

So eager were the passengers to be rescued that a boat was put over the side, swamping as soon as it hit the water and throwing four of its occupants into the surf. One by one they were dragged out, half drowned but still alive.

The pilot schooner stood nearby but was unable to get in close enough to rescue the party of the wrecked ship. Suddenly the *Jenny* began bumping over the reef. She covered about 1,000 feet, then drifted into deep water. Her stern post was stove, her fittings knocked loose, and five feet of water slopped in her bilge. Undaunted, Captain Jones, a typical sea dog, hoisted a water-soaked sail on the mainmast and got his rudderless schooner under way.

Three hours later, the *Jenny* dropped her anchor off Astoria, where all hands except the skipper were removed from the vessel.

"Better get ashore and get warmed up," hollered the master of the pilot schooner.

"It's all in the day's work," retorted Jones nonchalantly, spitting deftly over the taffrail.

This same Jimmy Jones was likely the most erratic skipper to operate in Pacific Northwest waters. Legends have grown up about him but the wildest tale is based on fact.

While running his ship between Portland and British Columbia, he was thrown into jail in Victoria because of a bad debt. His beloved *Jenny* escaped to the American side in command of the mate, but was seized and held at Olympia by the U. S. marshal.

The jail was frail — no match for the redoubtable Jimmy. With the aid of friends and disguised in women's clothing, he made his way to Olympia. There he learned that his ship was to be sent to Seattle for auction. Still bedecked in the bustle, bonnet, and veil of the times, "Miss" Jones shipped as a passenger.

When the *Jenny* stopped overnight at Steilacoom, the captain was delighted; he well knew the unsavory conditions of the sleeping quarters and the heavy insect population. Just as he figured, the marshal spent the night ashore in a hotel. Jones hijacked his own ship.

With the Canadians to the north and the Americans to the south both after him, Jimmy happily shoved off for the open sea. He carried only enough fuel for a forty-mile run; a sack of flour, a pound of tea, and two pounds of sugar. At Port Ludlow he picked up a few cords of wood, and at Nanaimo several tons of coal dust. He planned to get wood to mix with the coal dust north of Burrard Inlet. On the way, he chanced upon a leaky sloop loaded with provisions.

Sick of his flour-tea diet, Jones took the crew aboard, in return for their supplies, and again steamed happily off, this time for San Blas, Mexico. There he paid off the crew, plus $625 for the provisions; then once more sailed away, this time with freight for Mazatlan. But his troubles were mounting.

At Mazatlan, the crew demanded money. "Black Dutch" Albert pressed for $1,000. Another crewman unshipped and hid the *Jenny*'s rudder. The captain had had enough. Selling his precious ship for $10,000 he headed for San Francisco, where he was promptly arrested for taking his ship away from the marshal. On trial, Jones carefully pointed out that the ship did not leave the marshal—the marshal left the ship! The judge agreed and dismissed the case.

In his last years, Jones went on the road as a lecturer, but bad luck and bad health hounded him. He died at Victoria in 1882, aged 52, penniless and—some say—mentally unbalanced.

British Sloop of War *Raccoon*

A ship which the Columbia River bar did not claim for its own but one that left a profound mark in history was the British sloop of war *Raccoon*. The 250-ton vessel arrived off the mouth of the Columbia River, November 30, 1813, where adverse weather and bar conditions forced her to stand off the river entrance. She did not drop anchor at Astoria, until December 12, necessitating a long and frustrating wait by the crew of the ship.

Some accounts say that, while in transit, the *Raccoon* struck the bar and was hung up for several hours, but that change of tide and kedging efforts managed to get her free before any serious damage was incurred.

The close call from a major stranding might have been to blame for the ill temper of shipmaster Captain Black, when the *Raccoon* finally reached the little settlement at Astoria. His prime mission was to capture the fort, which he thought to be still in American hands. When he arrived, however, he found that the Americans had sold out to the North West Company of Montreal. Furious to find that the fort and all its contents had been sold to a British subject, the captain declared, "Great God, I could batter it down with a four-pounder in two hours." He referred to the simplicity of the little Astor-founded colony, set up by the Pacific Fur Company.

The War of 1812 being on, Black had intended to seize the fort as a prize of war. Now all that he was able to do was hoist the British flag and change the name from Astoria to Fort George. After reprimanding the British subjects for making his voyage a fiasco and defrauding himself and his officers, he hastily sailed away to the South Pacific.

Captain Black must have fumed even more when he learned a few years later that the United States got Fort George (Astoria), back. He could, though, take consolation in one thing—his ship escaped the clutches of the Columbia River bar.

French Brig *Sidi*

Leaving San Francisco on February 14, 1874, the brig *Sidi* ran into a succession of dirty weather. It was not until March 1, that she arrived off the mouth of the Columbia. Her charterers, Morgan & Sons of Portland, were greatly worried over her whereabouts.

A soupy fog hung over the river entrance. Captain Cometoux, making his initial trip into the river, was concerned about the position of his command. Dead reckoning informed him that he was dangerously near the river opening. With an unfavorable breeze approaching, he ordered the helm hard up and crossed the bar.

At the far end of Sand Island, the wind died and the vessel was forced to drop both anchors. The current started her dragging, and towards evening the tug *C. J. Brenham,* under Captain J. Hill, came to her aid and attempted to get a line aboard. The seas had kicked up considerably and the tug was unable to get close enough to make the line fast. At 10 p.m., the *Sidi* struck, at slack tide, and within a few hours was left high and dry on a shelf of sand. The crew walked ashore without getting their feet wet.

The following day, the tug returned to investigate salvage possibilities. The tug's crew observed that the stranded vessel rested in a precarious position, but found that the underwriters were willing to sell her as she lay. Captain Hill and his crew, consisting of George Warren, George Woods, and G. W. Raymond, joined forces with Captain William Koerner and F. C. Carr of Astoria, and purchased the wreck for a meager sum.

The men set to work immediately, their skill and determination motivated by the fact that the *Sidi* was insured for $50,000, and was only eight months out of the builder's shipyard. Day after day the work continued, the men divided between patching the hull and digging the sand from around the vessel. Several weeks later, with the aid of a high tide, the 276-ton brig was refloated and towed to Astoria for further repairs.

The venture was a financial success. Immediately the vessel was booked to carry lumber from Knappton to San Francisco. She was accepted under American registry, renamed *Sea Waif,* and sold to George Hume, shipping magnate of San Francisco.

American Steamship *Queen of the Pacific*

Averting what could have been a major disaster, the palatial passenger liner *Queen of the Pacific* was successfully refloated from Clatsop Beach in the fall of 1883.

The big steamer made her triumphant entry on the Pacific Coast in the late summer of 1882, and Californians hailed her as she passed through the Golden Gate. She was just out of the yards, where her Philadelphia builders had spared nothing in making her the finest afloat. Her owners, the Pacific Coast Steamship Company, had paid a substantial amount for her because competition demanded the best.

The *Queen of the Pacific* was placed in charge of Captain Ezekiel Alexander, and entered coastwise service in the fall, arriving at Portland from San Francisco, September 18, 1882, with 300 passengers and a sizable cargo.

The following year when destruction threatened, no efforts were spared to save the money-making liner.

It was to have been a celebrated voyage when the *Queen of the Pacific* departed San Francisco. Among her large passenger list were several members of the fashionable world and a collection of railroad executives en route north to witness the driving of the famous gold spike for the completion of the Northern Pacific Railroad.

When the steamer reached the mouth of the Columbia, pilot A. D. Wass boarded from the pilot schooner, but shortly after he took command, the vessel was enshrouded in a heavy fog. She drifted from the channel range, going hard ashore on Clatsop Spit, September 5. Immediately the screws went into reverse, spinning violently, but the vessel remained fast on the sands.

When the news reached Astoria, crowds of townsfolk set out for the beach to view the liner and to watch the evacuation of 230 passengers.

A dispatch from the vessel's owners in San Francisco said that the steamer must be saved regardless of the cost.

Five of the most powerful tugs in the area were summoned for salvage work. They included the *C. J. Brenham, Astoria, Columbia, Pioneer,* and *General Miles,* all of which got lines on the stranded steamer and proceeded to churn the waters. Hawsers became tight as fiddle strings, and billows of smoke belched from their stacks. Several hawsers were severed, but the stocky tugs kept going back for more punishment. The job went on hour after hour.

Fortunately the weather conditions remained mild and the work was able to continue. Finally with the aid of a high tide, the vessel loosened her grip on the sands. On the flood tide they finally got her free. The five tugs and the liner all gave prolonged blasts of their whistles, and the valleys for miles around echoed the good news that the *Queen of the Pacific* had been saved.

After a debated litigation, the combined salvage force was awarded $65,000 for services rendered, and the steamer continued a long and prosperous career after extensive bottom repairs were made.

Several years later, her name was shortened to *Queen,* and she was operated on the California, Puget Sound, and Alaska runs. On February 27, 1904, she suffered a fire off the Oregon coast, where fourteen lives were lost before the vessel finally reached Puget Sound. The *Queen* was purchased by the Japanese in 1938, and sailed across the Pacific to be broken up for scrap.

Columbia River Lightship No. 50

Columbia River Lightship No. 50 was the first lightship stationed on the U.S. Pacific Coast. The vessel was built by the Union Iron Works of San Francisco and towed north by the tug *Fearless.* She took her station off the mouth of the Columbia River in 1892, and maintained her vigil for seventeen years—except for a few months ashore near McKenzie Head.

The *No. 50* was 112 feet long with a twenty-six-foot beam and a depth of twelve and one-half feet. She was constructed with steel frames and oak planking. Her heavy construction enabled her to brave the most severe weather. The stem, sternpost, keel, and rudder were of white oak.

Her arrival on the Columbia was received with great ceremony. Mariners recognized the lightship as a welcome and comforting sight in fair weather or foul.

The vessel was not engined and was dependent on her jury rig for propulsion. She was equipped with two horizontal return tubular boilers which furnished steam to blow a twelve-inch foghorn and to raise lights on the mast by nightfall. The night lights on her two masts consisted of six lamps placed in a circle around the crosstrees to afford visibility from any direction. By day the lamps were lowered, but the vessel was easily recognized by her name painted in large letters on her sides. She was equipped with comfortable quarters for a small crew, and her compartments were thoroughly watertight and seaworthy.

The lightship was stationed southwest of the river entrance, but, in 1894, was moved still farther south to facilitate traffic.

On November 28, 1899, the *No. 50* was buffeted by terrific winds and unusually high seas which caused her to slip her anchor cables and drift toward shore in the blackness of the night.

At the crack of dawn, the tugs *Escort, Wallula,* and the lighthouse tender *Manzanita* raced to the side of the drifting lightship. The *Wallula* arrived first and managed to get a line on her. The tug had nearly gained the river entrance with its troublesome tow, when the hawser parted. The *Manzanita* then maneuvered in and put her line on the lightship, but it got tangled in her propeller and also broke. Next came the *Escort,* but she no sooner had begun to tow the vessel than her hawser also snapped.

Fear was felt for the eight crewmen aboard the lightship, but all rescue efforts had proved futile. The

Charles Fitzpatrick

Columbia River Lightship No. 50, carried ashore near McKenzie Head in 1899, is shown here being hauled across the spit on skids, to be relaunched in Baker Bay.

Escort stood by till 7 p.m., when the lightship went aground on the sands inside McKenzie Head.

When the tide receded, the *No. 50* was left high on the beach. From her position, salvage appeared a virtual impossibility. Captain Joseph Harriman and his crew were removed from the vessel, little the worse for their experiences.

The lightship remained on an even keel for several months, but her presence off the bar was badly missed, and the experts were figuring some way of getting her off the sands. The solution for salvaging the lightship proved to be a unique operation.

It was determined that, because of shoals and currents, she could not be launched back into the ocean; consequently, engineers of the Lighthouse Board decided to attempt to move her across the peninsula and launch her into Baker Bay. It was a journey of a mile, across beds of loose sand, through a forest, and over several elevations; a big job for which there was hardly a precedent. But they got to work, jacked the vessel up out of the sand, put enormously heavy trucks under her, rigged windlasses to haul the trucks, and got stout teams of horses to turn the windlasses. At the same time they cut a road through the woods and built a timber roadbed strong and smooth enough for the trucks to travel on. Then they started her and eventually she went. Cables broke and had to be replaced with stronger ones. Some days she progressed only a few feet. It took months to cover the distance, but it was done, and finally the *No. 50* lay broadside to Baker Bay.

There the salvage crew built an incline of planking down into the water, greased it as the ways are greased at a launching in a shipyard, stretched lines from bow, stern, and masts, to powerful steam tugs, then steadied her with guy ropes. Presently, with a long pull, a strong pull, and a pull all together, the land-locked ship slid down the beach and was afloat once again after sixteen months of imprisonment.

The lightship was then towed to Astoria, where she was repaired and eventually returned to her station. Three lightships have been assigned to this station at varying dates since the old *No. 50* was retired in 1909.

Many similar salvage ventures have been attempted on the ocean shores of the world, but most of these have ended in complete failure. The *No. 50*'s land

Here the picturesque *Poltalloch* proudly cuts through the seas under full sail—but the greedy sands awaited her.

Stranded on the north spit of Willapa bar in November 1900, the *Poltalloch* remained captive several months, but eventually was refloated.

voyage was a notable performance, novel and successful.

British Ship *Poltalloch*

The 2,250-ton British ship *Poltalloch,* owned by Potter Brothers, of London, was en route to Puget Sound to load grain for the United Kingdom on November 26, 1900. Off the Washington shore a heavy fog shrouded the coastline and the vessel's position was erroneously charted. She went on the sands north of the entrance to Shoalwater Bay, opposite North Cove, where the outgoing tide left her high and dry. After several anxious moments, the crew dropped the Jacob's ladder over the side and walked ashore.

Hopes of refloating the vessel ran high as her position was not dangerous. Hundreds of spectators were attracted by the spectacle, and the wreck was promptly labeled, "the ship on a voyage to nowhere."

After several months, the *Poltalloch* was removed from the sands, but the interesting incident of the stranding occurred in February 1902, when the German bark *Professor Koch* was making her way towards the Columbia River. Her helmsman sighted a large square-rigger dead ahead. He set his course for the ship, unaware that he was inbound for Shoalwater Bay and that the vessel by which he had set his course was the *Poltalloch,* aground on the sands.

With the crew aloft shortening sail, the bark was edging toward the bar when, all at once, churning through the swell came the steamer *Fulton,* which pulled up alongside the German sailer, waving a white flag.

"Where ya heading?" shouted a voice from the wheelhouse of the steamer.

A huge, ruddy-faced German leaned over the side and informed the inquirer that he was following the ship dead ahead across the bar.

"Ya darn fool," was the retort, "that there ship's aground and the tide ain't right for you to cross."

"Is not der Columbia bar?" bellowed the *Koch's* skipper.

" 'Not der Columbia bar' is right!" shouted the steamboater. "You're off Shoalwater."

As a red hue fell over the German captain's face, his ship came slowly about and stood out to sea.

British Bark *Pinmore*

During the storm season of the year 1901, the handsome four-masted British bark *Pinmore* was beating her way up the coast. From Santa Rosalia, Mexico, the weather had been unpleasant and the crew quarrelsome. The skipper was glad when his ship reached the latitudes of the Columbia River, with the worst, he thought, behind him. The vessel was traveling in ballast to Portland for a cargo of grain for the United Kingdom.

Then suddenly, as dusk began to encompass the ship, a fresh squall with heavy winds struck the vessel. The weather closed in and the sea became irascible. As the seas grew angrier, all hands were sent aloft to shorten sail. Then, without warning, the ship heeled far over to one side and refused to recover. The decks slanted at a precarious angle, and a fearful rumbling issued from the depths of the ship as the ballast began

Abandoned at the Columbia entrance in 1901, the *Pinmore* was picked up and safely towed in—to the wonderment of her crew.

to shift. The panic-stricken crew were certain that the vessel was about to roll over and succumb to the elements.

"Abandon ship," the captain ordered. Without even returning to their quarters for their personal belongings, the crewmen struggled desperately to get the boats into the water on the lee side. Soon the boats were in the raging waters, tossing like corks. Quickly they were swept away from the giant sailing ship, which was now almost touching her yardarms to the water.

There in the inky, storm-tossed sea, the pitiful little band of men, chilled to the bone, grimly pulled at the oars through the long night, struggling to reach the entrance to the river. In the early light of the following day, their straining eyes sighted a passing steamer. The ship altered her course slightly, rescued the men from the heaving waters, and took them into Astoria.

Another shock awaited them. As they looked about the tall vessels at anchor in the harbor, they spotted their old ship, the *Pinmore.* No question about it—there she was, large as life. They soon learned that another ship had sighted the abandoned *Pinmore* off the river and taken her in tow as a coveted prize of salvage. She was a handsome 310-foot craft, one of the world's longest sailing vessels of that day, and she tipped the scales at 2,358 tons. On boarding their ship, they found still another shock awaiting them: the salvagers had made off with all their personal belongings.

The *Pinmore* was repaired and went back to sea—eventually to become the World War I victim of Count Felix von Luckner, the Sea Devil, master of the German raider *Seeadler.*

Von Luckner recognized the *Pinmore,* when he sighted her from the decks of his raider that fatal day—February 19, 1917. He had voyaged many a mile in her as a common sailor, before joining the German merchant marine. Now he was in command of a raider operating in the Atlantic and Pacific. Before he was captured in 1918, he was destined to destroy some $25 million worth of Allied shipping.

He took the *Pinmore* as he had taken others, but it was not easy. No sailor with any sailor's soul in him will lift a hand to harm his old ship. But the *Pinmore* had to go. Still, he would pace her decks once more.

When the *Pinmore* crew had joined the *Seeadler,* the Sea Devil boarded the old sailing vessel alone, walked along the familiar passageways, visiting his old

The tug *Tatoosh* pulling the steamer *Washington* from sure destruction on Peacock Spit, November 17, 1911, in one of the most daring feats of skill ever seen in this area.

bunk and the stern rail where he had once carved his name, P-h-e-l-a-x L-u-e-d-i-g-e.

Returning to the raider, Luckner gave orders, then shut himself in his cabin. In the distance he heard the roar of a bomb. The proud old *Pinmore,* after thirty-five years at sea, had departed on her final voyage.

American Steam Schooner *Washington*

One of the most remarkable feats of daring in the history of the North Pacific occurred on November 17, 1911, when Captain C. T. "Buck" Bailey of the tug *Tatoosh* gambled with death in shoal-infested waters to get a line on the steam schooner *Washington,* fast aground on Peacock Spit.

The *Washington* was heavily laden with lumber when she went on the spit, and her delicate position had shoreside bets running ten to one that she would be a total loss.

For twenty endless hours the steamer was buffeted by nasty seas while, aboard, an unsung heroine, Mrs. Mary Fullmer, the only woman among the passengers, kept up the courage of all hands with humor and song.

Certainly under the circumstances it would have been an extremely dangerous task to attempt to rescue the passengers, but Bailey wasn't content with that, for he planned to save all or nothing, and when he accomplished the former, it proved the feat of the decade.

In his own modest words, Captain Bailey explained the deed after the *Washington* had been towed to safety:

"As I approached the *Washington*," said Bailey, "I could see twelve or fifteen passengers huddled together on the after end of the ship, with life-preservers on.

"I asked the captain if he had any steam to use in heaving the hawser aboard. He told me no, that the fires were out. Then I called to the passengers huddled aft and asked them to go forward and help get the hawser aboard. They did so, all of them running over the deckload of lumber and the debris like scared sheep.

"In about ten minutes' time we got the hawser aboard and it was made fast. Finally we started out with the *Washington* in tow. We came slowly through the breakers. I arrived down off the whistling buoy with the *Washington* at 3:45 o'clock. The passengers and crew acted like they were mad when we got started—threw up their hands, gesticulated and yelled at the tops of their voices. I looked over to North Head, and at the lifesaving station, and there must have been a thousand people there watching the rescue."

Later it was revealed that the *Washington* did not have a cent of insurance on her when rescued by the *Tatoosh.*

In writing to George Plummer, manager of the Puget Sound Tow Boat Company, owners of the *Tatoosh,* Bailey said that he did not care if he received a cent of salvage money for saving the *Washington,* but wished that his crew could be rewarded. The tug was valued at $91,000, a considerable gamble on such a venture. Olson & Mahoney of San Francisco, owners of the *Washington,* settled with the tug's operators in a case that commanded the attention of many shipping men.

American Schooner *North Bend*

Here is the amazing story of a schooner that saved herself. This vessel was the *North Bend;* she gained her freedom after resting on a sand spit for thirteen months.

While inbound from Adelaide for Astoria, eighty-nine days at sea, the four-master, commanded by Captain Theodore Hansen, attempted to cross the Columbia bar without a pilot. As he turned on the ranges at the mouth of the river, the wind suddenly died, and the windjammer stranded on Peacock Spit, at 2:30 a.m., January 5, 1928.

At daybreak the diesel tug, *Arrow No. 3,* plowed her way across the bar and made a gallant effort to pull

Woodfield Photo

American schooner *North Bend*, driven onto the beach near Peacock Spit, January 5, 1928, did the impossible—she worked her own way through the spit, refloating herself in the calm waters of Baker Bay.

Charles Fitzpatrick

Deck view of the *North Bend*, aground on Peacock Spit.

Looking down from the heights of Cape Disappointment on the path cut by the *North Bend* to free herself, after having been landlocked thirteen months.

the schooner free. The tug got a hawser on the vessel, but while taking up the slack, the line parted. On the second attempt the tug got the *North Bend* off the spit, and for a moment she was moving into deep water when a terrific sea struck her, breaking the hawser and tossing the schooner back on the spit.

While the salvage attempt was being carried out, the Cape Disappointment Coastguardmen removed the crew of the schooner.

During the ensuing days, heavy seas and high winds put the *North Bend* higher on the beach where she remained intact, free from the danger of breaking up. The crew returned and stood by for several days, until all attempts to salvage the vessel were abandoned.

For an entire year the schooner braved the elements, remaining virtually undamaged, and the position of the ship's hull aided the sands in playing one of those freak pranks of nature. The winter gales drove in seas that washed the sand away from the vessel and helped form a half-mile channel leading into the waters of Baker Bay. With little aid of the human variety, the vessel refloated herself and was edged down the channel to the bay on February 11, 1929, thirteen months after the stranding had occurred.

The Arrow Tug & Barge Company of Astoria, owners of the tug *Arrow No. 3*, purchased the schooner and converted her into a barge, after finding her hull in excellent condition.

Except for the dying era of sail, the *North Bend* might have returned to the sea lanes with a new suit of canvas but instead was reduced to a barge.

Norwegian Motorship *Childar*

Averting the fate that befell the *Laurel,* the Norwegian freighter *Childar* was saved from complete destruction by the uncanny salvage job performed by the Coast Guard cutter *Redwing,* off Peacock Spit, in a southwest gale that wreaked havoc along the coast on May 3, 1934.

The night was stormy along the lower reaches of the Columbia River as the motorship *Childar* moved cautiously through the drizzling rain and fog that filtered the river mouth. The *Childar* was down to her marks with a deckload of several million feet of lumber. The pilot called for constant course changes. Soundings were ringing in his ears and the ship's telegraph was jingling every few minutes. A gale was blowing outside and the wind whistled in weird crescendos through the rigging. Without warning a wall of pyramiding water poured against the side of the vessel, rolling wildly and smashing in her number one lifeboat.

That the vessel was working herself into shallow water was indicated by the terrific rolls that picked her up and plunged her into deep troughs. Losing all headway, the ship stood motionless for a brief moment and then was struck by a lunging comber that almost raised her keel completely out of water. The chain gripes which held the deckload snapped like rubber bands and the lumber began to sway wildly as though it were not sure of its freedom. Then with a thundering crash it let go and spread itself all over the decks like kindling. With each breaker the timbers smashed against the fo'c'sle and then against the superstructure,

U. S. Coast Guard

Close-up of the Norwegian Motorship *Childar*, driven ashore on the southwest end of Peacock Spit, by a heavy gale in 1934.

battering and gouging. The ship labored as the surf poured over the deck, while the crew rigged lifelines.

The careening timbers carried all loose gear over the side. Navigation was all but impossible. The howling of the storm was suddenly broken by the rending of steel plates and parting rivets. The *Childar* was aground on the southwest tip of Peacock Spit.

"Hard aport," was the command, but the vessel failed to come off her perch. She was hung up on the spit and an immediate call for help was sent out.

At Astoria the *Redwing* picked up the message at 7:07 a.m. and immediately got under way. Attempts at further contact with the *Childar* proved unavailing, for immediately after sending the distress message, her foremast was carried over the side, taking with it the aerial and the antennae.

In a phenomenal run under command of Lieutenant A. W. Davis, the cutter battled her way against the gale until she located the wreck in the murk of the new day. On the leeward, the *Redwing* was surrounded by the ship's wreckage. She edged in as close as possible and shot a pilot line over the stranded freighter, but the crew of the *Childar* was too weak to haul the wire rope aboard. Another line was shot. This time the crew was successful in hauling aboard a manila hawser. The line was made fast, and the *Redwing* moved cautiously ahead until the slack grew taut. The *Childar* appeared to be sinking, and four of five boats had been carried away. The sand and rocks had punctured her plates, and a gashing rip at No. 4 hold was evident.

Her smashed bulkheads had stood the onslaught of the sea too long; many of them had given way.

In spite of all this, the *Redwing* risked the tow, for to leave the vessel aground in her condition would have meant the lives of the entire crew. At first the freighter refused to move. Then two mountainous breakers came roaring in, lifting the vessel and enabling the cutter to get her off and begin the pull. The tow handled awkwardly, as the *Childar's* rudder had been stove, but the job had to go on.

Installing an auxiliary wireless set on the *Childar,* her Nordic skipper informed the cutter's commander that the first and second officers had been washed overboard and drowned, and that two seamen were dead and others badly injured. In turn, the *Redwing's* master called for assistance from the lifeboats at Cape Disappointment and Point Adams. These promptly came out to remove the injured and dead from the freighter. The boats removed the three most seriously injured by coming up under the *Childar's* counter while the crew lowered their shipmates over the stern in slings.

While the rescue was being carried out, one of the lifeboat crew broke four of his ribs; but the task was finally completed, and the injured were taken to Astoria while the cutter continued the tow.

Fearing that his ship would founder if the *Redwing* took her back across the bar, the *Childar's* master requested that he be towed to Puget Sound. It was a long haul, but Davis realized the danger of negotiating the bar under such circumstances.

Weakened by the terrific pounding, the vessel's bitts—to which the towing line was secured—ripped out, but fortunately hung up in the bow chocks. If the line had been lost, the *Childar* would have gone back on the spit. Already the cutter had been under way for over an hour and was not yet a safe distance from the shore. Toward afternoon the *Redwing's* course was set for Cape Flattery, commencing one of the toughest towing assignments the Coast Guard has ever been called on to perform.

The *Childar's* No. 4 hold was entirely flooded, and No. 5 hold was half full of water. The vessel had a sharp list to port, and her decks ran free with water. Cargo was strewn all over the ship, both masts had been carried into the sea, and the funnel had been knocked from its fittings.

At 8 p.m. that evening, the *Redwing* was off Grays Harbor, forty-seven miles from where the tow had begun. The *Childar's* captain expressed fear for the lives of his freezing crew. Davis wired the Grays Harbor motor lifeboat to come out and remove them. Meanwhile the freighter gave signs of breaking up.

The lifeboat came out across the bar and fell in company with the two vessels. Eighteen men were removed from the *Childar,* each by jumping into the sea and being pulled aboard the lifeboat and then transferred to the cutter. Only five men remained on the freighter, while the motor lifeboat stood by through the night to remove them should the vessel break up.

The following day, the *Redwing* was joined by the cutter *Chelan* and the steam tug *Roosevelt,* which convoyed the two vessels into Victoria, B. C., where the task ended after fifty-eight hectic hours.

The *Childar,* owned by Wiel & Amundsen of Halden, Norway, was pumped out and repaired at a cost almost equal to the value of the ship. Most of the cargo of lumber, which had been destined for Capetown, South Africa, was lost. Her faithful skipper, Captain J. Matthiasen, who stayed with his ship until she reached safe haven, was given another command after a long-deserved rest.

CHAPTER 9

FIRE, EXPLOSION, AND COLLISION

Not all disaster occurs in contrary weather. Nothing is more tragic to the mariner than to have his ship engulfed in flames, to hear the tearing of rivets and steel in a collision at sea — or to see his ship destroyed because of his own foolhardiness.

American Sternwheeler *Telephone*

By 1887, Columbia River commerce had shown signs of great progress, and river steamers shuttled to every whistle stop along its banks. The route between Portland and Astoria was highly competitive with only the swiftest and most luxurious steamers vying for the trade.

The biggest money-maker on the river was the vessel that combined the greatest speed and luxury; and

Joe Williamson

re gutted the sternwheeler *Telephone* near Astoria in November 1887, but from her charred hull was born an even more lavish vessel.

that honor rightfully fell to the steamer *Telephone,* built at Portland in 1885. Her owners claimed that she was the fastest sternwheeler in the world, and her record upheld her right to that boast. Her glory never faltered until a fire gutted her near Astoria on November 20, 1887.

Captain U. B. Scott, master and builder of the *Telephone,* was a former Ohio River skipper who took delight in showing his heels to the slower river boats. He had become wealthy by collecting bets from challenging steamboat captains who had tried in vain to outspeed the *Telephone.*

On November 20, the *Telephone* was darting toward Astoria, well ahead of schedule, when fire broke out amidships throwing pillars of flame and smoke in every direction. Panic broke out among the passengers, and Scott, who was acquainted with the peril of fire, quickly grabbed the wheel, giving it full left rudder and heading directly for the river bank. The steamer scraped over the beach doing nineteen knots. The jolt sent the passengers sprawling.

The crew attempted to restore order to protect the 140 passengers from being trampled to death, but the decks were so hot that the tourists stampeded to the railings and scrambled over the guards in droves. One by one they dropped to the mud on the beach and struggled to reach higher land.

As flames engulfed the bridge, Captain Scott was forced to jump through the pilothouse window—having discovered that the ladder had burned away. By the time he had reached safety, Astoria's horse-drawn fire wagons were winding their way over the washboard road leading down to the river bank. Spectators, startled by the blaze, came from miles around to see the steamer burn.

Oblivious to the blazing inferno, an inebriate had remained aboard, groping his way about until he was overcome by the fumes. The ashes of his body were found among the remains of the ship. Fortunately he proved to be the only casualty, though several persons suffered from burns and other injuries.

The housing of the steamer burned like tinder while hoses played streams of water on her from every angle. Only through the ceaseless work of the firemen was the vessel's hull saved, but nothing more.

The charred remains lay abandoned for several months, but later from them was born a new *Telephone*—more lavish than her forerunner but unable to break the speed record of the original boat which had to her credit a spectacular run between Portland and Astoria of four hours, thirty-four and one-half minutes.

American Ship *Silvie de Grace* or *Sylvia de Grasse*

The old proverb, an ounce of prevention is worth a pound of cure, undoubtedly held true in the case of the aged American packet ship *Silvie de Grace,* sometimes referred to as the *Sylvia de Grasse.* Because her owners did not take that ounce of prevention, her story had a sad ending.

The ship had taken on an overload of lumber, far more than a ship of her size was certified to carry. Inspection laws in those days were nonexistent, however, and every shipowner or master was his own guide. Some gambled and won. Others gambled and lost.

In the year 1849, the *Silvie de Grace* was at anchor off Astoria, awaiting a pilot. She rode very low in the water under her burden—lumber picked up from little mills along the river bank. Her destination was San Francisco, where gold fever ran high and lumber was an extremely valuable commodity. Aboard was the shipowner, William Gray, who had come with her all the way from New York, and was bent on making a killing with his cargo when he reached the Bay City.

When the pilot finally arrived, the ship's wooden-stocked anchor was lifted from the river mud. The crew was aloft preparing to drop the canvas, when the vessel drifted into a ledge of rock, where she remained fast a short distance from her anchorage.

To all indications she should have refloated herself within a few hours at most, but her weighty cargo shifted, causing her to become more tightly wedged on the ledge of rock which protruded from the river bottom just off Astoria.

The crew tried hard to kedge the vessel away from her imprisonment, but she would not budge. As the days faded into weeks, the situation grew worse. Gray decided to charter other vessels to carry his lumber to San Francisco in time to collect the inflated gold rush prices. He offered the master of the American ship *Walpole,* at anchor off Astoria, $10,000 to make the passage, but was refused as that ship was under charter to the United States government.

In desperation, Gray finally secured the services of three small schooners, and off-loaded the lumber from the wreck equally among these vessels. After long passages they finally entered the Golden Gate, only to be informed that the lumber market had taken a drastic drop. What might have been a highly successful venture ended in financial failure for William Gray—all because of overload. He lost his ship, and every red cent he could get from the sale of his cargo was paid to the masters whose schooners he had chartered. And he still owed more.

Years before her loss, the old *Silvie de Grace* is said to have brought the first news of the French Revolution to the United States. Forty-five years after she was wrecked, an Astoria boat builder visited the scene and removed some of her timbers, which he placed in the boat he was building. The old packet had been constructed of durable woods, mainly live oak and locust, unsurpassed in shipbuilding.

Parts of her rusted anchor chain are on display at the Oregon Historical Society. A buoy which marked the wreck of the *Silvie de Grace* was carried away by ice in the river three times before the turn of the century.

American Schooner *Challenger*

Near South Bend, on the Willapa River, the schooner *Challenger* reposes on the river bottom in fourteen feet of water, where she was sunk, November 7, 1904, to quell a blaze that had licked at her for eleven days.

The story of the hardship endured by the crew of the *Challenger* is best related by her master, Captain H. Nelson.

"I left Port Blakeley, October 24, 1904, for San Francisco and was becalmed four days in the Strait. After passing Cape Flattery, we had a northeast wind for twelve hours, when the wind suddenly changed to the southeast and blew up a hurricane. The ship labored heavily.

"On October 29, two seamen were washed overboard; but although the sea was high, they were picked up. The gale kept on increasing till November 4, when I discovered smoke issuing from the cabin. I found that the ship was on fire.

"We crowded on all sail to make port and lost much canvas. At noon on November 4, we were off Tillamook Bay, but could not get in because of mountainous seas. We then steered for the Columbia River. By this time no man could stand at the wheel because of the smoke and fumes from the lime cargo. We signalled for a Columbia River tug, but the bar was too rough for one to come out. I hailed the lightship but could get no help, so I made for Willapa Harbor.

"The tug *Astoria* was inside but was afraid to cross till I hoisted distress signals. Then Captain Chris Olsen of the tug came out and towed me to South Bend. Two hours later, flames broke through the cabin and the schooner had to be scuttled. I later found out that, in crossing the bar, the sea washed over the tug and Captain Olsen was knocked down and badly hurt."

Captain Nelson and his crew were all treated for burns, congested lungs, and internal injuries, at the town hospital. They had been without water for six days after the fresh water tanks had become flooded with sea water.

What little equipment remained aboard the *Challenger* was salvaged; but unfortunately the vessel's owners, the Pacific Stevedoring and Ballasting Company, of San Francisco, carried no insurance on the schooner. She was loaded with 3,800 barrels of Roche Harbor lime and 150,000 feet of lumber, which constantly fed the flames.

When the government dredge was working on the Willapa River, in April, 1934, it scooped up parts of the old schooner from the river bottom where she had reposed undisturbed for thirty years.

Collision of the *Welsh Prince* and *Iowan*

It was 11:10 p.m., May 28, 1922, and the lower Columbia was blanketed by a persistent fog which reached in from the Pacific. Inside the Columbia entrance off Altoona Head, two large freighters were cautiously feeling their way. One was the British steamer *Welsh Prince* and the other was the American freighter *Iowan*.

The night was still but for foghorns issuing mournful cries. Suddenly the stillness was broken by the sickening crash of cold steel, tearing and grinding. The *Iowan,* commanded by Captain L. LaVerge, had rammed her prow into the side of the *Welsh Prince;* and the night air was filled with human cries of agony.

It was so foggy that neither ship was visible to the other until an orange flame suddenly loomed up from the British vessel.

"We're afire!" came a voice from out of the haze.

Without hesitation the hoses of both ships were at-

The *Iowan* in drydock at Portland, May 1922, after she had sunk the *Welsh Prince* and badly crumpled her own bow during a fog-blanketed midnight inside the Columbia entrance.

tached and trained on the location of the flames. Bit by bit the blaze was extinguished. Then all hands were assembled to survey the extent of the damage. The *Iowan* had nearly severed the *Welsh Prince* forward and had badly crumpled her own bow in the process. Aboard the *Welsh Prince* the situation was far more serious, for seven seamen had been crushed to death in the fo'c'sle, and the vessel was settling fast.

Receiving the distress calls, the tug *Oneonta* set out from Astoria and felt her way through the fog till she reached the scene of the collision. Five bodies were removed from the water-filled fo'c'sle, but the remaining two were not found until the extreme tide.

The vessels were separated, and the *Iowan* was taken upriver to Portland for badly needed repairs.

When the fog lifted, the *Welsh Prince* was at the bottom of the river with only her upper works above water.

After several attempts to raise her had failed, Frank Waterhouse & Company, agents for the sunken ship, notified her owners, the Furness Prince Line, of London, that she must be considered a total loss. The wreck became a hazard to navigation, and the only way to remove her from the river bottom was through the use of high potency dynamite.

M. Barde & Sons were employed by the government to remove the wreck; but being unable to accomplish the task, they employed a dynamiter to finish the job. Accordingly, ten tons of super-power gelatin dynamite were ordered from the DuPont plant near Olympia. The deck of the *Welsh Prince* was blown off to remove the cargo of steel, and later the hull was blasted to pieces in a thundering explosion that was felt for miles around the mouth of the river. When the geyser of water had cleared away, the hazard to navigation was nonexistent.

Danish Motorship *Erria*

Tragedy once again struck inside the mouth of the Columbia River at 2:30 a.m., December 20, 1951.

The yacht-like, cargo-passenger liner *Erria,* owned by the East Asiatic Company of Copenhagen, Denmark, was afire. The 8,786-ton ship was at anchor off Tongue Point, awaiting a favorable tide for crossing the Columbia River bar, when she suddenly broke out in a blaze of smoke and flame. Eerie fingers of fire spiraled upward from the big white ship, casting dancing reflections over the dark waters.

Everything had happened so quickly aboard the ship that Captain Neils Agge, her master, was immediately forced to order hasty abandonment by all hands. Overpowering fumes filled the passageways as heroic crewmen, with gas masks and wet towels wrapped about their faces, pounded on stateroom doors in a frantic effort to awaken sleeping passengers and lead them to safety.

Suddenly the city of Astoria became a beehive of activity. As boats were swung over the side, laden with survivors, Coast Guard vessels and privately owned rescue craft rushed out to take them aboard. Eleven failed to make it. Three crew members and eight passengers were trapped amidships. Later some of these passengers were found burned to a crisp, sitting in chairs in the ship's lounge as if awaiting instructions. The death toll was tragic, but could have been much worse with its total 114 persons aboard the vessel.

The ship was pushed aground a few hundred yards from shore. There two Coast Guard cutters pumped thousands of gallons of water into her, but still she

Eleven persons perished in the tragic fire which gutted the Danish passenger-cargo vessel *Erria*, just east of Astoria, December 20, 1951.

burned furiously, assuming a decided port list. The intense heat caused some of the hull plates to pop their rivets. Then the ship's bridge collapsed. The wood burned; the steel melted away.

In desperation, the Coast Guard firefighters cut fire holes into the *Erria's* side and pumped in great quantities of carbon dioxide, yet several days later the ship was still smoldering and none could board her. Smoke still filtered into the air from the No. 2 hold, where lumber was stored, and from the engine room where oil was leaking from the ship's tanks.

While the ship smoldered, the underwriters marked her off the books as a total construction loss. Finally she cooled down, was pulled free, and towed upriver to Portland. There the remains of her cargo, including pulp, wheat, steel, lumber, and general freight, were unloaded. The ship remained idle for many weeks awaiting her fate. Should she be rebuilt or scrapped?

Because of high replacement costs, her owners finally elected to rebuild the *Erria.* In a surprise move they contracted with L. Smit & Company, a world-wide towing firm headquartered in Holland, to send the *Zwarte Zee,* one of the most powerful tugs afloat, to tow the charred vessel from Portland to Rotterdam for rebuilding. The 8,900-mile tow required 51 days, averaging about 170 nautical miles per day. The *Erria* departed Portland, May 16, 1952.

More than $1.5 million went into the rebuilding of the ship, after which she emerged as a trim freighter, minus her passenger accommodations. She was placed on another route and at this writing has suffered no other mishaps.

Following the tragic fire, inspectors of the *Erria* reasoned that the blaze started from a shorted wire amidships.

CHAPTER 10

MYSTERY SHIPS

Nothing so arouses man's imagination as the tale of a ship that sails out to sea and disappears with all hands. Theory and fantasy often act as a substitute for what cannot be explained. From these have come tales of the "Flying Dutchman," so widespread that each maritime nation has its own story of specter ships that sail the lonely seas.

As ill luck supposedly follows sight of the ghostly Dutchman's ship near the Cape of Good Hope—so did misfortune follow in the wake of the *Vandalia*.

American Bark *Vandalia*

She was sighted by Captain Phillips of the brig *Grecian* on January 9, 1853. He stated that she appeared to be laboring but was in no need of assistance. That was all that was heard of the *Vandalia* till a week later when she was carried ashore, bottom up, near McKenzie Head.

Four bodies floated ashore near the wreck, one of which was identified as Captain E. N. Beard, master of the *Vandalia*. His remains drifted into a rocky indentation which since that day has been known as Beard's Hollow.

Among the three other bodies was that of a fourteen-year-old boy.

The cause of the disaster was never known, but the supposition was that the vessel had missed stays while beating in towards the bar and had drifted into the breakers. She probably fouled her bottom, filled, and capsized—which may or may not be the missing link in the tragic loss that caused the death of twelve seafarers.

Three days later, the barks *Mindora* and *J. Merithew* also perished there at the mouth of the Columbia, followed in September of the same year by the *Oriole.*

American Schooner *Sunshine*

The *Sunshine* was constructed at Marshfield (now Coos Bay), Oregon, and completed in September, 1875, by Holden & Company for E. B. Deane and Associates, at a cost of $32,000. She was a three-masted schooner of 326 tons and was hailed as a shipbuilding triumph on Coos Bay.

The vessel was placed in command of Captain George Bennett, who shared an interest in the ownership of the schooner. On her maiden voyage from Coos Bay, she arrived at San Francisco, October 8, 1875, to discharge a cargo of lumber. For the return passage the *Sunshine* carried machinery and general cargo. In addition, several passengers were booked, her complement numbering twenty-five in all.

Captain Bennett had an excellent record as a mariner and carried two officers of equal repute: John Thompson and Joseph Johnson.

On the return leg of her maiden voyage, the *Sunshine* passed through the Golden Gate on November 3, and was not seen again till fifteen days later when sighted, bottom up, off Cape Disappointment. On November 22, the derelict washed ashore on the peninsula, but no clue to the disappearance of her company was found among the wreckage.

Some experts claimed that, owing to the newness of the schooner, she was stiff and perhaps difficult to operate, but her builders countered with the fact that she had been built structurally sound and was easy to handle. They held to the hope that some of her complement might be picked up at sea to answer the query, but the sea refused to give up its dead.

It is recorded that the *Sunshine's* cargo was valued at $18,000. In addition she carried more than $10,000 in gold coin, which was being sent to her builders at Coos Bay from interests in San Francisco, that shared a part ownership in the vessel.

As is the case with all mysteries of the sea, fantasy is bound to creep in and add its tantalizing flavor. There were some who claimed that the schooner was purposely destroyed by conniving passengers who escaped in a boat with the keg of gold after first killing the others. Estimates as to the loot ranged from $30,000 to $60,000—undoubtedly exaggerations.

Then there was another story hinting that the vessel had previously gone aground fifteen miles north of Coos Bay, and that a barrel of coins was buried in the sands by an officer. Later the schooner was said to have been carried back to sea and left at the mercy of the winds, before capsizing and going ashore again on the North Beach Peninsula. This tale is actually known to have started people digging in the sands north of Coos Bay in search of the gold – which, incidentally, has yet to be found.

Not the slightest clue to the fate of the twenty-five souls aboard the schooner has ever been forthcoming.

Pilot Schooner *J. C. Cousins*

The mighty Pacific holds many unsolved mysteries and tales of intrigue, but none is more baffling than the drama that was enacted in the waters of the Pacific Graveyard within view of the shore on October 7, 1883. It involved the wreck of a pilot schooner and the disappearance of her crew.

The pilot schooner was a craft of excellent lines, with cabins of the finest hardwoods and elaborate fittings. She was a two-masted vessel and bore the name, *J. C. Cousins.* Her beauty resulted from her originally having been built to the orders of a wealthy Californian as his private schooner-yacht. Several months later he was forced to sell her. The vessel was purchased at San Francisco in 1881, and brought to the Columbia River in March of the same year to run in opposition to Captain Flavel's monopoly in bar piloting. The schooner was operated as a pilot boat by the State of Oregon for two years prior to her mysterious loss.

When the *J. C. Cousins* first arrived on the Columbia, she was commanded by Captain George Woods, and was jointly operated by Captain Charles Richardson, H. A. Matthews, Thomas Powers, and Henry Olsen, all of Astoria.

The schooner loaded supplies at Astoria on October 6, 1883, and as usual stood out to sea to meet incoming vessels. Aboard were four men in charge of the boatkeeper, whose name is remembered only as Zeiber.

It was near noon when the schooner passed Fort

Stevens. Later in the afternoon she was sighted at anchor off Clatsop Spit. On the same day the tug *Mary Taylor* sighted the *Cousins* sailing out through the breakers near Clatsop Spit, and at dusk reversing her course to stand in for the bar. She continued those strange antics until she was lost in the darkness.

At daybreak other ships reported sighting the pilot vessel, sometimes standing in towards shore and then again tacking offshore and moving out to sea. At 1 p.m. on October 7, the *Cousins* was reported nearly three miles at sea when suddenly the wind changed and she came about, heading for Clatsop Spit. About 2:15 p.m., she reached the surf, but this time she failed to come about. Instead she came in through the breakers and was swept hard on the beach.

Several persons who had been following the strange course of the pilot schooner hastened to the scene but were unable to get near the wreck until low tide.

Not a living soul nor a dead one was found aboard the schooner. A further search revealed that the boat was missing, as were the logbook and papers. Everything else appeared to be in proper order.

A few days later the seas broke up the vessel, leaving no further clue to the disappearance of her crew.

When the ensuing weeks failed to divulge any word of the missing seamen, the maritime sleuths and yarn spinners settled down to some deep thinking. One theory was advanced that gained considerable acceptance.

It was claimed that Zeiber had been engaged to wreck the *Cousins,* kill his shipmates, and then disappear, thus destroying competition against the Flavel monopoly. This story was backed by mariners from Astoria, who in later years were said to have actually seen Zeiber in Oriental ports.

Such a scheme seems highly improbable, however, as the operators of the *Cousins,* immediately following her loss, chartered the centerboard sloop *City of Napa* to continue the opposition until the state could build the pilot schooner *Governor Moody.*

Other theories of sea monsters and mutiny were advanced. One demented old beachcomber told how a great ghost ship had borne down on the *Cousins* and frightened the crew so badly that they took to the boat for fear of being rammed. He claimed that he had once seen this same ghost ship coming across the bar.

When the waterfront folk of Astoria would laugh at the old-timer, a sinister look would come over his face and he would shake his bony finger at them.

"It is real, I tell ye," he would frown. "A ship of the dead that sails the sea, with a ghostly crew. In the tempest she appears, and before the gale or agin' the gale, she sails without a rag of canvas and without a helmsman at the wheel." Then down he would hobble to the river bank, cursing his unappreciative audience.

Perhaps the only logical solution given was that the schooner struck on the bar while outbound, frightening the crew, who in turn took to the boat. The heavy swell probably swamped the craft, throwing the men into the water and drowning them.

How long the schooner sailed without a crew was never established. The case has remained unsolved to this day.

American Steamship *Drexel Victory*

An air of mystery still hangs about the maritime courts concerning the loss of the steamship *Drexel Victory.*

At 5 p.m., January 19, 1947, the freighter — outbound from Portland for Yokohama with 5,000 tons of grain and general cargo — either structurally collapsed, struck Peacock Spit, or rammed the remains of a sunken wreck, while in transit across the bar.

The vessel, carrying forty-nine officers and men, was in charge of bar pilot E. P. Gillette, and her master was Captain Canute Rommerdahl.

While crossing the bar, the *Drexel Victory* suddenly cracked between holds Nos. 4 and 5. Water gushed through the break and her plates bulged from her frames like water blisters—seepage was everywhere. The crew were at the pumps but were unable to control the influx of sea water.

The situation became hopeless, and Rommerdahl had to give the order to abandon ship.

The Coast Guard motor lifeboat *Triumph,* the pilot ship *Columbia,* the cutter *Onondaga,* and the liberty freighter *Joseph Gale* all stood by. In spite of the blackness of the night, the crew was taken off without mishap.

When the sinking freighter drifted over the bar, the cutter *Onondaga* took out in pursuit in an attempt to get a line on her and beach her in shallow water. Darkness closed in all around, and at 1:30 a.m. the freighter plunged to the bottom in deep water, one-quarter mile due west of buoy No. 6—after drinking up tons of ocean water.

The survivors were landed at Astoria.

Following the hearing over the loss, the Oregon State Board of River Pilot Examiners exonerated Captain Gillette of any responsibility in the sinking of the vessel. The board held that Gillette, while piloting the ship over the bar, had discharged all his duties in a competent manner.

Gillette in turn suggested that structural failure might have caused the trouble, but expressed doubt that the vessel had actually grounded.

"When she struck," stated Gillette, "she was in fifty-nine to sixty-one feet of water—that is, if she did strike."

According to further reports at the hearing, it was brought out that the *Drexel Victory* was drawing twenty-nine to thirty feet of water when her hull cracked. She was in the proper ship channel and had taken some heavy swells though the bar was not rough.

Following the incident, Colonel O. E. Walsh, of the Corps of Engineers, ordered a further survey of the spot where the freighter was said to have struck; but the investigation revealed that the channel was as deep and unobstructed as the charts indicated.

The *Drexel Victory* was operated by Oliver Olson & Company and was owned by the U. S. Maritime Commission. She was a Victory-type vessel of 7,607 gross tons and was built at Richmond, California, in 1945.

CHAPTER 11

AGROUND IN THE FOG

Fog is the persistent enemy of the mariner. It is a ghostly vapor that creeps in silently, obscuring the headlands and closing the boundaries of the world.

Before the advent of radio and radar, now so vital to mariners, the Pacific Graveyard was a shore of ill-repute. Fog spread in from the sea, blotting out flashing lights, while storms pressing shoreward muzzled the most insistent foghorns, which were none too plentiful fifty years ago. Even in our space age, ships still occasionally fall victim to fog.

American Bark *Harvest Home*

If it is possible for a shipwreck to be a happy affair, perhaps the loss of the bark *Harvest Home* would fall under this classification. The date was January 18, 1882, and the bark was beating up the coast under a pleasant breeze in a calm sea shrouded by a white sheet of fog. Her destination was Port Townsend, and she rode low in the water with a full load of general cargo.

Under the command of Captain A. Matson, the bark was skirting along in a northwesterly course in the early morning hours, while most of the crew were asleep. Only the sea water caressing the hull of the vessel broke the silence of the nearing dawn. Then came another sound, a sound quite divorced from that of the sea. The helmsman cupped his hand to his ear—had he heard a rooster crowing or was he dreaming?

Suddenly the vessel began to pitch and roll as though it had been struck by a tidal wave. The crew were tossed from their bunks, and loose gear rolled over the deck. In a matter of minutes the ship was deposited on the sands and suddenly became motionless.

Captain Matson stormed up on deck and leaped up on the poop; but before he could get his mouth open, the helmsman informed him that the vessel was aground.

"Aground, you say, Mister? Why, we're six miles to sea. I set the course myself," bellowed the Old Man.

Though fog was all about the stranded ship, there was little doubt about her being aground. Before the flood tide had decided to go back to sea again, the

A defective chronometer was responsible for the grounding of the American Bark *Harvest Home*, on North Beach Peninsula, January 18, 1882. The crew walked ashore.

Harvest Home was bogged down in the sand up around the driftwood area.

Several hours later the bewildered skipper discovered that he had been navigating with a defective chronometer, which was responsible for the stranding.

When the fog lifted around noon, the helmsman sighted a big barn a few hundred feet from the beach. It was then that he knew that the rooster he had heard crowing had not been a figment of his imagination. The wreck was lying eight miles north of Cape Disappointment, on the sandy beach of the peninsula.

Later the crew walked ashore, the wreck remaining stationary while the tides swished around her, more firmly entrenching her in the sands. The cargo was salvaged, but the bark was left to die a slow death.

In the months that followed, tourists paused at the wreck to have their pictures taken under the summer sun or to picnic on her rotting timbers. Some of the shipwrecked sailors found for themselves pretty peninsula belles and tied the legal knot of matrimony.

Meanwhile Preston & McKinnon of San Francisco, owners of the *Harvest Home,* collected $14,000, the amount for which the vessel was insured.

Pilot Schooner *Governor Moody*

It will be recalled that the loss of the pilot schooner *J. C. Cousins* prompted the chartering of the sloop *City of Napa* until the State of Oregon had completed the building of the pilot schooner *Governor Moody* at Astoria, in 1885. The new sixty-four-ton vessel operated until September 20, 1890, when she was cast ashore on the rocks off North Head.

In command of Captain Peter Cordiner, the *Moody* moved silently through the fog-filtered waters off the river entrance. It was early morning and daybreak was awaited to meet an inbound vessel seeking pilotage.

At 4 a.m., the schooner was tossed about violently. The crew rallied forward to discover that the craft was trapped in dangerous waters frequented with swirling eddies. The sails were put aback, but the wind refused to fill them; and the currents swept the vessel onto the rocks, badly fouling her hull.

The men sprang to the shrouds as the seas came over the weather rail, covering the decks. Her bow dropped, reappearing with gallons of green water rolling aft. The foremast, knocked from its fittings, plummeted into the water, wedging itself against a rock that jutted from the sea a short distance from the schooner. Sloshing around in knee-deep water, the frightened seamen straddled the fallen mast, inching their bodies across to the rock to gain temporary refuge from the rampaging surf.

When the fog cleared, the wreck was sighted by the lighthouse keepers at Cape Disappointment, who in turn passed the word to the Fort Canby lifesaving crew. The surf boat put out from the station and picked up the shivering sailors from the rocks; then took the fallen mast in tow. The pilot schooner swamped within the day to become a total loss.

The schooner *San Jose* was later purchased at San Francisco by Pilot Commissioner P. W. Weeks, to fill the vacancy left by the *Governor Moody*.

The *Cairnsmore* was inbound for Portland from England, with a cargo of cement, September 26, 1883, when her captain lost his bearings in pea-soup fog.

British Bark *Cairnsmore*

When salt water mixes with 7,500 barrels of cement in a ship's hold, that vessel will become preserved in the sands of time.

The British bark *Cairnsmore* – Captain B. Gibbs, master—was inbound for Portland from London, but was hampered by a veil of fog which had made navigation difficult. Though Gibbs knew he was in the vicinity of the Columbia River entrance, he was unable to gain his bearings until after breakers were sighted at 10:30 a.m. on September 26, 1883. Down to her marks with a heavy load of cement and machinery, the vessel labored in the surf, defying all efforts to head her into the wind.

"Aloft and get 'em in!" yelled the bucko mate. The crew scurried up the rigging and strung themselves along the yardarms, standing in the swaying footropes. With bleeding fingers clutching and clawing at the stubborn acres of canvas, they struggled to haul them in and wrap the gaskets around them.

But it was too late; the vessel struck the sands with a thud. Signal flares that soared into the air were swallowed by the fog.

For fifteen hours the sailors worked to free the ship, but they were finally forced to man the boats and row out to sea, rather than risk their lives in the heavy surf. The boats bobbed in an ocean that seemed to set them apart from the rest of the world.

Suddenly from out of the fog came the sound of a deep-throated whistle which gradually grew louder. Oars were shipped and all eyes peered into the murk. Parting the strands of fog, the bow of a steamer appeared, knifing her way through the sea. Less than a hundred yards away, the whistle blasted again; and the men stood up in the boats, yelling at the tops of their voices.

Fortunately their cries were heard by the watch on the bridge wing; the engine room bell clanged, and the ship's forward motion decreased when the vessel veered off to starboard. As the lifeboats rowed toward the steamer, the crew made out the name *Queen of the Pacific* scrolled on her bows; the same ship had been ashore on Clatsop Spit three weeks earlier.

The shipwrecked seamen were taken aboard, and the liner crept on towards the bar, fading into the fog.

The following day a salvage crew went to the scene of the wreck to investigate possibilities of saving the ship and her cargo. They soon discovered that water had leaked into the hull and that the cement was seeping through the barrel staves. The ship lay in an exposed position, and the situation grew more hopeless as, day by day, the cement escaped from the barrels and hardened. Several months later, the hull was consumed by the sands, sealed in her casket of cement.

The *Cairnsmore,* a 1,300-ton bark, was valued at $48,000; her cargo was insured for $18,000.

British Ship *Glenmorag*

The ship *Glenmorag,* of Glasgow, departed New York, August 16, 1895, arriving at Melbourne after a lengthy run of 103 days. In the South Atlantic, she was trapped in an icefield frequented by more than a

Mabel E. Thompson

The tall British *Glenmorag* made a picturesque sight on North Beach Peninsula after wrecking in a thick fog, March 18, 1896.

hundred bergs, which nearly spelled her doom. She set sail in ballast for Astoria via Chile, arriving off the Columbia River on March 18, 1896. The following day the vessel was fog-bound and becalmed except for the prevailing northerly drift. At 3:30 p.m., the lookout sighted breakers, and the big square-rigger went on the beach seven miles north of Ilwaco.

The thick fog obscured the ship's grounding from the shore.

Two hours later a knock was heard at the door of a resident on the peninsula. A man answered and was met by a ragged seaman who requested help for his shipmates on the wrecked ship.

When the *Glenmorag* struck at high tide, broadside to, two boats were lowered and cleared away. The mate in charge of one boat attempted to pull out to sea but the surf drove him toward shore, forcing the craft to weather the breakers. The other boat, in rounding the stern of the *Glenmorag,* was caught by a tremendous sea and dashed up under the counter, killing two seamen and injuring the others. Though badly damaged, the boat was kept afloat by the air-tight tanks and was eventually carried up on the beach.

Captain Archibald Currie, master of the *Glenmorag,* later lowered another boat and, with the remainder of the crew, reached the shore in safety.

In all, twenty-seven persons were aboard the vessel at the time of the wreck. The dead were John Reedy and James Adams.

Among the injured was a seaman named William Begg. When he reached the shore, a young lady from Oysterville removed his wet shoes and gave him warm blankets. Several months later he married her and the

Charles Fitzpatrick

The *Glenmorag* spent her remaining days on the peninsula. Inset shows the stately figurehead she bore during her time of glory.

couple settled down on the peninsula in a stately house built by Begg himself.

Visiting their home in later years was like stepping into the past, for such items as the dinner bell and kitchenware salvaged from the galley of the *Glenmorag* were still in use. William Begg died a few years ago, not long after his children had built him and his wife a new home on the peninsula.

After the wreck, Captain Currie conferred with the British Consul concerning the possibilities of salvage. Because the *Glenmorag* had received only minor damage in the mishap, several attempts were later made to refloat her. In December, the ship was moved forty feet and local authorities reported that she would soon be afloat. On the day of the scheduled refloating, the tide was full, the cables and winches in place, and tugs were standing by. The *Glenmorag* was pulled to freedom momentarily, but was struck by a series of wicked breakers which carried her back on the beach, this time for good.

The ship was then dismantled by Kern & Kern of Portland, with everything of value stripped from her. The remains were abandoned and eventually devoured by the sands. About sixty feet of her steel hull was uncovered by shifting sands in the winter of 1948, but was covered again within the month. It still occasionally appears. The *Glenmorag*'s memory is kept green by the existence of her figurehead representing a stately goddess, now in the possession of William Begg's son at Vancouver, Washington.

German Bark *Potrimpos*

A strong wind and heavy sea prevailed as the Ilwaco lifesaving crew trudged along the beach to reach the wreck of the German bark *Potrimpos* on December 19, 1896. A large white horse was pulling the cart that carried the surf boat, but in the severe storm the animal became frightened and balked, refusing to pull the load any farther. Despite the whip, the horse would not go on. In desperation the lifesaving crew struggled with the cart, pulling it up to the track of the pioneer Ilwaco-Nahcotta Railroad, which ran the length of the peninsula. They awaited the arrival of the engine; when it came, they halted it and loaded the equipment on a flatcar, then continued to the scene of the wreck—minus the horse.

The lifesaving crew found that six seamen had already made the beach in a boat, but that their services were urgently needed in rescuing twelve others. The surf boat which put out from the beach succeeded in bringing the rest of the shipwrecked sailors ashore.

When the tide had receded, the steel bark was fully a hundred yards from the surf. Salvage work was begun immediately. After several months of unsuccessful attempts to get her off the sands, the big chance came, but ended in near disaster. The Spreckles tug *Relief* was standing by, and the hawsers and donkey engines were placed in strategic places for easing the hull into the surf. With the salvage crew aboard, the vessel was inched over the sands at the given hour, but the ballast had been removed from her hull and she floated high. When they got her into the breakers, she suddenly careened over on her beam ends, putting the lives of the salvage crew in grave peril.

The *Potrimpos'* bell was washed up on the beach at the feet of young Gilbert Tinker, who had played hooky from school to watch the salvage operations. Startled by the sudden turn of events, he picked up the bell and ran into town to get aid for the stranded salvage crew. Later the trapped salvagers were brought ashore and treated for their injuries.

Tinker lived near Long Beach, until his death a few years ago. He often recalled how he found the *Potrimpos'* bell on that fateful date in the spring of 1897. He remembered the straining donkey engines, the taut

Charles Fitzpatrick

Inbound for the Columbia from Manzanillo, Mexico, the German bark *Potrimpos* fell victim to strong winds and cross currents, stranding on North Beach Peninsula, December 1896. Salvage attempts failed when the vessel careened over on her beam ends.

hawsers, the smoking tug a quarter of a mile offshore—and also that tragic moment when the vessel flipped over on her side.

At a hearing concerning the stranding of the *Potrimpos,* Captain Hellwegge, her master, stated: "My ship, the *Potrimpos,* was out of Hamburg and had made a call at Manzanillo, Mexico, to discharge. Booking no cargo there, we were ordered to sail for the Columbia River in ballast to pick up a cargo of grain at Portland. When near the river, I was aware of the proximity of land and was sure I was off the mouth of the Columbia. I was constantly on the lookout for the pilot boat or a tug; but the vessel drifted northward with the wind and current, becoming helpless before we could bring her back to sea."

American Schooner *Solano*

A vessel that might well be referred to as the ghost ship of the peninsula, is the four-masted schooner *Solano* which grounded four miles north of Ocean Park, February 5, 1907. For several years her hull arose and disappeared in the sands; and then, in 1923, it vanished for nearly ten years.

The *Solano* had almost been forgotten when the shifting sands uncovered her hull once again. It has remained visible ever since, becoming a landmark on the beach. The hatches are banked with sand where shellfish move around in deep pools formed by high tides. The back is broken and only stumps stand where once tall masts shot skyward. The timbers have been bleached almost white by the salt water, wind, and sand.

In the summer of 1947, vacationers built a bonfire inside the old craft; then neglected to smother it on their departure. The sparks ignited the timbers, and the local firefighters were summoned to extinguish the blaze.

Fog, storm, surf, and fire have failed to put an end to thc old wreck. She languishes on amid her strange surroundings in a sea of sand.

The most common question of the visitor to the peninsula is, "How did she get there?"

It was early morning on that winter day in 1907, when the North Beach lifesaving crew received word that a schooner had gone around. The lookout in the station tower sighted distress signals several miles down the beach, rising above the low-hanging fog. Within a

Charles Fitzpatrick

The *Solano*, four-masted ghost ship of North Beach Peninsula, grounded February 1907, a total loss.

few moments the men in their storm gear were plodding their way toward the scene of the flares with their beach equipment. As the surf was exceptionally calm for a winter day, they encountered little difficulty in getting the shipwrecked seamen ashore.

At low water, the schooner was found to be undamaged, so plans were immediately undertaken to refloat her.

Ten months later, the scene was set. A large salvage crew, under the direction of W. H. Wood of the Hart-Wood Lumber Company, had worked ceaselessly to prepare the vessel for relaunching; and on the high tide of December 1907, the task was successfully accomplished with the aid of the flood tide.

Wood had made arrangements with the owners of the tug *Daring*, of Astoria, to be there at the designated time of the schooner's refloating so that she could be towed safely to port. All went according to schedule except that the tug failed to make an appearance. Anxiously, Wood scanned the horizon but the tug was nowhere in sight. The *Solano* wallowed in the surf, bucking a strong south wind which created an angry surf. Hour by hour the breakers mounted until she was finally driven back on the beach with tremendous force.

Bewildered, Wood watched his efforts fade before his very eyes. Further attempts to save the *Solano* were abandoned.

At the subsequent litigation, Wood was awarded half of the appraised value of the schooner, less half the tug-boat rate that had been agreed on.

When the schooner first went aground, she was en route to Grays Harbor from San Francisco. As she lay on the beach, a constant watch was kept over her to prevent looting. It was not an uncommon sight to see a large washing hanging from the rigging—strange, indeed, for a landlocked vessel.

Gazing at her gnarled bones today, one can hardly believe that she was once a graceful windship which had to her credit, in 1902, a record passage from Shanghai to Port Townsend, in the remarkable time of twenty-four days.

Canadian Freighter *Canadian Exporter*

It was just another case of fog that caused the *Canadian Exporter* to go aground at the entrance to Willapa Harbor, August 1, 1921. She was bound for Portland from Vancouver, B. C., to complete loading lumber

Charles Fitzpatrick

The *Solano* is still visible, more than half a century since she ran aground. Now shellfish move around her bleached timbers in the deep pools formed by high tides.

for the Orient, when she drove up on the sands and defied all efforts to be backed off. After the fog lifted, the tug *Wallula* went to the aid of the steamer but failed to get her off the shoal. The tug returned later in the day in company with the salvage steamer *Algerine*. After removing the crew of the freighter, both vessels got lines on the ship and put on a great show of power, which failed to produce results.

On the following morning, it was discovered that the *Canadian Exporter* was working on the shoals and showing signs of breaking up. The salvage crew of the *Algerine* boarded her to remove the loose deck equipment. Satisfied that refloating the wreck was a virtual impossibility, the *Algerine's* party made preparations for sailing home within the day, but their plans were interrupted when suddenly the whistle on the freighter began to blast. Because not a soul was aboard her, the ghostly sounds chilled the observers, as they stood on the deck of the salvage steamer.

T. W. Allen, superintendent of the salvage operations, immediately ordered a boat over the side to investigate. When the craft drew closer, Allen found that the freighter was breaking up before his eyes. A large crack aft the bridge widened as it traveled down to the waterline. As the swells struck against the ship's hull, the wave action on the sagging bow would tighten the whistle cord, causing a blast until the cord grew limp.

Allen would have liked to board the ship again to use the remaining steam to salvage cargo, but considered the ship's condition too dangerous to risk the lives of his crew.

At 7:30 a.m., the *Canadian Exporter* sounded her own death knell with one final blast of her whistle followed by the parting of rivets and the rending of steel. A few minutes later, the ship broke in two. With no further hesitation, the salvage steamer sailed out over the horizon, returning to her home base.

The story might have ended here but for two adventurous gentlemen from Vancouver, B. C., who purchased rights to the wreck from the underwriters for $2,000. Their names were H. R. McMillan and Percy Sills.

With each passing day, the position of the wreck grew more dangerous, but the two Canadians gathered machinery and equipment to salvage the lumber and made arrangements with Hugh Delanty, prominent Grays Harbor stevedoring executive, to supply fifteen of his best longshoremen.

Carl Christenson

The *Canadian Exporter* broke in half on the Willapa bar, August 1, 1921. Wave action on the sagging bow tightened the whistle cord till, at 7:30 a.m., she sounded her own death knell with one final blast.

The purchase of the wreck caused considerable comment up and down the coast and wagers were placed as to whether or not the salvage effort would prove successful.

With a string of barges and other conveyances, the work got under way on September 2, 1921. Only the steering engine was salvaged from the after section of the wreck, now well imbedded in the sands. From the forward section, refrigeration equipment, deck gear, and a quantity of lumber stowed in the holds was salvaged through tenacious efforts.

Lighters were constantly standing by, and a launch brought the workmen to and from the wreck. When the weather was bad, the job could not be carried on, for the Coast Guard placed tight restrictions on the operation, fearing loss of life.

Near the end of October, the wreck had to be abandoned.

When McMillan and Sills added up the accounts, they discovered that they had spent $20,000 in wages and equipment. They sold the lumber and machinery for $17,500, and were left with a deficit of $4,500, along with the rights to the wreck. Financially the venture had failed, but the partners agreed that the job was one of the most interesting they had ever undertaken.

The only money makers on the loss of the vessel were the lawyers, there being a protracted litigation over the insurance on the vexing question of deviation. Clearly the *Exporter* had not traveled the regular course for which she was insured. But where should the balance of blame be placed—on fog or faulty navigation?

American Steamship *Admiral Benson*

What was first reported on February 15, 1930, as a minor stranding, turned out to be a major steamship disaster.

With thirty-nine passengers, sixty-five crew members, and a cargo of citrus fruits and general freight, the liner *Admiral Benson,* of the Pacific Steamship Company, stranded on the sands near Peacock Spit. It was 6:45 p.m., and the vessel was inbound for Portland when she shoved her nose onto the spit in the foggy channel entrance. The stranding appeared so minor

Relief tram on its way to the stranded *Benson*. The ship's master was the last to leave the liner.

that Captain C. C. Graham did not send out an urgent appeal for help but asked assistance only.

The Coast Guard cutter *Redwing* was ordered out to stand by the *Benson,* but her boilers were cold and she was unable to clear from Astoria until several hours later. The freighter *Nevada* also received the call for assistance. She stood by the liner while the Coast Guard lifeboats from Point Adams and Cape Disappointment handled the evacuation of passengers. Many of the tourists were compelled to slide down wet ropes to the rescue craft.

By noon on February 17, most of the passengers had been removed and all efforts were directed towards saving the crew, who had remained with the ship hoping to refloat her. The situation appeared less hopeful as a high wind approached, kicking up a nasty surf. By 9:06 a.m. the following morning, the five remaining passengers were taken off, followed by the steward's staff and the ship's orchestra.

The wreck was located 400 yards west of the north jetty, directly in view of the remains of the *Laurel,* which served as a grim reminder to those still aboard the liner.

The following day, Captain Graham watched the last of the crew go ashore by breeches buoy, while he

Joe Williamson

The liner *Admiral Benson* stranded near Peacock Spit, at the mouth of the Columbia, February 15, 1930. No lives were lost but the vessel became a total wreck. Note the surf boiling around her.

Joe Williamson

Bow up, stern down, the *Benson*'s 3,049 tons yield to the sea.

alone remained aboard the vessel. The holds had been pumped full of water to keep the ship from pounding, but when a forty-mile gale arose, the *Benson* was given a salt bath by mountainous breakers. On the morning of February 20, the riveting began to pull loose, and the ship showed signs of breaking up. The decks cracked, the engine room was flooded, and the surplus water saturated the cargo in the holds.

On February 21, the redoubtable captain was still aboard, his spirit warmed by the friendly bonfire that was kept burning night and day at Cape Disappointment. It wasn't until four days later that Graham abandoned his vigil, signalling the Coast Guard for assistance.

A line having been made fast between the wreck and the shore, the shipmaster began an arduous journey through the air on a lifesaving conveyance.

The passengers and crew had been landed at Astoria, and each had a version of the disaster. Several agreed that the wreck of the *Laurel* had been mistaken for a range buoy, which may have misled the liner to the spit in the fog. The ill-fated liner had taken a course from the Columbia River Lightship, but veered northward in a heavy mist, circled past the masts of the wrecked *Laurel*, and struck the sands near the jetty. Though the loss of the *Benson* was attributed by some to faulty navigation, existing conditions on the Columbia bar can be confusing to the most experienced navigators.

The first passenger to be evacuated was Mrs. A. B. Reynolds of Portland, who rode a breeches buoy placed on a line between ship and shore by the Coast Guard.

She had a hectic trip, swallowed plenty of salt water and lost her new hat. It was then that boats were used to evacuate passengers. But the Reynolds woman was a good sport, and in spite of all, said, "I always did want to ride in one of those things."

After the captain was evacuated, a salvage crew, using Coast Guard lines, ran a tram gear to the wreck to remove some of the cargo, which was trucked to Astoria.

The *Benson* was sucked into the sand, stern first, but part of her bow was still visible at extreme low tide, two decades after her loss.

American Steamship *Sea Thrush*

In the summer of 1962, Captain Ernest J. Landstrom and his wife marked their 50th wedding anniversary at their Seattle home. Retired, the captain looked back on nearly a half century of seafaring with most of those years spent as a master mariner. Except for one incident, Captain Landstrom had had a remarkable record at sea. As it later turned out, that one blemish was not his fault. The wreck happened in a fog during a crossing of the Columbia River bar, because the charts were wrongly marked. At a hearing following the wreck, Captain Landstrom was cleared of all blame.

The ship, of which he was both master and pilot at the time of her loss on Clatsop Spit, was the American freighter *Sea Thrush,* a steamship of 5,538 gross tons.

She was inbound for the Columbia River from Puget Sound, December 4, 1932, to complete loading for East Coast ports. As a thick fog dropped its veil over the river entrance, the cargo ship felt her way cautious-

All lives were saved, but the freighter *Sea Thrush* was a total loss when her keel snapped on Clatsop Spit and she broke in two, December 1932.

ly. Her skipper was well acquainted with the personality of the river entrance, having crossed and recrossed it many times. Aboard was a crew of thirty-one, plus one youthful stowaway and a woman passenger.

Despite the thick fog, Captain Landstrom had the situation well under control—at least he thought so—when the ship suddenly stopped with a fearful jolt. She was hard aground on the sands of Clatsop Spit. Immediately distress calls were sent out.

Quickly the Coast Guard cutter *Redwing* and two Coast Guard motor lifeboats put out for the wreck. As a precaution on the following day, they rescued all but the captain. It was still hoped that the freighter might be pulled free, but on December 6, her keel snapped and she buckled amidships, breaking her back. Later that same day the Point Adams lifeboat made a spirited run out to the wreck and managed to remove Captain

Landstrom. On December 8, after salvagers had managed to pull the wreck 1,700 feet from where she stranded, she broke in two and became a total loss.

Captain Landstrom was certain that his calculations were right; at the hearing he told his account in detail. The decision handed down exonerated Captain Landstrom as well as all navigation officers of the ship. Here is part of a signed statement by U. S. Inspectors Donald S. Ames and Thomas Short, following the hearing:

"The *Sea Thrush* grounded, December 4, 1932, at a point north of the line between No. 10 and No. 12 buoys and near where No. 10 A buoy is now situated, where she had a right to be, according to the latest chart prior to the date of the disaster. We find no grounds for preferring charges against the navigation officers of the vessel."

The *Sea Thrush,* owned by the Shepard Steamship Company, was built at Portland, Oregon, by the Northwest Steel Company in 1917, as the initial vessel of the U. S. Shipping Board fleet to be constructed on the Pacific Coast. Her original name was *Westland,* a title suggested by Mrs. Woodrow Wilson, then first lady of the land.

DAVY JONES'S LOCKER

What becomes of the hulks rotting in the sands of the Pacific Graveyard? Why do they disappear so quickly, and how durable are the materials of which they are composed?

Wooden hulls survive the rigors longer than those of iron or steel construction when they become buried in the beds of sand or sink to the bottom of the ocean. It is hard to determine the length of time it takes for either to disintegrate completely, but it is known that wooden vessels have been dug up after centuries, not yet wholly decayed. However, iron and steel vessels seem unable to resist the elements for any great time because of the chemical effects of sea water.

When a wooden vessel sinks, the rate of progress to the bottom is very slow. It is thought not to be faster than 100 fathoms in fifteen minutes, unless the vessel is laden with some weighty cargo such as coal or mineral ore. Thus when she touches bottom, especially if the material be mud or sand, the impact is gentle and no damage is done to the structure beyond what it received at the surface. Neither is there any mechanical agency to interfere with it.

Currents are frequently harmless, and the movement of bottom waters slow, so there the wreck lies where it has fallen, with little to disturb its quiet world but the myriad sea animals, mostly teredos and other wood borers.

The action of sea water is not very rapid either, and paint protects the shell and the metal work that hold it together. The wreck is gradually overlaid with barnacles and marine growth, layer upon layer, until it is covered completely, while sea and river sediment slowly settles down over it. It is claimed that wrecked ships lying at the ocean bottom have been the beginning of a reef, shoal or similar obstruction.

When an iron or steel ship sinks, especially a steamer with heavy boilers and engines, and a closely packed heavy cargo, she is apt to go down very rapidly. Her collision with the ocean floor may go far to break her up.

Whatever happens, she has the corrosive effects of the salt water and electrolytic action to withstand as well as all or most of the factors that affect the wooden ship. Vegetation and animal life settle on her wooden parts; and barnacles, teredos and other marine growth are the cause of further chemical change. Every scratch in the paint is an opening for electrolysis. Presently the paint scales off, and after many decades there will be little more than a rust stain at the bottom of the sea to mark where the vessel found her resting place.

It is interesting to note that of all the vessels that have stranded on the shoals of the Pacific Graveyard, the remains of about a half dozen show a vestige of themselves. Yet probably deep under the sands and offshore, parts of old wrecks still remain intact. The bones of ships buried in this area have frequently been uncovered by the shifting sands along the beaches and then completely buried again within a short period of time. Offshore, areas of quicksand prevail; often ships have been doomed by settling on one of these quagmires.

The Graveyard of the Pacific has also played host to many minor accidents which have cost ship owners many thousands of dollars in repairs. Between 1910 and 1912, before the construction of the north jetty, more than thirty ships stranded or struck the sands along these shores, with damages ranging between $1,000 and $15,000 per ship. Many of these vessels were heavily laden when they struck.

To estimate the amount of ship damage and total destruction in this area would be a difficult problem, but it is a known fact that it would run into the hundreds of millions of dollars, a far greater sum than has been expended to make the area safe for navigation.

Cape Disappointment has fittingly become the tombstone over this maritime cemetery. Standing as a massive bastion against the marauding swell of the ocean, it has witnessed a grim chapter in the chronicle of Pacific Northwest ship disaster. The sandy spits crowned with precipitous cliffs and beetling crags have provided a fit setting for the tragedies enacted here.

Losses total well over 200 deep-water ships with damages inflicted on an additional 500. The fishing fleets alone have suffered about 500 losses and another 1,000 fishing craft have been damaged. Predictability is not a byword in the Pacific Graveyard and the toll in men and ships bear that fact out to the utmost. Sometimes gales can erupt with very little notice, or widow-maker and sneaker waves can build like watery avalanches sending green water over a ship's pilot house.

History is deeply inscribed in the sands, reefs and rocks of this most unusual portion of the North Pacific Rim, and for well over a century names like Peacock Spit, Clatsop Spit and Cape Disappointment have become household words in maritime circles.

This great battleground, where the mighty Columbia meets the surging Pacific head-on, is a constant turmoil of sand, silt, and waterpower; and man will never be able to relax his efforts to keep the bar safe and deep as long as he wants ships from around the world to trade with the vast inland empire up the Columbia and Willamette rivers.

CHAPTER 13

SHIPWRECK LIST

Major Marine Disasters in and around the Pacific Graveyard

A star (★) preceding the name of a ship indicates a full-length story elsewhere in the book. See index.

Abbey Cowper, British bark, 699 tons, stranded at Leadbetter Point, near Shoalwater Bay, January 4, 1885. No lives were lost in the wreck but the ship was a total loss. She was carried ashore by the currents in a thick fog, while in command of Captain William Ross. The wreck occurred while the vessel was en route to Portland from Mollendo, Peru, in ballast.

Abe Lincoln, schooner, said to have been a sunken wreck at Astoria in 1870. She reputedly operated out of Shoalwater Bay and was built in 1861.

★ *Admiral*, American schooner, 605 tons, was driven into the south jetty of the Columbia bar, January 13, 1912. The crew was rescued but the vessel drifted across the river mouth and capsized, becoming a total loss.

★ *Admiral Benson*, American steamship, 3,049 tons, stranded near Peacock Spit, at the mouth of the Columbia, February 15, 1930. Passengers and crew were saved but the vessel was totally wrecked.

★ *Alice*, French ship, 2,509 tons, wrecked in gale one mile north of Ocean Park, January 15, 1909. Total loss.

Allegiance, British ship, stranded on Sand Island, in May, 1879. No lives were lost and the vessel was later refloated, repaired and returned to service.

Alpha, American gas screw, 20 tons, wrecked near Ocean Park, Washington, September 19, 1924. The craft was wrecked while trying to land an illegal cargo of liquor on Klipsan Beach. The crew narrowly escaped with their lives and the vessel was leveled by the surf.

Alsternixe, German bark, 3,039 tons, stranded in heavy weather at dusk, February 9, 1903, one and one-half miles southwest of Cape Disappointment Light. Complement of the vessel, including Captain Richard Auhagen, were rescued the following morning by the lifesaving crew. Several weeks later, the vessel was safely refloated after having been considered a total loss. The four-masted bark, valued at $90,000, hailed

Charles Fitzpatrick

Stranded inside the north entrance to the Columbia River bar near Chinook, February 9, 1903, the German bark *Alsternixe* was one of the few early-day sailing craft salvaged from that area.

from Hamburg, and was one of the few large ships to escape the sands of Peacock Spit. The stranding was attributed to the vessel getting out of the marked channel.

Americana, American schooner, 900 tons, went missing with all hands (11 souls) after clearing the Columbia bar, February 28, 1918. She was believed to have foundered in a gale, but no trace was ever found. The *Americana* was en route to Sydney, Australia, from Astoria, with lumber. This 204-foot vessel was built at Grangemouth, Scotland, in 1892, for Hawaiian interests.

Andrada, British bark, 1,200 tons, vanished with all hands several miles west of the Columbia bar, December 11, 1900. She is believed to have foundered in a gale off the Washington Coast on December 15, but no trace of her has ever been found.

Anna C. Anderson, American schooner, vanished at sea with her party of seven men, under Captain W. H. Stapleford in January, 1869. The vessel was outbound from Oysterville with a cargo of oysters for San Francisco. She was last seen crossing the Shoalwater bar. Some speculated that the master of the schooner had crowded on superfluous sail for a fast passage south due to the perishable cargo. The craft was perhaps struck by a heavy blow before her canvas could be taken in, causing her to capsize and sink. The vessel was owned by John and Thomas Crellin, of Oysterville, and S. Morgan of San Francisco.

Architect, American bark, 279 tons, stranded on Clatsop Spit, March 28, 1875. She was in ballast from San Francisco en route to Cementville on the Columbia. As she followed the ship *Pactolus* across the bar, the wind failed, causing her to go on the sands. After spending the night in the rigging in refuge from the surf, Captain Mertage and his crew were rescued by a lifeboat manned by Lieutenant Samuel Jones and the Allen Brothers of Astoria who were towed to the scene of the wreck by the tug *Astoria.* F. C. Carr, of Astoria, purchased the wreck for $52, but salvaged little of value. The *Architect* was built at Rockland, Maine, in 1865, and was insured for $8,000 at the time of the wreck.

Ariel, American schooner, wrecked on Clatsop Spit in 1886. The crew is believed to have been saved. No record appears to have been kept as to which schooner *Ariel* was lost at the river mouth. It was claimed by some of the old-timers to have been the 99-ton schooner *Ariel* built at Baltimore in 1853, and registered at San Francisco; while others say she was the 43-ton schooner-yacht *Ariel* built at New York in 1873, later becoming a unit of the Pacific sealing fleet.

★ *Arrow, U. S.* Army transport, 2,157 tons, wrecked at Cranberry Road, a few miles north of Long Beach, February 13, 1947. She parted her tow line and was carried ashore with nobody aboard.

Arrow No. 2, motor tug, 15 tons, owned by the Arrow Tug and Barge Co., of Astoria, Oregon, exploded and burned off Astoria, January 21, 1949. One life was lost.

Artemisia, American schooner or sloop, was wrecked south of Klipsan Beach in 1889. No lives were lost. The vessel was one of the early-day units of the Shoalwater Bay mosquito fleet. She first made her appearance in the area in 1875, under Captain E. G. Loomis.

Aurelia, American steam schooner, 424 tons, stranded at Buoy No. 8, on the Columbia bar, August, 1911. The vessel was later refloated and repaired.

Aurora, American ship, 346 tons, stranded on the sands off Grays Bay inbound from San Francisco in June, 1849, in ballast. Aboard were twenty-six passengers, all of whom were rescued by John Hobson on his flat barge from Astoria. The *Aurora* was skippered by Captain H. Kilbourn, formerly of the brig *Henry.* A short while after the passengers were rescued, a gale arose and destroyed the vessel. All hands were saved. This ship was in quest of lumber for the return trip when disaster occurred. Built at Baltimore in 1823-24, the *Aurora* was owned throughout most of her career by Robert Kermit and James Mowatt of Baltimore, and was classed as a packet ship.

Avalon, American steam schooner, 881 tons, stranded April 29, 1925, off Cape Shoalwater, at the entrance to Willapa Harbor. With great effort the vessel was finally refloated but was so badly damaged that she was never put back into service. Instead, she was scrapped in 1927. The steam schooner was owned by Hart-Wood Lumber Company. Built by Matthews Shipyard at Hoquiam, Washington in 1912, this coastwise lumber vessel was powered with a 650-horsepower steam engine.

Baby Doll, freight boat, 140 tons, stranded at the Columbia River entrance, March 1, 1955, but was later refloated.

BARGE Ex-*Nichols I,* unnamed steel oil barge, was carried up on the beach north of Long Beach, after being cut loose from the tug *Tidewater Shaver* off Columbia bar buoy No. 5, when she and the barge *Intrepid* threatened to carry the tug into dangerous waters. Cut free February 22, 1954, at 9 p.m., the barge drifted up on the beach the following day. The 100-foot barge was being towed to Portland from Honolulu when she came to grief.

Barge No. 16, 45,000 gallons capacity, 260 feet long, went aground on Clatsop Spit, after breaking loose from tug *Sea Lion,* November 24, 1953, with 16,600 tons of benzol. The Devine salvage tug *Salvage Chief* pulled her free two days later. The petroleum barge was operated by the United Transportation Co.

Barge 91, stranded at the mouth of the Columbia River, May 14, 1909. She was later refloated.

Battle Abbey, British bark, lost at sea off the Columbia River, December 18, 1914. The crew was rescued by the German ship *Eilbek* and landed at Astoria. The ill fated vessel was built as the *Royden* in England in 1875.

Beaver, gas-powered boat, 15 tons, wrecked on Clatsop Spit August 3, 1940.

Bell Buoy, fishboat, about 15 tons, foundered, August 19, 1960, 196 degrees true from Cape Disappointment. This crab trawler, built in 1949, was owned by the Bell Buoy Crab Company, was oil powered, and operated out of Astoria.

Bettie M., tuna seiner, owned by Bumble Bee and Castle & Cook, wrecked near jetty A at the north entrance to the Columbia River, March 20, 1976. The vessel failed to turn into the Sand Island range. The vessel and 900 tons of tuna

Sam Foster

The sleek tuna seiner *Bettie M.* reaches her port of no return. She ran onto the sandy outcroppings of the Columbia River bar near Jetty A, on March 20, 1976. The crew of ten was lifted to safety by Coast Guard helicopter.

were a total loss. She was 997 gross tons and 172 feet long. Built at Tacoma in 1972, she was powered with a 3,600 horsepower diesel.

Biddle, U. S. dredge. See *General John Biddle.*

Bonnie, fishboat, sank off the Columbia River May 2, 1985. Two men drowned.

Bordeaux, American brig, 250 tons, was wrecked on Clatsop Spit, December 13, 1852. The disaster occurred while the vessel was bound for San Francisco from Puget Sound. She ran into the Columbia River for an unscheduled call and fell victim to the currents when the wind died on the bar. The crew walked ashore on dry sand, but the vessel was later demolished in the surf.

Brodick Castle, British ship, 1,820 tons, disappeared with all hands after departing the Columbia River, December, 1908. She is believed to have foundered in a gale.

Buster, barge, 230 tons, foundered on the Columbia bar, October 17, 1940. Built in 1920.

Cadzow Forest, British bark, 1,116 tons, pounded unmercifully by heavy seas while attempting inbound crossing of the Columbia River bar, January 4, 1896. The pilot had been taken aboard. The vessel suffered heavy damage and the seas were so ugly that the pilot could not be removed by the pilot schooner. Instead, the damaged Britisher drifted northward at the mercy of the elements and was lost with her entire crew. The derelict later drifted as far as the British Columbia coast where she foundered. Built at Port Glasgow, Scotland, in 1878, the ill-fated bark had been in command of Captain McInnis.

★ *Cairnsmore,* British bark, 1,300 tons, stranded on Clatsop Spit, September 26, 1883. All hands were rescued; the vessel was a total loss.

★ *C. A. Klose,* American schooner, 401 tons, drifted ashore bottom up, on North Beach Peninsula, March 26, 1905.

★ *Canadian Exporter,* Canadian steamship, 5,400 tons, stranded in the fog on Willapa bar, August 1, 1921. No lives were lost but the freighter eventually broke in two.

★ *Caoba,* American steam schooner, 683 tons, wrecked north of Ocean Park, February 5, 1925. The crew abandoned her at sea.

Cape Wrath, British bark, 2,140 tons, vanished off the mouth of the Columbia River, January 16, 1901 with her crew of fifteen. The vessel was sighted off the river, seventy-five days out from Callao for Portland, and was never heard of thereafter. It is believed that she was a victim of a terrific storm that struck the area on the day she was last reported. The big bark was registered at Glasgow, and was owned by the Lyle Shipping Company.

Capt. James Fornance, American steamer, 153 tons, stranded in a gale four miles east of the Fort Canby Lifesaving Station, December 21, 1917. Forty-seven passengers were removed and landed safely at Ilwaco.

Captayannis S., Greek cargo vessel, while standing into the river signalling for a Columbia River pilot, stranded on Clatsop Spit, October 22, 1967. Captain Ioannis Markakis and his 22-man crew were removed by Coast Guard helicopter. Her cargo of fishmeal was salvaged, but although the freighter was pulled free of the shoals nine days later, she was found to be badly damaged and was eventually sold for scrap.

Carlina, troller, wrecked at the river entrance, June 8, 1978.

Carrie B. Lake, American schooner, 36 tons, stranded near the present location of Long Beach, January 3, 1886. Three lives were lost, including Captain John Exon and two seamen. Two others struggled ashore in the surf. The schooner was built on Puget Sound in 1883, and was valued at $3,000. She was completely destroyed.

Casco, troller, wreck found on the north side of the entrance to Willapa Bay, December 1966. The owner-operator was missing.

Castle, American river steamer, exploded and sank off Tongue Point, Oregon, in 1854. No reported loss of life.

Cavour, Italian ship, 1,354 tons, stranded on the sands two miles south of Cape Disappointment Light, on the night of December 8, 1903. The twenty-two-year-old vessel had been at anchor on the bar awaiting favorable winds, when a strong breeze came up suddenly from the south and swept her ashore with anchors dragging. The tugs *Wallula* and *Tatoosh* were unable to free the vessel, but the lifesaving crew from Point Adams rescued the complement of sixteen men and Captain Telemore Sofianos. The *Cavour* was the first Italian ship lost on the bar. She was owned by G. Bucelli and Domingo Loero of Genoa, and was valued at $15,000. The ship was built at Nova Scotia in 1881.

CG-40564 and *CG-36454,* motor lifeboats. See *Triumph* incident.

★ *Challenger,* American schooner, 279 tons, caught fire off the Oregon Coast and burned for several days until towed across Willapa bar and scuttled in the Willapa River, November 7, 1904.

Champion, American schooner, driven ashore on the north spit of the Columbia bar, April 15, 1870. The vessel was en route to Shoalwater Bay from the Columbia River and was swept ashore by the currents when the wind failed while outbound. The six-year-old vessel, in command of Captain Dodge, was under charter to a Mr. Mudge of Astoria. After the schooner stranded, she was swept on her beam ends and the crew took to the boat. The boat, however, swamped. As they attempted to return to the wreck, a tremendous breaker struck and tossed them out of the boat. Two were drowned and the remaining survivor, an Indian, was carried to sea on the overturned lifeboat to which he had lashed himself. The following morning the boat and its occupant were carried ashore on the North Beach Peninsula. The *Champion* was built by Capt. Quick at Tillamook in 1865.

Chatham, His Majesty's Ship (tender) British, 135 tons, stranded on what is now part of Peacock Spit, October 20, 1792, in command of Lieutenant William Broughton. Though the stranding was at first believed to be of a serious nature they got her off on the change of the tide.

★ *Childar,* Norwegian motorship, 4,138 tons, grounded on the southwest end of Peacock Spit, May 3, 1934. Four lives were lost but the freighter was pulled to safety in one of the most remarkable salvage feats of the decade.

City of Dublin, British ship, 814 tons, wrecked on Clatsop Spit, after the currents carried her on the shoal when the wind failed on the bar, October 18, 1878. The vessel was en route to Portland from Port Chalmers, and was forty-nine days at sea. She was in command of Captain David Steven who, being unfamiliar with the landmarks, stood in too close to the bar and was helpless to bring his ship about after the breeze failed. The anchor cables parted and the vessel was dashed hard on the sands. The crew made shore safely. Two weeks later, salvage attempts were commenced but proved unsuccessful. The *City of Dublin* was valued at $40,000.

Columbia, gas-powered fishboat, about 15 tons, burned to the water's edge off Long Beach, Washington, February 10, 1928. The vessel was built in 1909 and was a veteran fishboat in the area.

★ *Columbia River Lightship No. 50,* American, 296 tons, was carried ashore inside McKenzie Head at the north entrance of the Columbia, November 29, 1899. The crew was saved and several months later the vessel was refloated in one of the most interesting salvage feats ever performed.

Corrie P., fishing vessel, 86 feet, vanished with her crew of four between Grays Harbor and the Columbia River. Last reported January 16, 1981. She was to have landed her catch at Astoria but is believed to have foundered off the Columbia bar.

Corsica, British bark, 778 tons, foundered twelve miles southwest of the Columbia bar, February 21, 1882. The vessel was bound for Queenstown, N.S.W., from Portland, with a full cargo of grain. She was drawing twenty feet when she passed over the bar in tow of the tug *Astoria.* The heavy swell caused her to strike the sands on three occasions and she commenced to take water rapidly. Captain W. H. Vessey fearing for the lives of his wife and child, ordered the *Astoria* to come

Charles Fitzpatrick

The *Deneb* was en route to Alaska when her main water pump failed and she was tossed ashor on North Beach Peninsula May 1950.

alongside and take them ashore, while the tug *Fearless* stood by. The pumps were manned continuously, but the vessel settled deeper and deeper. The *Fearless* tried to get a line on her, but Vessey refused to take it. At midnight the vessel had taken ten feet of water in her hold and the pumps were choked with wheat chaff. Finally she was abandoned and the crew rescued by the *Fearless*. The bark plunged to the bottom at 5 a.m. The cargo was valued at $50,000 and the vessel at $30.000. The *Corsica* was built in 1869.

★ *C-Trader,* motor vessel (freighter), 2,392 gross tons, struck bottom while outbound over Willapa bar, Dec. 6, 1963, because of steering troubles. Began leaking badly five miles offshore. After the crew was removed, the ship was towed across the Columbia River bar by the salvage tug *Salvage Chief.* She settled lower in the water and struck inbound, necessitating her being pushed higher on the sands where she became a total wreck December 17.

David E. Day, Atlantic-Richfield tanker grounded at the north entrance to the Columbia River, 300 yards off buoy 9, December 7, 1967. A Coast Guard helicopter removed part of the crew. The 572-foot tanker had 150,000 barrels of gas aboard. Fortunately the tanker refloated herself a few hours later while being slammed by 20-foot seas. A major accident was narrowly averted.

Decorah, American gas schooner, 39 tons, stranded on Clatsop Spit, July 15, 1915, but was later salvaged and repaired.

Deneb, American, converted landing craft, en route to Alaska, was driven ashore four miles south of Ocean Park on May 15, 1950, when the main water pump failed. She was salvaged and towed to safety by Fred Devine's 3600-hp *Salvage Chief,* of Portland. The *Deneb's* master was John Niemi.

★ *Desdemona,* American bark, 331 tons, stranded on Desdemona Sands, so named after the wreck, January 1, 1857, with the loss of one life.

Detroit, American brig, 141 tons, stranded on the middle sands of the Columbia bar, after missing stays, on December 25, 1855. Later she drifted free but her bottom had been fouled and she took water rapidly. In twenty minutes, seven feet of water filled her hold, and the frightened crew refused to work. The brig's master lashed the wheel hard over and squared the sails and then gave the order to abandon ship. The men were picked up by the pilot boat *California* and taken to Astoria in time for Christmas dinner. The *Detroit* drifted about the mouth of the river for twenty-four hours, and was finally carried ashore near Tillamook Head. James Cook, a resident of Astoria, purchased the wreck and stripped her remains. At the time of the accident, the *Detroit* was en route to San Francisco from Astoria. The eighty-four-foot vessel was built at Guilford, Connecticut, in 1836.

Devonshire or *Dovenshire,* British, rig unknown, wrecked on Clatsop Spit in 1884. Very little is known concerning this wreck, but the vessel is said by some to have been an early British tramp steamer.

Dewa Gungadhar, British bark, 594 tons, went aground in the fog near Leadbetter Point, south of Shoalwater Bay, January 18, 1885. The bark was in command of Captain John Battersby, and was inbound for the Columbia River from Magdalena Bay. Over-running the Columbia entrance, she was trapped by the currents and carried northward. Despite the dropping of both anchors, the vessel dragged on to the beach and became a total loss. A rescue crew got a line on the wreck and rescued the thirteen men aboard.

Dilharree, British bark, 1,293 tons, met disaster while outbound from the Columbia bar in tow of two bar tugs. She carried a full grain cargo from Portland destined for Queenstown, N.S.W. In transit, the bark veered toward the shore and ran aground on the tip of Peacock Spit, March 10, 1880. The two tugs and a revenue cutter tried in vain to pull her to safety, but under her heavy load the vessel refused to oblige. The crew abandoned, and after a narrow escape in the boats was rescued. The composite vessel was valued at $65,000 and the cargo at $78,000. The respective skippers of the tugs were exonerated of blame when it was learned that the bark had failed to answer to her helm after the steering mechanism became jammed. The vessel was owned by John Lidgett, of London, and all the ships of his fleet had name prefixes beginning with "Dil," a Hindustani word meaning heart. The name *Dilharree,* for instance, means "Heart's Delight."

Dolphin, U. S. Navy brig, mounting ten cannon, was wrecked on Clatsop Spit in 1852, while attempting to enter the river. The vessel was carried onto the beach and demolished, but the crew reached shore safely.

Donna, American fish boat, 20 tons, wrecked with the loss of her three crew members, near Ocean Park, April 14, 1944. The wreck was removed from the beach via the overland route.

Douglas Dearborn, American schooner, 1,024 tons, was discovered, bottom up, several miles off the mouth of the Columbia River, January 4, 1890. No trace of her crew has ever been found. The vessel's hull was salvaged and rebuilt.

Dovenshire, see *Devonshire.*

Dreadnaught, American sloop, also referred to as "Unknown Sloop of 1876," built on Tillamook Bay near Bay City, was wrecked February, 1876, on Clatsop Beach, in command of Capt. Wm. Terwilliger. All hands, seven in number, were drowned.

★ *Drexel Victory,* American steamship, 7,607 tons, foundered outside the Columbia entrance, one-quarter mile due west of Buoy No. 6, January 19, 1947. The crew of forty-nine were all rescued.

Drumcraig, British bark, 1,979 tons, went missing with all hands en route to Manila from Astoria in 1906. The iron vessel was last seen crossing the Columbia bar well freighted with a load of lumber. The 280-foot square rigger was built in 1885, and was owned by Gillison & Chadwick as a unit of the famous "Drum" fleet.

Eagle, gas-powered fishboat, foundered near Tillamook Rock, March 8, 1942.

Edith Lorne, British bark, 805 tons, stranded on the middle sands of the Columbia bar, November 17, 1881. The vessel was bound for Queenstown, N.S.W., from Portland with a cargo of wheat. She was crossing the bar in company with the ship *Napier* when she brought up on the shoal. The stranding occurred with a pilot aboard. The vessel was in command of Captain William Watt. As she yawed on the sands, the bark's stern post cracked and the rudder was unshipped. Shortly the vessel began to break up. The Fort Canby surfboat crew, led by Captain Albert Harris, maneuvered to the scene and rescued the ship's company. The vessel, which ultimately became a total loss, was valued at $58,000, and her cargo at $44,000. She was drawing eighteen feet of water when she struck the sands.

Ediz, American, gas propelled, burned September 16, 1951, three miles above the mouth of North River, Pacific County.

Efin, American, river freight boat, 196 tons, was destroyed by explosion and fire at 9:30 p.m. after departing Ilwaco for Astoria, May 11, 1937. The fire was caused by a fuel tank explosion. Capt. Alfred Babbidge and his crew of ten took to the lifeboat and were picked up, half-clothed, by the motor lifeboat from Cape Disappointment. Among the crew was a woman cook. The *Efin* burned to the water's edge and her remains drifted to Sand Island. The vessel, built at St. Helens, Oregon, in 1914, was owned by Babbidge & Holt, of Portland.

Eine, launch, lost on the Columbia River bar, in September, 1914, without loss of life.

Electra, American fish boat, 72 tons, stranded on Clatsop Spit, inside the river bar, January 26, 1944. All hands were rescued. The Coast Guard cutter *Nemaha* attempted several times to pull the craft to safety, but was unsuccessful. A year later only the *Electra's* mast remained above the sand and surf.

Ellen, American schooner, wrecked on Shoalwater bar, April 20, 1870. The vessel was loaded with lumber when she was destroyed at the bar entrance. Her crew members were saved, after a narrow escape in the surf. The *Ellen* was a small coaster that was built for the Tillamook-Shoalwater Bay trade in 1865.

Elsie Faye, fishboat, oil-powered, about 15 tons, collided with buoy No. 12, near the entrance to the Columbia River bar, in 1960, and was lost.

Emily Stevens, American schooner, 100 tons, stranded on Clatsop Spit, February 8, 1881. She was given up as a total loss and abandoned by her crew, who were picked up by the tug *Columbia.* Later the schooner drifted off the shoal and floated out to sea where it was picked up comparatively undamaged by the tug *Columbia,* which towed it to Astoria, and collected $950 in salvage money. Master of the tug was Captain Eric Johnson. The 87-foot schooner was built at Westport, Oregon, in 1879, by Captain Alexander Henderson for service as a halibut schooner. At the time the *Stevens* struck Clatsop Spit, she was inbound from Eureka for Portland with a cargo of lumber.

Empire, American schooner, missed stays and stranded on the Shoalwater bar in 1854. The schooner was outbound for San Francisco from Oysterville, well freighted with oysters. Her crew struggled to safety through the surf.

Enterprise, American steamer. Some old accounts say a vessel of this name was wrecked at the entrance to the Columbia River, in July 1858, but this cannot be confirmed.

★ *Erria,* Danish cargo-passenger motor ship, 8,786 tons, suffered a severe fire while at anchor near Tongue Point, Oregon, December 20, 1951. Eleven persons lost their lives.

Fanny, American sloop, was dismasted and waterlogged off Shoalwater Bay in 1864. Her crew took to the boats and were later picked up at sea. The wreck capsized and became a menace to navigation. Her remains were rammed and sunk by the steamship *Pacific.*

Fern Glen, British ship, 818 tons, was cast ashore on Clatsop Spit when Captain F. Budd, her master, mistook Tillamook Rock Light for Point Adams Light, and ran his ship onto the beach at 4 a.m., October 16, 1881. The vessel was en route to Portland in ballast from Wellington, New Zealand, to load grain. The following day the twenty crew members were employed in removing the ballast to lighten the vessel's burden, but that evening a southwest gale arose and put the vessel in a serious situation. The steamer *General Canby* attempted to rescue the seamen, but was prevented from getting near the wreck by the heavy surf. Later the ship began to heel over when the ballast shifted, but the crew managed to launch a damaged lifeboat, and row to the side of the tug *Columbia* which was standing off the wreck. The *Fern Glen,* a ship of graceful lines, was classed as a medium clipper, and was valued at $40,000. Captain Budd was criticized over the loss of his ship as the accident occurred in perfect weather on a starlight night.

Firefly, American steam tug, was carried ashore near Tansy Point while towing logs at the mouth of the Columbia February 24, 1854, with a loss of four lives. The tug was en route to Welsh's Sawmill from Young's River in command of Captain Thomas Hawks. As she rounded Smith's Point she was met by a strong ebb tide and was unable to make any headway against the currents. Her low-power engine could not stand the strain and the tug was carried on the sands at Tansy Point with her tow drifting aimlessly behind. Hawks refused to cut his tow loose, fully expecting to get off on the next tide. The mounting surf, however, carried the log raft ashore and pulled the tug after it, causing her to capsize and sink, taking the Captain and three crew members to a watery grave. Aboard the tug was I. Welsh, owner of the mill for which the logs were destined. He was thrown clear of the wreck and managed to scramble up on the log raft. He succeeded in severing the hawser with his knife and was carried all the way to Astoria astride the raft. When a salvage party returned to the scene of the wreck only the tug's tall stack rose above the surface, but to it they found clinging the tug's fireman, whom they rescued. The stubby tug was brought to the river from San Francisco only a year prior to her loss.

FISHING FLEET, May 4, 1880, met with tragedy. Research by author Don Marshall has uncovered facts that dispute the long-lasting tales of the wipe out of the fishing fleets of Astoria and Ilwaco and the loss of 200 lives. In actuality, though one of the most devastating storms recorded in the area did destroy several of the craft, the recorded death toll was between 15 and 20. The big hero was Captain W. L. Harris whose little steamer *Rip Van Winkle* rescued numerous fishermen from their capsized craft, as did the operators of other powered vessels that fought the fury of the storm with winds exceeding 100 mph.

Flora, trawler, lost near the Columbia River south jetty, March 26, 1954, with the loss of two lives.

Foss No. 2, American scow, 495 tons, parted her hawser while under tow and drifted ashore, near Tillamook Head, where she was dashed to pieces in the year 1931. The scow was built at Seattle in 1926.

Francis H. Leggett, American steamship, 1,606 tons, foundered in a gale sixty miles southwest of the Columbia River, September 18, 1914, with a loss of sixty-five lives. Only two were saved after a terrible ordeal in storm-tossed seas. The vessel carried a cargo of railroad ties, which several days later drifted ashore on the Tillamook and Nehalem beaches, along with some bodies. The revenue cutter *Bear,* the Japanese cruiser *Idzimno,* and the tanker *Frank Buck* answered the distress calls, but when they arrived at the scene, the *Leggett* had foundered. She was outbound from Grays Harbor for San

Salvage attempts were soon abandoned on the 292-foot steel bark *Galena*, after she crashed ashore on the sands of Clatsop Beach, November 13,1906. In a few years she was swallowed by the hungry sands.

Francisco. The steamer was built at Newport News in 1903 for the Hammond Lumber Company.

★ *Frank W. Howe,* American schooner, 573 tons, was carried ashore near Seaview, just north of North Head, February 22, 1904, after becoming waterlogged at sea.

Friendly, fish boat, 17 tons, foundered off the mouth of the Columbia, August 15, 1945.

Galena, British bark, 2,294 tons, stranded on Clatsop Beach at night, on November 13, 1906. She was inbound from Junin, Chile, in ballast to load grain at Portland. The weather had been severe and the vessel was beating off the mouth of the river waiting opportunity to pick up a pilot. She got in too close to shore and was carried onto the beach by the surf. Captain Howell and two of his officers stood by the vessel in hopes of salvaging her, but with the storm season coming on, the sands built up around the hull of the 292-foot steel vessel, and salvage prospects were abandoned. A few years later the ship was devoured by the sands. She was one of the largest and finest of the grain fleet and was owned by S. Galena & Company of Liverpool, for whom she had been built at Dundee in 1890.

Gamecock, American sternwheel steamer, damaged severely and structurally disabled on the Columbia River bar and towed back to Astoria in 1898. The vessel was built at San Francisco for Alaska river service.

Gary Denn, fishboat, wrecked 500 yards off the north jetty of the river on Peacock Spit, August 31, 1966.

G. Broughton, British bark, 803 tons, stranded at Leadbetter Point just south of the entrance to Shoalwater Bay, November 1, 1881. The vessel, inbound for Portland from Brisbane, Australia, was in ballast, and struck the beach at

Sternwheeler *Gamecock* was heading for the Yukon gold rush country when she was battered and badly damaged by a ground swell on the Columbia River bar in 1898.

night in thick weather. Off the mouth of the Columbia the vessel had drifted northward with the prevailing currents before taking to the beach. Captain Payne ordered the masts chopped down in an effort to lighten the vessel, but she failed to relinquish her place in the sands, and the crew of sixteen had to be rescued. She remained on an even keel for three days and then careened over and dug her grave in the sands. The vessel was owned by Peter Iredale & Porter of Liverpool, and was valued at $40,000. She grounded one day after the *Lammerlaw* went ashore in almost the identical spot, and both ships became total losses within a few feet of each another.

General C. H. Muir, U. S. Navy transport, suddenly sank at dockside, February 1955, while berthed at Astoria. Shallow water kept her from going down beyond her superstructure. She was hastily patched and pumped out, temporarily repaired, and later dry-docked at Portland.

General John Biddle, U. S. Corps of Engineers' huge seagoing hopper dredge, ran aground on the north jetty of the Columbia River bar while working in the area on July 1, 1964. Captain Ernest Williams, master, jumped from his bunk and ran to the bridge, to find the 351-foot ship hung up on the rocks. There she remained for a terrifying twenty minutes while the breakers licked at her steel hull. With skillful maneuvering, the captain got the vessel to back off under her own power, but sharp jetty rocks had punched a sizable hole in her port side just aft the midship section, and she was taking water into her hull. Pumps controlled the inflow as the *Biddle* headed across the bar for Portland, escorted by the Coast Guard. There a survey showed she had damaged a hull plate also compartments, floors, and bulkheads. Northwest Marine Iron Works was successful bidder for repair work at $84,082. After nine days the mammoth dredge was back at work in the graveyard area—one of the few large sea-going ships ever to escape from a jetty, on the entire Pacific Coast. More than thirty crewmen were aboard her at the time of the stranding.

★ *General Warren,* American steamship, 309 tons, put aground on Clatsop Spit, in sinking condition, January 28, 1852. Forty-two lives were lost when the vessel was leveled by the surf. The *Warren* was built for the Portland Steam Packet Company, of Portland, Maine, in 1844. She was one of the early sidewheel steamers seen in Maine. She came to the West Coast during the California Gold Rush, and eventually entered coastwise service.

It is interesting to note that in October, 1854, two years after the *Warren* was lost, the whole stern frame of the vessel was found on the beach sixty miles to the north of the wreck—an example that shows the prevailing littoral current around the Columbia bar.

George Olson, 3,321 tons, lumber barge, broke loose from the Tacoma tug *Mikimiki* while crossing the Columbia River bar with a load of lumber at 1:20 a.m., January 30, 1964. Coast Guard vessels from Cape Disappointment—a 52-footer and a 40- and 36-footer—went to the aid of the runaway barge and managed to get lines on her. They began the tow in rough waters toward Astoria, but the 321-foot barge, one of the largest on the coast, had been damaged in crossing the bar and began sinking fast. To prevent her from sinking in the channel, the boats ran her aground on the seaward side of Jetty A, about 1,350 yards off Cape Disappointment Light. The Coast Guard cutter *Yocona,* on arriving at the scene, reported a third of the barge was broken off at the stern and lumber was breaking loose. Total cargo was 3.5 million feet of lumber.

The *Olson* was later abandoned as a total loss, though much of her lumber was rounded up. She was owned by Oliver J. Olson Company of San Mateo, California pioneer shipping firm in the haulage of coastwise lumber. Only a short time earlier, she had been converted from a steel steam schooner. The *Olson* was originally built (1919) by Pusey & Jones at Gloucester City, New Jersey and launched as the *Castle Town* for the U. S. Shipping Board. Sold to

Burkharts-Meier

'rothing waves scattered lumber like toothpicks when the barge *George Olson* grounded at the mouth of the Columbia, January 30,1964.

Charles Nelson Company of San Francisco, she was purchased in 1936 by John Rosenfeld's Sons, also of San Francisco, and later re-sold to the Coos Bay Lumber Company of Coos Bay, Oregon. They renamed her *Lumbertown* and later *Coos Bay*. When purchased by Oliver J. Olson, the vessel was given the name of *George Olson*, retaining that name until her loss. She was in the lumber packing trades for virtually her entire career

George W. Prescott, schooner, foundered off the Columbia River, March 9, 1902. She was built at Irondale, Washington in 1893.

Gleaner, American, river steamer, capsized off Tongue Point, en route to Astoria from Deep River at 11 a.m. January 28, 1888. The loss was caused by a gale that swept the lower river. The cargo shifted and the craft heeled over, drowning one man and two women passengers. The remaining twenty-seven passengers took refuge in a fishing boat that the steamer was towing. The *Gleaner* was commanded by Captain Peter Jordan. The vessel was a propeller steamer that was built at Grays Bay in 1883.

★ *Glenmorag*, British ship, 1,567 tons, stranded north of Ocean Park, March 18, 1896, with the loss of two lives. The vessel was built in 1876, for the J. & A. Allen fleet.

Go-Getter, American tugboat, 79 tons, out of Garibaldi, Oregon, in the service of Sause Bros., Ocean Towing Company, ran aground on the south jetty at the mouth of the Columbia River at high tide at 3 a.m., June 12, 1952, punching holes in her hull. The crew of six waded ashore. The tug was towing a steel barge with a $25,000 cargo of logs, which also grounded but was pulled free by the Coast Guard and the tug *Chahunta*. Three days later the salvage of the 1,000-hp *Go-Getter* got underway, with the services of the Sause tugs *Klihyam* and *Chahunta* aided by a Coast Guard cutter. The damaged tug was pulled free and escorted into safe haven, completing a splendid and speedy salvage undertaking, under supervision of Curtis Sause.

Gotoma, American two-masted schooner, 198 tons, lost at Willapa Harbor, Washington, on Christmas Day, 1908. She was built by John Kruse, in 1872, at the Simpson yard in North Bend, Oregon, at a cost of $16,000. She was last owned in San Francisco, by A. M. Simpson, James Madison, and Samuel Perkins. The 119-foot craft was employed in coastal service.

★ *Governor Moody*, American pilot schooner, 65 tons, was wrecked at North Head, September 20, 1890. The crew were saved but the vessel was a total loss.

Grace Roberts, American barkentine, 286 tons stranded two miles south of Leadbetter Point, December 8, 1887, without loss of life. The vessel, commanded by Captain M. Larsen, was feeling her way along the coast in a thick fog when she drifted into the breakers, knocking several holes in her hull. The crew had to take to the boats. Shipbreaker Martin Foard purchased the wreck for a small sum and salvaged the cargo and equipment. The *Roberts* was built at Port Orchard, Washington, in 1868, at a cost of $30,000. It was said that the owners of the barkentine had run the vessel hard, overlooking badly needed hull repairs which may have caused her to bilge on the sands. Parts of her barnacle-encrusted remains could be seen on the peninsula as late as 1964. They are the oldest visible ship's remains in the Pacific Graveyard.

Charles Fitzpatrick

Remains of the American barkentine *Grace Roberts*—wrecked December 8,1887—could still be seen on the peninsula three-quarters of a century later.

★ *Great Republic,* American sidewheel passenger steamer, 4,750 tons, stranded on Sand Island, April 19, 1879. The passengers were safely evacuated, but eleven crew members were drowned in the last full lifeboat to clear the wreck.

★ *Harvest Home,* American bark, stranded four miles north of North Head, January 18, 1882, without loss of life. The vessel was beyond salvage.

Hazard, American brig, commanded by Captain Benjamin Swift, in 1798, lost the chief officer and four crewmen in a small boat while the men were trying to sound the Columbia bar depths.

Helen M., charter fishing vessel, smashed against the south jetty of the Columbia River, July 9, 1967, after her engine broke down. Six aboard rescued.

Henrietta, omitted from records, was said to have been a French bark that stranded on the south side of the river entrance near Astoria, in 1860.

Henriette, French bark, 735 tons, grounded on a reef of rocks just above Astoria, on the south side of the river in a gale on December 27, 1901. She settled on both anchors, which forced a hole in her bottom, causing her to sink. Her master filed suit against the crew of the tug *Walulla* for leaving him at anchor when he was told that the bar was all right for crossing. The twenty-seven-year-old iron vessel was salvaged several months later and purchased by Simon McKenzie, for use as a barge. Later she was converted to a steamer, and then

Grace Kern

A major salvage job was required to refloat the 735 ton French bark *Henriette*, after she settled on her anchors and punched a hole in her hull, December 27, 1901.

Grace Kern

For several weeks the *Henriette* rested on the river bottom. This on-board photo shows that she swallowed a considerable amount of river water because of broken plates. Astoria is seen in the background. Daniel Kern raised the vessel and gave her a new lease on life.

After wrecking at the mouth of the Columbia in 1901, the bark *Henriette* was salvaged and rebuilt as a schooner. During her busy career she sailed under the flag of three different countries.

to a four-masted schooner. During her career she flew the flags of France, the United States and England. The vessel was lost in the South Seas in 1922.

Ida Mae, American fish packer, 26 tons, struck bottom and went down off Cape Disappointment on October 27, 1953. The Astoria crew of three swam to safety.

I. Merrithew, see *J. Merithew.*

★ *Industry,* American bark, 300 tons, stranded on the middle sands at the Columbia's entrance, March 15, 1865, with a loss of seventeen lives.

Intrepid, American barge, 1,110 tons, carried up on the beach and abandoned, February 23, 1954, just north of Long Beach, after she and a smaller oil barge were cut loose from the tug *Tidewater Shaver.* The barges were cut loose when they threatened to carry the tug onto treacherous Peacock Spit.

Charles Fitzpatrick

American barge *Intrepid* washed up on the shore north of Long Beach, February 23, 1954—cut loose from the tug *Tidewater Shaver*, when she threatened to carry the tug onto treacherous Peacock Spit.

The barges were being towed from Honolulu to Portland without cargo. The *Intrepid* was built at Mare Island, California, between 1903-07 as a U. S. Naval bark and for many years served as a naval training vessel, her only mode of power being sail. In the latter "20s" she was sold out of the service and cut down to a barge by the Hawaiian Dredging Company. Under ownership of Independent Iron Works of Oakland, Calif., she was being towed to Portland to go on the block when she went on the beach. She and the companion barge were cut loose from the tug near buoy No. 5 and were carried by the prevailing currents and breakers to the peninsula beach.

Inveravon, British bark, en route Callao—Portland, went missing off the Columbia River with all hands, October 1914.

★ *Iowa,* American steamship, 5,724 tons, stranded and foundered off Peacock Spit, January 12, 1936, with the loss of her entire crew of thirty-four.

★ *Isabella,* British brig, 195 tons, stranded on Sand Island, May 3, 1830, without loss of life.

Jane A. Falkenberg, American barkentine, 310 tons, stranded on Clatsop Spit in 1872. At first it was feared that she would be lost but determined salvage efforts were rewarded, and the vessel was eventually refloated from her sandy perch. She was built at New Bedford in 1854, and came to the Pacific Coast the following year. She had clipper lines and seldom made a slow passage. Shortly after her arrival on the coast she was purchased by Captain Flavel.

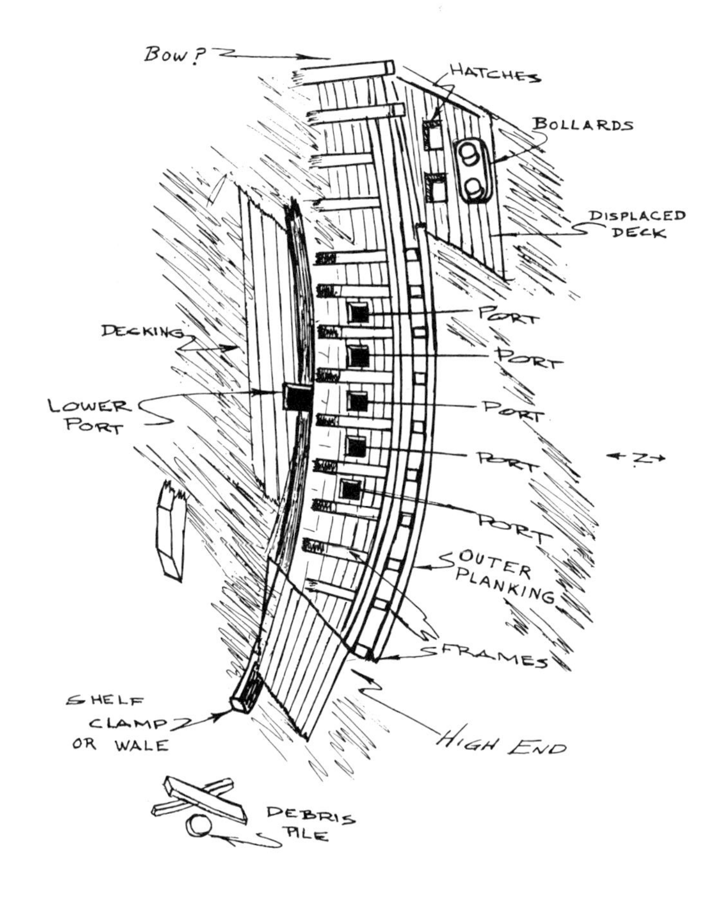

Sketch by Lt. Michael Monteith, courtesy Columbia River Maritime Museum.

On September 23, 1987, Daryl Hughes, a commercial fisherman, arrived at the Columbia River Maritime Museum in Astoria to report that he had discovered an old wreck near Ilwaco. Museum curator Larry Gilmore enlisted the assistance of a team of qualified divers and archaeologists. Shown here is a drawing of an overhead view of the wreck remains which has been identified as the Hudson's Bay Company brig *Isabella*, wrecked May 3, 1830.

JAPANESE JUNK, unnamed, drifted ashore on Clatsop Spit in 1820, after being carried across the Pacific Ocean with the prevailing current. The vessel was devoid of life.

JAPANESE JUNK, about 1905, name unknown, washed up in pieces along the beach by gale-whipped seas on North Beach Peninsula, between the Ocean Park and Oysterville sea approaches. Wreckage was deposited in the peninsula forest after high waters receded. Though the craft was not identified, it undoubtedly drifted across the Pacific with the strong Japanese Current that annually deposits hundreds of Japanese fish floats and other flotsam and jetsam on western shores. In earlier years, numerous junks were reported wrecked at various locations throughout the Pacific most of them victims of the sweeping ocean currents.

★ *J. C. Cousins,* American pilot schooner, stranded on Clatsop Spit, October 7, 1883. No trace of her crew of four was ever found.

Jennie F. Decker, fishing vessel (motorized schooner type) rammed and sunk by a Liberian freighter at the entrance to the Columbia River, June 28, 1981. The 65-foot *Decker* was split in half, but all aboard were rescued. She was built at Seattle in 1901.

Jennie Ford, American barkentine, wrecked on a rocky shelf off North Head, January 29, 1864. The vessel was beating up the coast in command of Captain McCarty, and was en route to Puget Sound from San Francisco in ballast. Out of the thick weather suddenly loomed a rocky promontory, and the vessel struck on the shelving undersea extension. She immediately began to break up, and the crew experienced difficulty in launching the boat. A passenger named Osgood was swept overboard and drowned. After several hours in an open boat the ship's party landed on North Beach, exhausted from their tribulations.

★ *Jenny Jones,* American schooner, stranded on Peacock Spit, May 14, 1864, while entering the river. The vessel and her party were miraculously saved. Famous Captain "Jimmy" Jones was in command.

Jessie Nickerson, American schooner, 184 tons, was wrecked at the entrance to Shoalwater Bay in 1880. The schooner was commanded and principally owned by Captain Samuel Bonnifield of San Francisco. No lives were reported lost in the wreck. The *Nickerson* was constructed by the Hall Brothers yard at Port Ludlow, Washington, in 1874, and shortly before her loss had a fine passage to her credit of ten days from Honolulu to Humboldt Bay, California.

★ *J. Merithew,* American bark, stranded on Clatsop Spit, January 12, 1853. She arrived off the Columbia, December 30, 1852, after a twelve-day passage from San Francisco, and due to unfavorable conditions was compelled to stand off the river several days. No pilot having come, on January 11 Captain Samuel Kissam started his command across the bar. When abreast of the red channel marker near Clatsop Spit, the wind died and the bark was swept onto the middle sands dragging both anchors. The masts were cut away and the cargo was jettisoned in an attempt to get her afloat. A gale was in the making and was soon lashing at the wreck with all its fury. The pilot boat set out from Astoria to rescue the crew but was unable to do so until the following morning. Lying abandoned on the shoal, the *Merithew* floated free and drifted seaward, only to be caught in a cross current and swept into the rocks near North Head. At the time of the wreck, the vessel was carrying 128 tons of general merchandise.

Josephine, British brig, wrecked on Clatsop Spit, in 1849. Very little is known of this wreck except that the vessel was totally destroyed. Some sources claimed she was of British registry, others French registry. No mention of loss of lives was made.

Jupiter, fish boat, 14 tons, foundered off Willapa Bay, April 14, 1918, with the loss of her crew of four. Her skipper was Captain Charles B. Ammerman.

Kake, gas-propelled salmon packer, American, 34 tons, was swept onto the spit at midnight near the south jetty of the Columbia bar, November 1, 1913. The craft was destroyed in the surf but the crew was rescued. The *Kake,* commanded by Captain Morzey, was inbound from Kake, Alaska, with 360 cases of packed salmon. She was owned by the Sanborn-Cutting Company of Astoria.

LaBelle, trawler, 15 tons, foundered off Peacock Spit, with the loss of one life, March 25, 1945.

Lammerlaw, British bark, 746 tons, stranded at Leadbetter Point, when her master, Captain Pringle, mistook Shoalwater bar for the Columbia bar, October 31, 1881. The vessel was bound for Portland from Newcastle, N.S.W., with a cargo of coal when she grounded. The lifesaving crew picked up the survivors, while the beachcombers picked up the coal to heat their homes. The officers' mess table and some silver service from the *Lammerlaw* are still in use at the home of Mr. and Mrs. Charles Nelson of Nahcotta. The bark was an iron vessel valued at $70,000, and was less than three years old at the time of the wreck. Captain Pringle was censured by the Board of Inquiry over the loss of his command.

★ *Laurel*, American steamship, 5,759 tons, stranded on Peacock Spit, June 16, 1929, with the loss of one life.

Lenore, trawler, 15 tons, stranded near Ocean Park, April 10, 1917, without loss of life.

Leonese, American bark, came ashore on Clatsop Spit, bottom up, December 27, 1860. Not a sign was ever found of her crew of nine.

L'Etoile du Matin, French ship, unable to get a pilot, July 11, 1849, attempted to cross the Columbia River bar unaided. She struck the shoals, badly damaging her keel and losing her rudder. Later she came off the reef and drifted into Baker Bay, where Alexander Lattie, of Astoria, took some Indians to her rescue. A box rudder was constructed, and the crews of several vessels helped pump and bail, so she could be worked upriver to Portland, where her cargo was saved.

Lively, oil-propelled fishboat, 25 tons, October 31, 1962, grounded on Clatsop Spit between buoys 12 and 14, at the Columbia River entrance, six or seven miles from Astoria. Owned by Edwin N. Goodrich of Astoria.

Louie III, Knappton tug, sank in 75 feet of water off Astoria, May 12, 1971, in command of Captain Erling Flats.

Lucky, American oil screw, 48 tons foundered six miles west of the Columbia River Lightship, July 16, 1950.

Lupatia, British bark, 1,300 tons, struck the shore and foundered off Tillamook Head, January 3, 1881, with the loss of her entire complement of 16 men. A dog was the only survivor.

Machigone, American schooner, disappeared with her crew of nine off the mouth of the Columbia, after departing Astoria for San Francisco, November 20, 1852. The windjammer—commanded by Captain I. H. Simpson—put out from Astoria with a heavy load of lumber and shortly after her departure a terrible gale roared across the latitudes of the Columbia's mouth.

Maine, American bark, 294 tons, was wrecked on Clatsop Spit, Aug. 25, 1848. She was a whaler that was originally out of Fairhaven, Massachusetts, but sailed around to the Pacific to scout our possibilities on the west coast. The master of the whaler elected to cross the Columbia bar for supply and recuperation for his crew. When his signal for a pilot went unheeded he endeavored to sound the channel with a small boat. His ship eventually ended up on the spit and became a total loss. Two of the ship's crew remained in Oregon, the others worked their way back to the east coast after sailing a small craft down the coast to San Francisco. No record exists of the disposition of the whale oil cargo and bone but it was presumed to have been lost. Only pioneer John Hobson benefitted from the wreck, equipping his cooper shop with materials from the wreck.

Makah, American barkentine, 699 tons, found, bottom up, off Tillamook Head, October 24, 1888, eighteen days after leaving Port Discovery, Washington, for Sydney, Australia, with lumber. No sign of her crew of eleven was ever found and the remains of the six-year-old vessel were rendered a total loss. She was commanded by Captain Larsen.

Marathon, American fish boat, 37 tons, burned one-fourth mile up the entrance to the North River, Pacific County, Washington, November 18, 1948.

Maria B., American fishboat, about 15 tons, owned by George P. Karl of Portland, burned at Warrenton, Oregon, May 4, 1955. The craft was built in 1945, as a pleasure boat at Holland, Michigan.

Marie, gas boat, foundered off Peacock Spit in the summer of 1913.

Marie, American brig, was wrecked in a fog two miles north of Cape Disappointment, November 29, 1852, with the loss of nine lives. The brig was en route to Shoalwater Bay from San Francisco. The fog blotted out all landmarks and the vessel's master was unaware of the proximity of the shore until breakers were sighted and the vessel carried on the shoals. A boat was put over the side but immediately swamped, drowning its occupants. By the following morning the *Marie* was reduced to a total wreck and nine men, including the captain, were dead. Two survivors struggled through the surf to safety and were later found on the beach suffering from exposure.

Martha, fishboat, capsized on the Columbia River bar March 20, 1984. One person drowned, two rescued by Coast Guard helicopter.

Mary Joanne, fishboat, sank April 23, 1969, 4½ miles southeast of the *Columbia River Lightship*. Three crewmen were rescued by the Columbia River pilot boat.

Massachusetts, U. S. Transport, 750 tons, stuck fast on a sand spit near Tongue Point, May 10, 1849. She was carrying 161 men of the 1st Artillery to Fort Vancouver. Her pilot was Alexander Lattie, perhaps the best known of the early-day pilots. The vessel was worked off the spit on May 12, after some anxious moments. She proceeded upriver with Lattie as pilot and successfully dropped anchor at Fort Vancouver, bringing the first American troops officially stationed in Oregon Territory. After a brief stay, she departed downriver and across the bar without further incident.

When the *Massachusetts* entered the Columbia, she was claimed to be the largest vessel that had yet crossed the bar. She carried both a full suit of sail and the Ericsson propeller, along with her steam plant, making her one of the more modern government vessels of her time.

★ *Mauna Ala,* American steamship, 6,265 tons, stranded during the coastal blackout off Clatsop Beach, December 10, 1941. All hands were saved.

★ *Melanope,* British bark, 1,624 tons, partially dismasted in a storm in December, 1906. Abandoned at sea by her crew, the derelict was later picked up off the mouth of the Columbia by the steamer *Northland.*

Mermaid, fishboat. See *Triumph* incident.

M. F. Hazen, launch, capsized off the Columbia River bar, in 1905.

Michigan, American steam schooner 566 tons, in November 1890, put into Astoria all ablaze en route to Portland from Puget Sound. The fire was finally squelched but repairs were costly. The vessel was wrecked off the West Coast of Vancouver Island, January 21, 1893. She was built in 1888 by Mortensen and Colwell at Skamokawa, Washington.

Midnight Express, fishing vessel, 86 feet long, wrecked near Ocean Park, November 30, 1981 with four crewmen missing. Only the skipper, Captain McMurrick made it safely ashore on a liferaft. The vessel was one of three sisters built at the same yard in Pascagoula, Mississippi, that were all lost off the Oregon coast, the others being the *Corrie P.* and the *American Express*. An investigation was launched.

So badly battered on the Columbia bar was the *Multnomah,* June 1929, that she never put to sea again. In this photo she is shown partially sunk inside the bar.

Mildred C., fishboat, 62 foot, out of Newport, Oregon, grounded on the south jetty of the Columbia bar at midnight, August 26, 1980. Valued at $300,000 and her fish cargo at $15,000, she slipped off the rocks and sank.

★ *Mindora,* American bark, stranded off Sand Island, without loss of life, January 12, 1853.

Mizpah, American motor craft, wrecked on North Beach Peninsula, with the loss of two lives in 1952.

★ *Morning Star,* French bark, stranded off Sand Island, with a loss of one life, July 11, 1849.

Multnomah, American steam schooner, 969 tons, damaged beyond repair in heavy seas June 16, 1929. She sent out a call for the Coast Guard after she had lost part of her deck load of lumber but the Coast Guard was attending the wreck of the *Laurel* on Peacock Spit. Finally the *Multnomah* was escorted over the bar, but her condition left her no longer fit for sea duty.

Nabob, British bark, disappeared with her entire crew after crossing the Columbia bar, outbound with grain for the United Kingdom, March 4, 1876. She was commanded by Captain Fetherstone.

Nemanosha, gas-powered fishboat, 22 tons, foundered June 25, 1925, near the *Columbia River Lightship,* with a loss of two lives. The 55-foot craft was built at Toledo, Oregon, in 1911. Her home port was Portland, Oregon.

Neptune, American diesel tug, 415 tons, was struck by the steamship *Herald of the Morning,* while maneuvering in to get a line on the vessel nine miles off the Columbia River, November 16, 1948. The *Neptune* was aiding in the towing of the freighter to Puget Sound from San Francisco, and the collision occurred in rough seas after the big steamship broke loose from the tug *Sea Fox.* The *Neptune* attempted to retrieve the tow. Her tanks were punctured in the subsequent collision and shortly afterwards she plunged to the bottom. The Coast Guard cutter *Balsam* picked up the survivors. One of the tug's crew died of a heart attack from immersion in the icy waters. The *Neptune* was a unit of the Puget Sound Tug and Barge Company, and was skippered by Captain Kelly Sprague.

Nightingale, United States Navy minesweeper, 225 tons, sank after colliding with Columbia bar buoy No. 11, December 26, 1941. After she struck the buoy she was run for the jetty sands to prevent her sinking in deep water. A big hole had been knocked in her side, however, and before the sands could be reached, she sank. The CG-402 removed 9 men and the CG-4315 rescued the remaining 7. There were no casualties. Only the tips of the *Nightingale's* masts remained above the water. Several weeks later, Capt. Loring Hyde, salvage master, raised the AMc type minesweeper, and the wreck was sold as surplus and rebuilt at Astoria. Cause of the disaster was listed as unknown.

Nimbus, American ship, 1,302 tons, struck the sands of the Columbia bar outward bound, and plunged to the bottom twenty-five miles northwest of the river, December 29, 1877. The vessel, under pilot Thomas Doig, crossed the bar at 8:30 a.m. with a cargo of wheat from Portland valued at $92,500. Following the south channel, the ship scraped over the middle sands. When the pilot departed the ship, Captain R. L. Leonard discovered his vessel was taking water at an alarming rate. The vessel was put about and headed for shore, but the wind died and she was becalmed. Leonard signaled the *Aberystwith Castle* and the *Pilgrim to* stand by. At 7 p.m., when the water reached the 'tween decks of the *Nimbus,* the crew abandoned and was picked up by the stand-by sailing vessels. The ship went down a few hours later. She was valued at $65,000, and had been built at Bath, Maine, in 1869.

American steel barge *Nisqually* on dock at Portland, Oregon, getting her plates repaired.

Nisqually, American barge, 1,251 tons, stranded on Clatsop Spit after breaking loose from the tug *Tyee* off the mouth of the Columbia, on March 26, 1938. The steel barge went ashore with 600,000 feet of peeler logs. The surf washed the deck-load off the barge. Several weeks later salvage efforts proved successful and the craft was refloated. The barge, owned by Allman-Hubble Towing Company of Aberdeen, was the former steamship *Suremico,* built at Newark, New Jersey, in 1920. On June 3, 1927, she had collided with the French freighter *Arkansas* off Cape Flattery, Washington, and was so badly damaged that she was reduced to the role of a barge.

Nola, gas screw, stranded on the north spit of Willapa bar, July 29, 1944, without loss of life.

★ *North Bend,* American schooner, 981 tons, stranded on Peacock Spit, January 5, 1928, without loss of life. Thirteen months later she refloated herself.

Nuny II, luxury yacht, 55 foot, en route San Diego–Seattle, skippered by Jim Vallentyne, was smashed to bits in a storm immediately off the Columbia River entrance, October 2, 1967. All three aboard perished.

Oleum, American oil tanker, 10,448 gross tons, suffered a serious structural crack while crossing the Columbia bar

Woodfield Photo

Six of the seven men aboard lost their lives when the *Oshkosh* capsized off the Columbia entrance, February 13, 1911.

January 2, 1951, and spilled oil all the way to Portland. Oil damage to the fishing industry was heavy. Repairs, including replacement of 19 steel plates and bulkhead work, totalled $118,700. The tanker was built at Portland in 1945, and was a unit of the Union Oil Company of California.

Orbit, American brig, stranded on Sand Island inbound from Puget Sound, March, 1850. Captain T. Butler and his crew, fearing that the breakers would make short work of the brig, abandoned her. Some Astorians with an eye for salvage later boarded the vessel and after herculean efforts succeeded in getting her afloat. She drifted to Baker Bay and was safely anchored. Michael Simmons, of Newmarket, Washington, paid off the salvagers and regained his vessel.

Oregon, launch, was lost on the Columbia bar, in the fall of 1914.

Orient, American brig, 324 tons, was wrecked at the south entrance to Shoalwater Bay, near Point Leadbetter May 7, 1875. No lives were reported lost. The brig, hailing from Boston, was operated in the coasting trades at the time of her loss.

★ *Oriole,* American bark, was destroyed on the south sands inside Clatsop Spit, September 19, 1853.

Orion, two-masted schooner, cut in half after being rammed by the German ship *Peru,* just north of the *Columbia River Lightship,* October 4, 1897. Captain P. Nelson and the crew of the 117-ton schooner were rescued. The ill-fated vessel was built on Humboldt Bay in 1878.

Oshkosh, American motor vessel, 145 tons, struck bottom off the south jetty of the Columbia bar, on February 13, 1911, with a loss of six lives. The vessel departed Tillamook for the Umpqua River, but ran into a strong southeast gale. Her fresh-water tanks became filled with sea water, and Captain Latham reversed his course and headed for the Columbia. The bar was in a disturbed condition for a crossing, and at 5 a.m., February 13, the vessel was tossed ashore and a few minutes later capsized, carrying six of the seven men aboard to their deaths. The one survivor struggled up on the jetty rocks and was found by the lifesaving crew blue with cold. His name was George May. The *Oshkosh* was owned by the Elmore Navigation Company and had been carrying freight out of Astoria to other bar ports prior to her loss.

Otsega, American steel barge, 643 tons, owned by the A. C. Dutton Lumber Co., parted her towing line from the tug *Columbia Queen* and went aground on the North Beach Peninsula one and one-half miles north of Long Beach, laden with 700 tons of explosives, destined for the Umatilla Ordnance Depot. The barge came ashore at 11:15 p.m., November 10, 1953. After several salvage attempts failed, the *Salvage Chief,* owned by Fred Devine of Portland, succeeded in pulling the barge free. The *Salvage Chief* utilized a pair of tow lines to jerk the barge loose. A light plane was used to fly lines to the barge,

Ackroyd Photography, Inc.

ıe super tug *Salvage Chief* shows in the distance, maneuvering in to pull the stranded barge *Otsega* off North Beach Peninsula.

Ackroyd Photography, Inc.

Here is the *Salvage Chief* in the foreground successfully pulling the barge *Otsega* free November 23, 1953.

while 600 spectators along the beach looked on. The barge was refloated November 23.

Palos, American brig, stranded on Leadbetter Point, at the south entrance to Shoalwater Bay, in November, 1853. The vessel was en route to Oysterville from San Francisco, and attempted to enter the bay in a thick fog. When the crew and passengers were abandoning the ship, the captain was swept overboard and drowned. The others reached shore safely, but the vessel was pounded to pieces.

Parker Barge No. 1, 85-ton barge, was lost at the mouth of the Columbia River, in 1934. She was owned by W. W. Parker of Astoria.

Pasolento, American gas-propelled fishboat, 17 tons, burned at Astoria, April 17, 1949.

★ *Peacock,* U. S. Naval brig (sloop of war), 275 tons, stranded on Peacock Spit, July 18, 1841, without loss of life.

Peacock, pilot boat. On September 27, 1962, the dory from the *Peacock* drifted forty miles from the Columbia bar, resulting in the loss of one life.

Pearl C., charter fishing vessel, radioed for help when a fuel line clogged and the vessel began leaking, September 13, 1976. A Coast Guard 44-footer took the vessel in tow at 6 p.m. south of the Columbia. A second 44-footer assisted in the tow when the three crafts gained an area between buoys 6 and 8, the *Pearl* heeled over and began to sink. Two were rescued, but eight others were missing. Despite an all night search by surface vessels and aircraft, the effort was to no avail. The skipper of the *Pearl,* William Cutting of Ilwaco, was among those who were presumed to have drowned. It was the worst charter fishing boat disaster in the Columbia River area, and an extensive investigation followed calling for stiffer regulations.

Permanente Cement, American freighter (cement carrier), 4,782 tons, owned by Permanente Steamship Company, sustained serious superstructure damage while crossing the Columbia River bar, November 1, 1954. The 400-foot steamship was struck by huge bar swells. A frequent caller at Portland, this ship was built at Nagasaki, Japan, in 1920.

★ *Pescawha,* American motor schooner, 93 tons, was carried into the north jetty and demolished, February 27, 1933, with the loss of her master.

★ *Peter Iredale,* British bark, 2,075 tons, stranded on Clatsop Beach, October 25, 1906, with no loss of life.

Picaroon, fishboat, wrecked on the south jetty of the Columbia River bar, August 17, 1945.

★ *Pinmore,* British bark, 2,134 tons, was towed in from several miles off the Columbia River entrance, after the crew had abandoned her in 1901. When her cargo shifted in rough seas, she went over on her beam ends. The *Pinmore* was brought into Astoria for salvage, and her crew—which had been picked up by another steamer and brought to Astoria—were amazed to find their ship at anchor in the harbor. She was repaired and went back to sea, to become a victim of Count von Luckner's *Seeadler* in World War I.

Point Loma, American steam schooner, 310 tons, grounded on the North Beach Peninsula, near Seaview, February 28, 1896. In charge of Captain Conway, the vessel was en route

Charles Fitzpatrick

Steam schooner *Point Lomo* was driven ashore near Seaview, on the North Beach Peninsula, February 28, 1896, during one of the worst gales of that year. Recipe for her wreck: flooded boilers, savage winds, high seas.

to San Francisco from Grays Harbor with lumber. The day prior to the wreck, one of the worst gales of that year struck the steamer. About midnight the engines broke down and water leaked into her hull and extinguished the fires in the boilers. The wind and high seas carried the ship toward the shore. Distress signals shot from her bridge were sighted by shore lookouts, and the Fort Canby lifesaving crew hustled down the beach to render aid. They launched a surf boat several times, but each time it was repelled by the breakers. Finally a line shot from the beach reached its mark. The crew of the wrecked steamer made it fast and then by means of a raft were successful in getting ashore without the loss of a man. Seventeen, in all, were saved. The vessel was pounded to pieces. The *Point Loma* was built at San Francisco in 1888, and was one of the pioneer steam schooners to engage in coastwise lumber trades. She was last owned by the Grays Harbor Commercial Company. Her remains could be seen on the beach at low tide until a few years ago.

★ *Poltalloch,* British bark, 2,250 tons, stranded north of Shoalwater bar, November 26, 1900, without loss of life. She was eventually refloated.

Potomac, American brig, wrecked on the Columbia bar, near the middle sands, in early May, 1852, outbound for San Francisco with lumber. The cargo was jettisoned after the vessel struck and she bumped the shoals constantly for several hours. Finally she drifted free and was carried to Astoria with the tide and currents. There she was surveyed and pronounced a total construction loss. Her master was Captain Addison Drinkwater.

Potrimpos, German bark, stranded on North Beach Peninsula, near Long Beach, December 19, 1896, without loss of life.

Primrose, wrecked on Clatsop Spit in 1882. Practically nothing is known concerning this wreck.

Battering breakers swept barge *No. 1684* against the precipitous rock walls of North Head in January 1947

Protection, American steam schooner, 281 tons, departed Seattle with a cargo of lumber for San Francisco. Off the mouth of the Columbia River she encountered a severe storm and plunged to the bottom with all hands, on New Year's Day, January 1, 1900. The vessel was owned by John S. Kimball, of San Francisco.

P. S. B. & D. Co. No. 14, American scow, 142 tons, foundered off the mouth of the Columbia River, November 15, 1943. The scow was built in 1913, and owned by the Puget Sound Bridge and Dredging Company.

P. T. & B. Co. No. 1684 and *P. T. & B. Co. No. 1685,* American barges, 1,007 tons each, were being towed to Honolulu from the Columbia River by the tug *Teton* of the Portland Tug & Barge Company, of Portland, Oregon. The barges were each loaded with $70,000 cargoes of lumber. Off the mouth of the river, heavy seas and high winds carried the tug and barges toward Peacock Spit, and in order to save the tug, the hawser had to be cut. Both barges went on the spit January 18, 1947. The surf made kindling of the cargo and the barges were a total loss. One of the barges was swept against the rock walls of North Head. The owners of the tug were exonerated in a $150,000 lawsuit involving the lost cargo.

★ *Queen of the Pacific,* American passenger steamship, 2,727 tons, stranded on Clatsop Spit, September 5, 1883. In an all-out salvage effort utilizing the services of a fleet of tugs, the liner was refloated.

★ *Raccoon,* British sloop of war, stranded briefly on the Columbia River bar, while inbound to the Astor Colony (Fort George) in December 1813. She refloated herself.

Racquette, barge, 643 tons, stranded off the main channel near Tongue Point, Oregon, September 23, 1953. The barge was later refloated. She was owned by A. C. Dutton Lumber Company and was registered out of Eureka, California.

Rambler, American schooner, came ashore on Clatsop Beach, bottom up, in March, 1860. The vessel had departed Neah Bay, Washington, December 21, 1859, en route to San Francisco with peltries and oil from a northern trading voyage, and is believed to have capsized off the mouth of the Columbia. No trace of her crew of four has ever been found. She was commanded by Captain A. J. Tuthill.

Red Star, American fish packer, 21 tons, burned at Warrenton, Oregon, October 14, 1947.

Republic, American shark boat, 25 tons, foundered off the mouth of the Columbia River, February 7, 1945, with the loss of her crew of four. Built in 1926, the vessel was a veteran of the Pacific Northwest fishing fleet. Part of her bow and forward deck drifted ashore on North Beach Peninsula several months later.

Rescue, American steam tug, 139 tons, said to have been wrecked off North Head, October 3, 1874. She was built at San Francisco in 1865.

Ricky, American fish boat, 25 tons, dragged anchor and was smashed against the rocks of the north jetty of the Columbia bar, in a storm, July 22, 1949. Skipper J. B. Price and his crew fortunately escaped death.

Rival, American bark, 299 tons, stranded on Peacock Spit, September 13, 1881, and became a total loss. With a pilot aboard, the vessel was outbound for San Francisco loaded with hay and shingles from Knappton. While she was on the bar the wind died, and after a lull changed to an easterly direction. The bark drifted onto the sands with both anchors dragging. The pilot schooner, nearby at the time, summoned the tug Astoria. The tug managed to get a line on the wreck several hours later, but while attempting to pull the *Rival* free, the line parted. Shortly, the starboard anchor cable broke, and the vessel swung abruptly about. The tug was unable to get another line on the wreck and at 1:30 p.m., September 13, the *Rival* parted her port anchor chain and was carried high on the beach between Cape Disappointment and McKenzie Head. Captain Thomas B. Adams, the *Rival's* master, his wife, and the crew took to the boats and landed safely on the beach. The bark was valued at $8,000, and her cargo at $6,000. The vessel was regarded as a veritable floating coffin, her hull being old and tender. She was a total loss.

Robert Bruce, American schooner, was burned to the water's edge by a mutinous crew at Bruceport, on Shoalwater Bay, December 16, 1851. As told in the pages of Samuel Snowden's *History of Washington,* "The small but exceedingly palatable oysters for which Shoalwater Bay has since become noted, had been found, and during the summer of 1850, Captain J. W. Russell had taken a small quantity of them to San Francisco by steamer where they were received with much favor. Captain Felstead also took a supply by sailing ship, but they arrived in bad order and were a total loss. Anthony Ludlam then fitted out the schooner *Sea Serpent* to engage in the oyster trade, and a

Woodfield Photo

As the *Minnie E. Kelton*, this steam schooner was badly battered off Yaquina Head and suffered the loss of eleven crewmen, May 2, 1908. Six years later, as the S.S. *Rochelle*, she was wrecked on the Columbia bar.

company was formed later which sent the schooner *Robert Bruce* to the bay for cargo, but while she was loading, the crew quarreled, and the ship was set on fire and burned to the water's edge. The crew, being unable to get away, became permanent settlers, near what has since been known as Bruceport, from the name of the ship." In another version of the story the ship's cook is said to have gone mad, set the *Robert Bruce* afire, and then to have disappeared. Survivors were Messrs. Garretson, Morgan, Tyson, Hanson, Wenant and Terry.

Rochelle, American steamship, 831 tons, wrecked on Clatsop Spit, near Buoy No. 12, October 21, 1914. On May 5, 1908, the steamer *Minnie E. Kelton* was towed to Astoria partially submerged, after having been buffeted by a storm that claimed eleven crew members off Yaquina Head, Oregon. At Astoria, the damaged vessel was stripped of her housing and used as a rock barge for the maintenance of the Columbia River jetty. Several months later she was rebuilt into a passenger steam schooner and renamed *Rochelle*. Ironically, the jetty which the vessel had helped maintain was the location of her loss. The steamer struck Clatsop Spit at night in thick weather. The engineer reported that the vessel was taking water fast and accordingly distress signals were shot into the air which alerted the lifesaving crews at Point Adams and Cape Disappointment. The bar tug *Wallula* also rushed to the wreck. Captain Simon Kildahl, pilot H. A. Matthews, and the crew of nineteen were rescued by the Lifesaving Service. An hour later, the action of the breakers caused the steamer's cargo of coal to catch on fire and the wreck became a torch. By morning she was on the bottom with only a few charred timbers breaking the surface. At the time of the wreck, the *Rochelle* was inbound to Portland from Boat Harbor, BC. The twenty-year-old vessel was valued at $40,000. The pilot blamed the stranding on inoperative channel lights.

★ *Rose Ann,* American fish boat, 51 tons, disappeared with her crew of four somewhere off the mouth of the Columbia River in February, 1948.

★ *Rosecrans,* American tanker, 2,976 tons, wrecked on Peacock Spit, with a loss of thirty-three lives, January 7, 1913.

Rose Perry, schooner, went aground on the south spit of Shoalwater bar, in September, 1872. The vessel operated in the coasting trades at the time she was lost. Some sources claim that she was of Canadian registry.

Rudolph, American fish boat, 27 tons, stranded on Peacock Spit, September 2, 1945, without loss of life. The gas-propelled vessel was built in 1911.

Samaria, full-rigged ship, en route Seatle–San Francisco, is believed to have foundered off the Columbia River, March 19, 1897. No survivors. A ring buoy from the ship was found at Cape Disappointment April 24, 1897.

Santa Adela, 6,507 gross tons, stranded at Youngs Bay, near Astoria, July 7, 1955. The 459-foot freighter was later pulled free. Owned by Grace Line, the ship was built in 1942 at Kearney, New Jersey, and was a regular unit in the West Coast-Latin American service.

SAUSE BROS. BARGE, (unnamed), 1,000-ton-log capacity, went ashore near Long Beach, March 30, 1950. The unrigged vessel was owned by Sause Brothers of Garibaldi, Oregon. She went aground after breaking away from the tug *Klihyam* during a heavy gale. A second barge also got away in the rough seas, but the tug's crew managed to "lasso" it. The tug, also owned by Sause Brothers, returned a week later and succeeded in pulling the barge off the beach. The salvage job was considered "remarkable" as most of the jobs of this kind have proved unsuccessful. Oftentimes small fishing craft that go aground on the peninsula are dragged up on the beach and hauled away on trucks.

S. D. Lewis, American brig, stranded on Clatsop Spit, March 16 1865, without loss of life. The vessel missed stays and went hard aground. She temporarily drifted free, but as the prow swung into the wind, a giant breaker carried her higher on the shoal. The crew took to the boats and managed to land in the surf. The brig eventually fell to pieces.

Sea King, trawler, radioed it was taking on water while near Peacock Spit the morning of January 11, 1991. The Coast Guard rescue boat *Triumph* took the 75-foot trawler in tow while four Coast Guardsmen were flown by helicopter to the *Sea King.* The tow was delayed by heavy seas for several hours. When a second attempt was made, the *Sea King* capsized and sank in 18-foot swells between bouys 8 and 9. Six people were rescued, but two of the *Sea King's* crewmen and one Coast Guardsman were lost. The following investigation led to the National Transportation Safety Board's ruling that poor communication about the flooding and the Coast Guard's failure to evacuate everyone from the *Sea King* before attempting the second tow contributed to the deaths of the three men.

Sea Lion, oil screw, stranded on the Columbia bar, October 5, 1939, without loss of life.

Sea Lion, trawler, disappeared with her two-man crew off Willapa Bay in calm weather in June, 1948.

Seaport, American gas-propelled fishboat, 36 tons, stranded one-half mile southeast of the south jetty of the Columbia River bar, June 22, 1950. The vessel was built the previous year.

Seaspan Barge 241, stranded inside the south jetty of the Columbia River in 55-mile-an-hour winds, March 20, 1976. Believed to be a total loss, the limestone carrying barge became the target of salvage by a small salvage outfit, Garrison & Divers, who to every professionals' surprise managed to free the battered barge after weeks of heavy labor. Cost of repairs came to $1.3 million.

★ *Sea Thrush,* American steamship, 5,538 tons, wrecked on Clatsop Spit, Oregon, December 4, 1932. Total loss. No loss of life.

★ *Shark,* U. S. Naval survey schooner 300 tons, stranded on Clatsop Spit, Oregon, September 10, 1846. Total loss.

★ *Sidi,* French brig, 276 tons, stranded near Sand Island, March 1, 1874. She was later salvaged and returned to trade-lanes as the *Sea Waif.*

Sil-Char, American, gas-propelled, foundered off Peacock Spit, April 27, 1951.

Silverside, crabber, out of Hammond, vanished off the Columbia River entrance, January 17, 1982, all three crewmen missing. A Coast Guard search turned up only bits of wreckage.

Silver Star, barge, sank off Willapa Harbor entrance, May 1974. Some wreckage was recovered by the *Salvage Chief* in June 1974.

★ *Silvie de Grace* or *Sylvia de Grasse,* American ship, wrecked on rock ledge near Astoria in 1849. Total loss.

Six-Pack, fishboat, 50 foot, capsized on the Columbia River bar, June 3, 1985. One life was lost, two were rescued.

★ *Solano,* American schooner, 728 tons, stranded five miles north of Ocean Park, February 5, 1907.

SPANISH VESSEL, name unknown, stranded on Clatsop Beach, supposedly in the year 1725, years before the Columbia River had been officially discovered by white man.

State of Washington, American sternwheel river steamer, 605 tons, destroyed by terrific explosion, June 23, 1920, off Tongue Point. The steamer was en route to Portland, towing oil barge *No. 93* from Astoria. Suddenly she was shaken by a terrific boiler explosion and six members of the crew were seriously injured and another scalded to death. The sternwheeler was so completely demolished that all that kept the wreck afloat was the hawser that remained fast to the oil barge. Nearby vessels came to the rescue and removed the injured men. The steamer was valued at $40,000. Her master was Captain H. L. Hill, but the vessel was in charge of the river pilot who had relieved the skipper a few minutes before the explosion occurred. The *State of Washington* was built at Tacoma in 1889, and was one. of the best known sternwheel steamers in the Pacific Northwest.

★ *Strathblane,* British ship, 1,300 tons, wrecked south of Ocean Park, November 3, 1891, with a loss of seven lives.

Sulphur, H.M.S. (British Naval Ship), 300 tons, stranded on Peacock Spit, while inbound on a surveying mission in 1839. No lives were lost and the ship was eventually refloated. The spot where she grounded was for many years known as Sulphur Spit. She was commanded by Captain Edward Belcher.

Arnold Harju

A tiller cable broke and the cannery tender *Susan* was forced by the heavy surf onto the sand of Peacock Spit, January 21, 1952. In less than one month she was swallowed by sand and se

Sundowner, fishboat out of Ilwaco, sank off the Columbia River bar, December 20, 1988, loaded with fish. Three crewmen were rescued.

★ *Sunshine,* American schooner, 326 tons, drifted ashore, bottom up, on North Beach Peninsula, November 22, 1875. To this day no trace has been found of her party of twenty-five.

Susan, American cannery tender, 52 tons, 72 feet long, drove aground on Peacock Spit in a snowstorm, January 21, 1952, after her tiller cable broke. Loss amounted to $30,000. The crew members, Thomas Delahunt and Jack Sheridan, waded ashore. George Moskovita purchased rights to the 32-year-old vessel and removed her engine and other equipment before the sands claimed their victim.

★ *Telephone,* American sternwheel river steamer, 386 tons, caught fire and was beached north of Astoria, November 20, 1887. One life was lost in the conflagration.

★ *Tonquin,* American ship, 269 tons, stranded momentarily on the Columbia bar while crossing inbound, March 22, 1811. Because of the captain's haste to cross the bar before a heavy sea had abated, he sent several of his men needlessly out to sound the bar in small boats. Eight of them were drowned.

Treo, American gas-propelled fish boat, 24 tons, foundered off Peacock Spit, December 2, 1940. The vessel was built in 1914. Captain George Moskovita and two crew members were returning from a fishing trip when, according to Moskovita, "We were hit by a big sea and she opened up and sank in about an hour. I had to burn a bucket of gasoline to attract the attention of John Lampi's boat *Washington,* which picked us up not a moment too soon and took us to Ilwaco."

★ *Trinidad,* American steam schooner, 974 tons, stranded on the north spit of Willapa bar between Buoys 6 and 7, May 7, 1937. One life was lost.

★ *Triumph,* Coast Guard motor lifeboats *CG-40564* (40-footer) and *CG-36454* (36-footer), and crab boat *Mermaid*–all lost on the Columbia River bar, January 14, 1961. Seven lives lost.

29 C 822, trawler, wrecked off Clatsop Spit in May, 1944, with the loss of her two crew members.

UNKNOWN SLOOP of 1876, (see *Dreadnaught),* was wrecked on Clatsop Beach in February, 1876, with the loss of her entire crew. The vessel was built new the same year at Tillamook, Oregon, and was commanded by Captain William Terwilliger, who was also her owner. Seven persons, including two eight-year-old boys, were drowned when the vessel was cast into the breakers. No registers carry the name of this craft though reliable sources claimed that it was named *Dreadnaught.*

U. S. COAST GUARD 41-foot training craft on maneuvers flipped over on the Columbia River bar at 7 p.m. November 15, 1977 throwing ten men into the sea. Coast Guard helicopters rescued seven, but three others were drowned. The men were practicing to be coxswains, and were on nighttime exercises. Out of the Cape Disappointment station, the vessel was not one of the self-righting types. Bar swells were up to 18 feet.

★ *U. S. Grant,* American steamer, 47 tons, broke loose from her moorings and was totally wrecked after grounding on Sand Island, December 19, 1871.

Vancouver, British bark, 400 tons wrecked on the middle sands of the Columbia bar, May 8, 1848, without loss of life. Pilot S. C. Reeves, the first officially appointed bar pilot in the lower Columbia, took charge of the ship when she arrived off the river mouth inbound to Fort Vancouver from London. Captain Mouatt, master of the *Vancouver,* had his men stand by the lead lines, but the pilot assured him that he could make the crossing with his eyes closed. The currents and the freshets were exceptionally strong on that day, and the vessel drifted from her course and hung up on the middle sands. That night, strong winds sent high breakers into the stranded bark. After every conceivable attempt to refloat her had failed, all hands finally abandoned her, and managed to reach the shore without serious mishap. The vessel was owned by the Hudson's Bay Company, and was loaded with agricultural machinery and general stores for the post at Fort Vancouver. Among the cargo was much finery and clothing that was salvaged by the natives. The ladies' gowns and trinkets were appropriated by the Clatsops, who were frequently seen picking berries in the latest London fashions of 1848. Captain Mouatt charged negligence on the part of pilot Reeves, but no further action was taken, and the insurance companies paid for the loss on the vessel.

★ *Vandalia,* American bark, washed ashore north of Cape Disappointment, January 9, 1853. Nine lives were lost in the tragedy.

★ *Vazlav Vorovsky,* Russian steamship, 4,793 tons, stranded on Peacock Spit, April 3, 1941, without loss of life.

Walpole, American Army store ship, struck the Columbia bar in the summer of 1849, severely damaging her keel. However, she made Astoria in safety.

★ *Washington,* American steam schooner, 539 tons, stranded on Peacock Spit, November 17, 1911, and was removed in a daring rescue attempt.

Washtucna, American barge, 710 tons, dragged anchor and drifted against the south jetty of the Columbia bar three-fourths of a mile southwest of the old lifesaving station, November 10, 1907. At the time she went aground she was being towed from Fort Stevens to Astoria. The barge, valued at $10,000, was finally pulled off by use of a kedge anchor and taken in tow by the tug *Sampson.*

Wavertree, British ship, 2,170 tons, out of Liverpool, and en route to Portland from Tocopilla, Chili, dragged anchors and was carried aground on Desdemona Sands at the mouth of the Columbia River, November 19, 1907. After being hung up on the spit for a considerable time, tugs succeeded in getting her off and escorted her to Young's Bay for repairs.

W. B. Scranton, American bark, stranded on the middle sands of the Columbia bar, May 5, 1866. The vessel, under Captain Paul Corno, was bound for Portland from San Francisco with 810 tons of cargo valued at $20,000. While sailing into the river, the wind failed and the vessel drifted onto the spit at 10 a.m. Captain J. D. Munson, lighthouse keeper at Cape Hancock (Disappointment), went to the rescue with a lifeboat and picked up Captain Paul Corno's wife and a woman passenger, but the crew remained with the ship until nightfall and then abandoned her. She broke up twenty-four hours after she struck the spit, and a few damaged threshing machines were about all of the cargo that was saved. The *Scranton* was valued at $25,000, but was insured for only $9,000, and her owner-master had expended $6,000 in repairs before departing San Francisco. Corno also owned the bark *Industry,* lost in the same area the previous year.

Web Foot, American barkentine, 361 tons, abandoned by her crew in sinking condition off Tillamook Rock Light, November 21, 1904, after being buffeted by a severe gale. The crew reached shore safely. The vessel, completely waterlogged, was towed into the Columbia and dismantled. She was built at North Bend, Oregon, in 1869, for A. M. Simpson of San Francisco.

Wellesley, American steam schooner, 907 tons, was en route to San Francisco from Willapa Bay when caught in a gale off Tillamook Rock. Beginning to leak, she put back for the Columbia River and on reaching Hammond, inside the mouth of the river, sank in 20 feet of water, April 11, 1926. Many months later she was raised and repaired.

★ *Welsh Prince,* British steamship, 5,000 tons, collided with the American freighter *Iowan,* off Altoona Head, near Grays Bay, May 28, 1922, with a loss of seven lives.

W. H. Besse, American bark, 1,300 tons, wrecked on Peacock Spit, July 23, 1886, without loss of life. Captain Gibbs, master, stood in for Cape Hancock, until, by cross bearings, the bar was three-quarters mile distant. Towards evening he

Formidable figurehead of the barkentine *Web Foot* abandoned off Tillamook Rock in 1904. With the disappearance of sailing vessels, these colorful carvings became practically extinct.

tried to stand out to sea, but before the wind filled the canvas, the vessel struck hard on Peacock Spit. Hundreds of persons gathered on the Cape to watch the operations as the rescue crews paced the beach below. The surf mounted, and fear was felt for the eighteen-man crew. The bark was loaded with rails, valued at $75,000, for the Northern Pacific Railroad. The vessel itself was valued at $45,000. Her crew finally managed to escape the wreck in the boats, but experienced a rugged ordeal before they reached the beach. The location of the wreck is still marked today with a channel marker, known as Besse Buoy. At the time of the loss, the bark was inbound from New York for Portland. Many observers claimed that Captain Gibbs was attempting to enter the river without the aid of a pilot. Part of the wreck later drifted onto the beach a mile north of Ocean Park.

Whistler American bark, 820 tons, wrecked on North Beach Peninsula, October 27, 1883. The vessel was bound for Astoria from San Pedro, in ballast. Her skipper was Captain J. F. Soule. Thick weather and strong currents caused the vessel to overrun the river entrance and go ashore at 2:30 a.m., on the sands of the peninsula, south of Ocean Park. In the inquiry over the loss of the vessel, Captain Soule testified that his unfamiliarity with the coastline and the natural forces of the area were responsible for the wreck. The vessel was valued at $18,000, and was built on the Atlantic coast in 1853.

Whitney Olson, American steam schooner, 1,558 tons stranded on Clatsop Beach, December 16, 1940, and was saved from destruction by the Coast Guard cutter *Onondaga,* which braved shallow waters and got a line on the lumber freighter. The vessel stranded after dragging her anchors with a jammed rudder. After three hours on the shoals, the cutter towed her off the beach, stern first, and took her to Astoria. At the time of the accident, the vessel was bound for Knappton from Los Angeles Harbor.

Willamette, American schooner, 180 tons, with its master and owner Captain John Vail, was wrecked at the Shoalwater (Willapa) Harbor entrance in 1861. She was en route to Shoalwater Bay from San Francisco. Two lives were lost when the crew attempted to reach shore. Bearing no malice at such an inhospitable reception on these shores, Vail homesteaded a claim where the city of Raymond is now located.

★ *William and Ann,* British brig, 300 tons, wrecked on Clatsop Spit, March 10, 1829 with an estimated loss of forty-six lives. Some accounts claimed the loss of life to have been twenty-six.

William Nottingham, American schooner, 1,204 tons, dismasted and waterlogged in a gale off the Columbia River, October 9, 1911. Her crew was picked up by the schooner *David Evans.* Later the derelict was found by the tug *Wallula* and towed to Astoria as a prize. She underwent extensive repairs and returned to the sealanes. At the time of the accident the *Nottingham* was outbound for Callao from Astoria. She was built at Ballard, Washington, for the Globe Navigation Company in 1902. Her latter years were spent as a cable barge, and in 1948, she was towed to the mouth of the Nisqually River, on Puget Sound, and sunk as a breakwater.

Windward, American ship, 818 tons, stranded momentarily near Sand Island, December 23, 1871, but was freed after anxious moments She was inbound for Portland from

Seattle when she got caught in a gale off the mouth of the Columbia, along with two other sailing ships. Braving the sou'wester, a tug put out from Astoria and took the *Windward* in tow. The tug towed the ship as far as Sand Island, where she dropped anchor while the towboat went out after the other vessels. The wind reached hurricane velocity and the *Windward* drifted toward the island over which a high sea was running. Both anchors were out, but regardless, the vessel went on the shoal. The three masts were cut away, which relieved the vessel's burden. She drifted free and was afterwards towed to Portland and fitted with new masts and rigging. She was wrecked for good on Puget Sound four years later.

Woodpecker, British schooner, 300 tons, stranded on Clatsop Spit, May 10, 1861, without loss of life. The vessel was outbound from the Columbia with flour, general freight and 104 head of cattle destined for Victoria, B. C. In transit the schooner missed stays, and the pilot, Captain Alfred Crosby, ordered the anchors dropped immediately to keep the ship from going on the sands. The starboard cable snapped and the *Woodpecker* swung broadside to the breakers, striking in ten feet of water. Over the side went the cattle and the cargo to lighten the ship's burden but the vessel had punctured her timbers and made water fast. The crew was forced to man the boats and was subsequently picked up by the pilot schooner *California.* Beachcombers reaped a harvest from the sea in the aftermath of the wreck. Only one cow reached shore alive, and she was landed through the efforts of William Chance, an early pioneer of the area. The cow lived for many years but was often accused of having salt water in her milk. The *Woodpecker* was a composite schooner built in England, and valued at $15,000.

W. T. & B. No. 3, barge, 194 tons, lost at the entrance to the Columbia River, about 1916. The vessel was built at Seattle, in 1910.

Zampa, American schooner, 385 tons, stranded on Point Leadbetter, just south of Willapa Harbor entrance, July 17, 1904, without loss of life. The schooner was buffeted by a gale off the Columbia, and lost her rudder. She commenced drifting at the mercy of the wind and was carried through the breakers. Grounding on the sands the vessel was 300 feet from the water when the tide ebbed. Captain Kellenberger, his wife and the crew of nine were all saved. For several months the schooner remained on the beach, and after being given up for lost on several occasions, was finally refloated and towed to port for repairs. After a hectic career, the *Zampa* was lost in 1926, near Honolulu. She was built in 1887.

The schooner *Zampa*, ashore on North Beach, opposite Oysterville, July 17, 1904. Refloated several months later, she outwitted the winds and tides for another two decades.

In addition to the foregoing list, many other ocean-going vessels have suffered minor and major mishaps in and around the Pacific Graveyard, either through stranding on shoals or from the action of the bar in extreme conditions. Scores of small craft have been lost, many with loss of life or injury. The elements have taken their toll from the days of the Indian canoes to the sports fishing craft of today.

The Coast Guard is constantly busy with distress calls or calls for assistance. Though the personnel of the Cape Disappointment base, the former Point Adams, Klipsam and Willapa facilities have saved many lives, this roll has cost the lives of many Coast Guardsmen.

It was a great advance when the Coast Guard Air Station was established at Astoria, Oregon, August 14, 1964. With the advent of Coast Guard search and rescue helicopters the perils at sea have been greatly reduced. Rescue helicopters are able to reach the scene of an accident more quickly than surface craft. Operators and crewmen in the helicopters have been responsible for saving many lives that otherwise might have been lost.

Competent Columbia River Bar Pilots have established an enviable record but caution can never be relaxed when approaching the graveyard of the Pacific.

WEATHER AND TIDE CONDITIONS

According to a survey by the Corps of Engineers, U. S. Army, the weather conditions at the mouth of the Columbia River vary in direction and velocity during different seasons of the year. During the months from April to August, inclusive, the prevailing winds in the vicinity of Astoria are from the northwest; for the remainder of the year southwesterly winds prevail. On the coast, northwest winds of high velocity, sometimes developing into gales which last several days, are not infrequent during the summer months. During the winter months, southerly gales may occur at any time, and a heavy southwest swell prevails.

The average wind velocity at the mouth of the river is high. Records of the United States Weather Bureau for a period of more than twenty-five years indicate the average to be fourteen miles, increasing from ten miles in July and August to nineteen miles per hour in December.

Though fog is most frequent off the mouth of the Columbia River in July, August and September, it may occur at any time. At times fogs extend many miles seaward and are very dense. During late summer and fall seasons they will often last over an extended period.

The average annual amount of precipitation at the port of Astoria is 77.24 inches a year.

Ice forms occasionally in the river, but is seldom heavy enough to seriously affect navigation.

In the entrance to the Columbia River the velocity of the currents is variable. On the flood tide a velocity of two knots is seldom exceeded but the velocity sometimes attains five knots during an ebb tide. This variation is due largely to the strength of the river discharge, the velocity of the tide alone being two and a half knots at strength of either flood or ebb. Above the mouth of the river the currents lessen to between one and two miles per hour, except during the freshet period, when they increase.

At the mouth of the Columbia River, the mean range of tide is seven and one-half feet.

A

B

C

D

E

F

G

V

W

Y

Z